Tackling the Tough Stuff

A Home Visitor's Guide to Supporting Families at Risk

Second Edition

by

Angela M. Tomlin, PhD, HSPP, IMH-E®
Professor and Co-Chief of the
Division of Developmental Medicine
Indiana University School of Medicine

and

Stephan A. Viehweg, ACSW, LCSW, IECMH-E®, CPC-P
Assistant Research Professor and
Associate Director of the Indiana LEND Program
Indiana University School of Medicine

Baltimore • London • Sydney

Paul H. Brookes Publishing Co.
Post Office Box 10624
Baltimore, Maryland 21285-0624
USA

www.brookespublishing.com
Copyright © 2025 by Paul H. Brookes Publishing Co., Inc.
All rights reserved.
Previous edition copyright © 2016.

"Paul H. Brookes Publishing Co." is a registered trademark of
Paul H. Brookes Publishing Co., Inc.

Typeset by Progressive Publishing Services, York, Pennsylvania.
Manufactured in the United States of America by
Integrated Books International, Inc., Dulles, Virginia.

All examples in this book are composites. Any similarity to actual individuals or circumstances is coincidental, and no implications should be inferred.

Purchasers of *Tackling the Tough Stuff: A Home Visitor's Guide to Supporting Families at Risk, Second Edition*, are granted permission to download, print, and photocopy the Appendices and Form 1: RSC Preparation Worksheet in the text for professional purposes. This form and the appendices may not be reproduced to generate revenue for any program or individual. Photocopies may only be made from an original book. *Unauthorized use beyond this privilege may be prosecutable under federal law.* You will see the copyright protection notice at the bottom of each photocopiable page.

Cover art © Strekalova/iStock.

Library of Congress Cataloging-in-Publication Data
Names: Tomlin, Angela M., author. | Viehweg, Stephan A., author.
Title: Tackling the tough stuff: a home visitor's guide to supporting families at risk / by Angela Tomlin, PhD, HSPP, IMH-E, Professor and Co-Chief of the Division of Developmental Medicine, Indiana University School of Medicine, and Stephan Viehweg, ACSW, LCSW, IECMH-E, CPC-P, Assistant Research Professor and Associate Director of the Indiana LEND Program, Indiana University School of Medicine, IN.
Description: Second edition. | Baltimore: Brookes, [2025] | Includes bibliographical references and index.
Identifiers: LCCN 2024014896 (print) | LCCN 2024014897 (ebook) | ISBN 9781681257877 (paperback) | ISBN 9781681257884 (epub) | ISBN 9781681257891 (pdf)
Subjects: LCSH: Home-based family services. | Developmentally disabled children—Services for. | Early childhood education—Parent participation. | Family social work.
Classification: LCC HV697.T66 2025 (print) | LCC HV697 (ebook) | DDC 362.82/53—dc23/eng/20240429
LC record available at https://lccn.loc.gov/2024014896
LC ebook record available at https://lccn.loc.gov/2024014897

British Library Cataloguing in Publication data are available from the British Library.

2028 2027 2026 2025 2024

10 9 8 7 6 5 4 3 2 1

Contents

About the Downloads v
About the Authors vi
Foreword   *Katherine Rosenblum* viii
Acknowledgments xi
Dedication xiii
Getting Started xiv

Chapter 1   Connecting and Keeping Connected:
            Relationships Matter 1

Chapter 2   Looking Inside: Reflective Practice and
            Relationships for Learning 19

Chapter 3   PAUSE—A Problem-Solving Framework:
            Blending Relationship and Reflective Skills 29
            Appendix 3A   PAUSE Worksheet 49
            Appendix 3B   Provider Reflection Worksheet 51

Chapter 4   What's Going On in There? Understanding
            Causes of Behavior 53
            Appendix 4A   Exploring Challenging
               Behaviors—Pulling It Together Worksheet 72

Chapter 5   When Caregivers Say . . . Calm Down!
            Early Regulation: Sleeping, Eating, and Soothing 77
            Appendix 5A   Tips for Calming Your Baby 105

Chapter 6   Stop That! Biting, Hitting, Throwing,
            and Meltdowns 107
            Appendix 6A   Timely Tips for Tolerating
               Challenging Behaviors 129

iii

Chapter 7	Why Won't You Listen? Cooperating and Following Directions．．．．．．．．．．．．．．．．．．．．．．．．．．．．．．．．	131
	Appendix 7A　Practice Reframing Commands．．．．．．．．．．	149
Chapter 8	Don't Be Such a Baby: Fears and Separation Issues．．．．．．．．．．．．．．．．．．．．．．．．．．．．．．．．．．．．	151
Chapter 9	What Else Might This Be? Family Challenges．．．．．．．．．．．．	175
	Appendix 9A　Practice Discussing Difficult Topics．．．	205
Chapter 10	You Can't Do This Alone: Boundaries, Self-Care, and Supervision．．．．．．．．．．．．．．．．．．．．．．．．．．．．．．．．．．．．	207
	Appendix 10A　Reflection on Work–Life Balance．．．．．．．．	227

Last Reflection．．． 229
Reflective Supervision and Consultation: What Is It,
　Why Do I Need It, and How Can I Use It Most Effectively? ．．．．．．．．． 231
Form 1: RSC Preparation Worksheet．．．．．．．．．．．．．．．．．．．．．．．．．．．．．．． 242

References ．． 247
Index．． 267

About the Downloads

Purchasers of this book may download, print, and/or photocopy the Appendices and Form 1: RSC Preparation Worksheet for professional use.

To access the materials that come with this book:

1. Go to the Brookes Publishing Download Hub: http://downloads.brookespublishing.com

2. Register to create an account (or log in with an existing account).

3. Filter or search for the book title *Tackling the Tough Stuff: A Home Visitor's Guide to Supporting Families at Risk, Second Edition*.

About the Authors

Angela M. Tomlin, Ph.D., HSPP, IMH-E®, Professor, Co-Chief of the Division of Developmental Medicine, Indiana University School of Medicine, Indianapolis

Dr. Tomlin is Professor of Clinical Pediatrics and Co-Chief of the Division of Developmental Medicine at Indiana University School of Medicine (IUSM). She is also Director of the Indiana LEND Program, a nationally recognized interdisciplinary leadership training program supported by the Maternal and Child Health Bureau at IUSM. Her credentials include endorsement as an infant mental health mentor in both clinical and research scopes. She is also a certified perinatal mental health specialist. Dr. Tomlin provides clinical services to very young children and their families, supports the training of interdisciplinary learners within the LEND, advances the knowledge and skill of medical learners rotating in her clinics, and promotes the professional development of the infant and early childhood workforce as a provider of reflective supervision and consultation. She is passionate about supporting and growing a diverse infant and early childhood workforce through scholarship and mentorship. Dr. Tomlin is the author or co-author of 30 publications on topics that include infant mental health, autism spectrum disorder, and workforce development. Dr. Tomlin has served the university and the infant and early childhood field, and her community by serving on boards, including leadership roles in Infancy Onward, Indiana's infant mental health association, committees and workgroups of the Alliance for the Advancement of Infant Mental Health, and other state and local groups. She was the 2022 recipient of the Alliance's Deborah J. Weatherston Award for leadership in infant mental health. With her husband of over 40 years, Dr. Tomlin is the proud parent of two adult daughters and two wonderful grandchildren.

Stephan A. Viehweg, ACSW, LCSW, IECMH-E®, CPC-P, Assistant Research Professor of Pediatrics, Associate Director of the Indiana LEND Program, Indiana University School of Medicine, Indianapolis

Mr. Viehweg is Assistant Research Professor of Pediatrics and Associate Director of the Indiana LEND Program, a nationally recognized interdisciplinary leadership training program supported by the Maternal and Child Health Bureau at the Indiana University School of Medicine, Department of Pediatrics, Division of Developmental Medicine. He is also Associate Director of the Center for Translating Research Into Practice at Indiana University–Indianapolis. He currently serves as the Centers for Disease Control's Learn the Signs. Act Early. Ambassador to Indiana. Mr. Viehweg is author or co-author of many publications, book chapters, and webinars on reflective practice, interdisciplinary education and service delivery, early childhood mental health, early detection, translational research, and open access. He is the founding chair of Infancy Onward, Indiana's infant/toddler mental health association, and founding president of Family Voices Indiana (now Indiana Family to Family). He is passionate about children and families and is a fierce advocate for policies and programs that support family-centered, community-engaged best practices. He volunteers on various boards and committees that focus on children and families at the local, state, and national levels. With his wife of over 35 years, he is the proud parent of an adult son and daughter, and Papaw to his amazing grandchildren.

Foreword

As a university professor and infant mental health mentor, I have spent many years teaching, researching, and advocating for the fields of home visiting and infant and early childhood mental health practice. At the core of this work is a commitment to relationship-based, reflective, and culturally responsive practice, and I have therefore always greatly appreciated the opportunity to share the work of Professors Angela Tomlin and Stephan Viehweg. The original volume of this book, *Tackling the Tough Stuff: A Home Visitor's Guide to Supporting Families at Risk*, helped countless numbers of professionals enter and engage in this critical field. And so it was with great delight that I learned that a second edition of their foundational book was in preparation. As the authors acknowledge from the outset of this volume, home visiting is both an intimate and an intense experience, and while this is most certainly true, this book, and the wisdom it holds, is certain to leave home visitors feeling more prepared, less alone, and more supported in their home visiting practice.

The work of the infant mental health home visitor is indeed profound. We are invited into the family's personal space, and to hear and see them in often very intimate ways as they navigate the incredible challenges of being human and being a parent. We hold the family's stories, both those we hear and those we see and feel. We keep the baby's experience at the center, but also the experiences of the parent, as well as the emerging dance that unfolds between parent and child. We often say that our work is two-generational—powerful because it has impact on both caregivers and infants and toddlers in the present. And it doesn't stop there. Our work touches on multiple generations, including experiences that parents have had that contribute to shaping the present. These experiences span joys and sorrow, hopes and dreams, suffering and grief, as well as current and historical experiences of structural oppression, including economic and racial oppression, marginalization, and trauma. The home visitor is called upon to both recognize these challenges and celebrate the strengths and unique beauty of each parent–child relationship.

Our work also spans relationships: infant with parent, but also infant and parent with the home visiting provider. With such a broad calling it is therefore not surprising that the challenges and questions we face as home visitors are many: how can we help parents and caregivers and their young children feel seen, heard, and supported as they navigate the myriad challenges that infancy and early childhood hold? How do we help parents respond to challenging child behaviors, hold developmentally appropriate expectations, cope with mental health challenges, and access resources? How do we embrace and celebrate culturally diverse parenting and relational experiences and maintain a commitment to anti-racist, anti-ableist, and culturally humble practices? How do we steward our own responsibility to care for ourselves in this work, sustaining our capacity to see and hear and respond effectively, and to feel efficacious and successful in our work?

Remarkably, this book covers all of this, and more, conveying a clear conceptualization of what is tremendously complex in a straightforward manner, offering highly relevant and relatable case vignettes (without dictating a one-size-fits-all approach) and specific and tangibly useful tools and strategies for the home visitor. The authors center their work around the foundational early relationships that are at the heart of home visiting and infant mental health practice, and make space for acknowledging the cultural stories that can vary and reflect the beliefs, practices, and values of families and communities.

There are so many things that make this book invaluable. It is clear and tangible, easy to access, yet rich and deep in content. Tables throughout provide incredibly useful summaries of content and offer a great reference for providers working with families. The case vignettes are respectful, thoughtful, highly relevant, and illustrate concepts clearly. The authors do not offer a simple, reductionistic "do this" approach. Instead, they offer concrete and clear but varied possibilities of things to do, reflecting a humble, culturally responsive approach. They introduce and use psychodynamic strategies such as parallel process and behavioral approaches to address challenging behaviors. Every chapter concludes with a clear summary of Key Points to Remember, a set of Tips for Practice, and suggestions for further reading and learning.

Importantly, this volume retains the authors' incredibly useful PAUSE framework for approaching challenges. PAUSE stands for Perceive, Ask, Understand, Strategize, and Evaluate. Ultimately, the PAUSE framework helps scaffold a reflective process for the provider. Worksheets provided offer a concrete way to think through a challenge, taking into account multiple layers of information, and ultimately helping the provider reflect and generate ideas for action. These worksheets are incredibly helpful tools to support the reflective process and help equip home visitors with a way to select strategies and approaches they believe will be most supportive of the infants and families they serve.

The authors suggest that three important functions of parents and caregivers are to 1) show interest and attention towards their infants and young children; 2) accurately read their child's signals and needs; and 3) respond in a timely and sensitive way. In writing this wonderful book, Professors Tomlin and Viehweg have offered home visitors the same; the authors 1) demonstrate clear interest and attention to the complex, intimate, and important work of the home visitor, 2) accurately read the signals and needs of the workforce; and 3) address many of the challenges providers face, responding sensitively and thoughtfully by sharing their accumulated wisdom generated through years of work in the field with all of us, the readers.

There are no simple answers to the complexities of this work, but this volume absolutely helps scaffold the work of the home visitor, validating that there are many ways providers can do the right thing. As the authors note, there is no one "right way" for all people across all situations, yet the home visitor can nurture and develop their skills and embrace a reflective practice approach to strengthen their thinking and enhance best practices. A great way to start that learning begins with reading this book!

Katherine Rosenblum, Ph.D., ABPP

Acknowledgments

This work is the result of many years of clinical experiences, research and reading, teaching, talking and thinking together and with colleagues, and—most important—spending time sitting beside and getting to know young children and their families. Recognizing our privilege, we are grateful to the families who let us hear their challenges and see their strengths. They have taught us much about the hard work that caring for young children can present and why support is so necessary.

We thank our many colleagues dedicated to infant/early childhood mental health and the development of a competency-based endorsement system through the Alliance for the Advancement of Infant Mental Health for their encouragement and feedback. Their explicit commitment to a diversity-informed and antiracist stance, along with their long-standing efforts to bring awareness to the importance of early experiences, a focus on relationships as key to development and lifelong wellness, and the value of reflection and reflective supervision/consultation in professional development provide a context for our ideas to flourish.

We appreciate the candid feedback from our colleagues and friends who took the time to review our work. Their strong suggestions made our book better and, we hope, more practical and useful to the important work that is done by home visitors, early care and education providers, and early interventionists. We especially appreciate recommendations to better capture the diversity of families and the workforce, use more inclusive language, and consider how a range of universal experiences in the last 5 years have affected us and those we serve. We acknowledge that recent years have brought many stressful experiences, including the COVID-19 pandemic, conflicts around the world, and challenges of balancing widely differing views about what to prioritize in our shared world. At the same time, positive results can and have grown from these troubles. For example, we have seen significant growth in the use of virtual means of providing services and receiving professional development. Through the voices of

BIPOC (Black, Indigenous, People of Color) colleagues we are growing in our understanding of the treasure that diversity brings to this work with families. We embrace efforts toward antiracism, join with our colleagues to honor the lived expertise of diverse families and providers, and look forward to a future in which all babies and families see themselves in both the workforce and its leadership.

Projects like this do not happen without the expertise, commitment, and guidance of brilliant editors like Johanna Schmitter, our first edition editor from Paul H. Brookes Publishing Co. Thank you for believing in our idea, providing thoughtful feedback that challenged us and improved our thinking, and keeping us on track! We also extend our gratitude to Melissa Solarz and Savanna Neubert, who guided our second edition. Your help in gathering input, conceptualizing changes, and integrating our new ideas is much appreciated.

We gratefully acknowledge the steadfast support of our spouses John (Angie) and Jan (Steve), who unselfishly gave up hours of their time with us to make this book a reality. They are our anchor and most ardent supporters in this project and many others.

Finally, we would like to send love and thanks to our own children and grandchildren; having you in our lives gives us the courage and encouragement to do this important work and to turn our passion into reality.

*To the children and families in whose care we share:
You inspire us to do the best we can to make things better.*

Getting Started

It is often acknowledged that the work of home visitors, although very rewarding and satisfying, can be challenging. Each child and family presents a different situation, which must be understood from many different contexts, including culture, race, and identity, as well as the values, beliefs, and experiences of all individuals involved. To work effectively and sensitively, home visitors must find ways to think broadly, remain flexible, consider multiple perspectives, and be prepared with reliable information and resources that can be shared. Furthermore, because it involves helping families with very young children, is provided in the family's home, and often addresses very personal information, home visiting can be an intimate and intense experience. It's not uncommon for home visitors to have many responses and reactions. Altogether, home visitors frequently find that they need more than just information; they also need strategies and supports.

In this book we will present the PAUSE (Perceive, Ask, Understand, Strategize, and Evaluate) framework, a set of strategies for partnering with caregivers that blends relationship-based practice, reflective skills, and concrete information in a way that home visitors can use in everyday interactions. Our goal is to take evidence-based strategies and translate them into practical concepts and actions you can use. Using the PAUSE framework to observe, listen, and ask questions, the home visitor can better understand child behavior and development, understand sources of challenging behaviors, recognize and respond to stressful family situations and needs, acknowledge and celebrate family and caregiver strengths, and find ways to manage their own reactions to this intense work.

Throughout the chapters you will find many vignettes, examples, and worksheets with opportunities to think and try out skills you can use in your everyday practice. Throughout the book, we invite you to recognize, respect, and honor the culture and identities of families, colleagues, and yourself and to consider how these similarities and differences play a role in our work. The first three chapters provide an overview of relationships and relationship-based practice, of reflective practice, and of how these two practices can work together. Chapter 4 covers how to understand and address common behavior problems in early childhood: a frequent reason for which families seek home visiting services. Chapters 5 through 8 explore specific typical and challenging behaviors. These include developing self-regulation, aggression, compliance, and anxiety. Chapter 9 focuses on stressful family issues such as parental mental illness and disability. Chapter 10 revisits relationship and reflective practice from the perspective of some of the more significant struggles that many families encounter. In this chapter we encourage recognition that home visitors can be affected by this work and consideration of how best to support the workforce as they support families The chapters end with Tips for Practice and suggestions for further reading and learning.

We hope this book provides a useful set of tools to help you continue to grow and thrive in your practice. Let's get started!

1

Connecting and Keeping Connected

Relationships Matter

Home visiting is exciting and challenging work. Who else has the opportunity to support young children and their families in such an intimate and meaningful way? When families invite us into their homes, whether in person or virtually, to support them in meeting their children's needs at such a young age, we have a unique opportunity to engage in and support early relationships that can significantly affect their lives. For more than 40 years and across many different types of services, the focus on relationships has been the foundation of home visiting with infants and young families (Ribaudo et al., 2022; Schafer, 2016; Weatherston & Ribaudo, 2020). During this time much has been learned! In this book we will discuss ways to build your skill as a home visitor. We will also consider challenges to worker physical and emotional well-being while engaged in this often demanding career (Eaves et al., 2022; Sparr et al., 2022).

In the field of early intervention, relationships matter, and different kinds of relationships are connected. Relationships of all kinds matter because relationship is the way we learn best (Guralnick, 2001; Norman-Murch, 1996; Slade et al., 2023; Watson et al., 2014; Weatherston & Ribaudo, 2020). A positive relationship supports learning at any level. Three interrelated relationships must be considered in home visiting and other early intervention fields: caregiver–infant/toddler; caregiver–provider, and provider–supervisor/consultant.

Because early intervention professionals are acutely aware of the benefits of early relationships, their work is often focused on supporting the caregiver–child relationship. For many of us, our work includes specific goals centered on improving relationships between caregivers and their young children. The Minding the Baby model, which centers relationship as the foundation for reflection, is a prominent example of home visiting work using this perspective (Sadler et al., 2006; Slade et al., 2023). For others, we attend to relationships less formally. Either way, attention to caregiver–child relationships is critical in early childhood (Jones Harden & Lythcott, 2005; Jeong et al., 2021; Rosenblum et al., 2019). A wealth of evidence stretching back more than 60 years supports the importance of parent–child relationships (Ainsworth, 1979; Ensher & Clark, 2020; Thompson et al., 2022; Weatherson & Ribaudo, 2020) and makes clear that:

- A positive relationship between a young child and their caregiver is necessary for healthy development.
- A positive relationship between caregiver and child can provide long-lasting benefits, including school readiness and better social skills.
- A positive caregiver–child relationship provides support in the face of challenging environments, such as exposure to traumatic events.
- Problems in the caregiver–child relationship may exacerbate difficult experiences and can lead to long-term problems such as behavior disorders, unhealthy relationships, and antisocial behaviors.

FIRST RELATIONSHIPS: ATTACHMENT

The first relationship that a baby forms, attachment, is developed over time when caregivers respond to babies' needs. Although specific caregiving practices clearly vary across cultures, researchers have come to recognize that babies and caregivers can form different kinds of attachments depending on the way that caregiving is delivered. For the most beneficial attachment to form, usually called a *secure* attachment, it is important for one or more primary caregivers to:

Be *interested and attentive* to the baby's needs and signals for help.

Be able to *read* the baby's signals accurately.

Respond to the signals in an appropriate, timely, and reliable way.

Attachment has been thought to be universal in the sense that all cultures need to ensure the safety and development of infants (Ensher & Clark, 2016, 2020; Thompson et al., 2022). However, it is also recognized that both caregiver behaviors and child attachment behaviors may look different across families while still accomplishing the goal of ensuring safety. Much of the original research on attachment was done with Western mother–baby dyads. However, we know that family configurations can vary widely and for many different reasons. For example, in some cultural groups it is typical for extended family members to be involved in daily caregiving

(Gopalkrishnan & Babacon, 2015). Lack of representation of families that are diverse in race, ethnicity, configuration, and culture in research means the results may not apply to all families. For example, in early childhood few caregiver assessment tools include consideration of race or ethnicity; this gap limits our understanding of how concepts about caregiving may apply to these various groups (Rodriguez et al., 2023).

Experiences that families and providers have related to their identities can have many ramifications for one's physical, emotional, and social well-being. Specifically in the United States, authors have recently linked historical and current racial trauma to caregiving interactions and have called for more attention to these experiences in attachment research (Coard, 2022). While we do not have a full understanding of how such experiences may impact caregiver beliefs and child-rearing practices, effective home visitors are aware of and make space for conversations about these topics with families. In home visiting practice, adaptations that make a program more "culturally congruent" may improve effectiveness (Luke, 2020, p. 21). Often, the best way to learn what adaptation will be best is to listen to the stories of the caregivers (Charlot-Swilley et al., 2022).

When babies have the ongoing experience of caregivers who consistently identify and fulfill their needs at the right time and the right level, they feel important and safe, and they learn to trust in relationships. Knowing that their basic needs will be met helps a baby stay calm or regulated in both an emotional and behavioral sense. In other words, babies come to count on the adults in their lives to help them calm down and learn to trust that the caregivers are there to help them navigate the complexities of life. When babies don't have to worry that these basics are covered, they are free to learn and develop in all skill areas. In this way, the kind of attachment that infants have affects what they learn about themselves, other people, their families, and their cultures. Over time, this knowledge contributes to a person's ideas about relationships in general, setting expectations about future relationships and even guiding behavior in future relationships.

What happens when babies do not receive sensitive caregiving? For many reasons, adults may not provide the kind of caregiving that creates a sense of safety and security, leading to attachments that are described as insecure. Insecure attachments occur when the caregiving is insensitive or inconsistent. A range of caregiver responses are possible, resulting in attachments that vary from mildly maladaptive to those that are highly disturbed or even not present at all (Ainsworth, 1979; Main, 1996; ZERO TO THREE Press, 2021). See Table 1.1 for examples of concerning behaviors requiring attention.

This book further explores the kinds of caregiver characteristics and experiences that may challenge early relationships. You may have learned about a range of methods to promote relationships, increase reflection, and improve practice with families. Over the course of this book we present

Table 1.1. Examples of concerning caregiver behaviors from an attachment perspective

Behavior	Examples
Pulling away from the child	Caregiver stays far away from baby; caregiver isolates baby in bouncy seat
	Caregiver encourages toddler to play alone and ignores bids for attention or comfort
	Caregiver often leaves child alone in playpen
	Caregiver does not speak to the child when returning from separation
Caregiver acts afraid or seems distant	Caregiver speaks in frightened or uncertain-sounding voice
	Caregiver interacts, but seems distant or unengaged
	Caregiver has trouble relaying information about his or her child, such as naming a favorite food or toy
Role confusion	Caregiver talks to or about the child as though the child is an adult
	Caregiver defers to child about decisions, begs child to comply
	Caregiver cries when trying to discipline child or asks child, "Do you want to make me cry?"
Confusing communication	Expression, tone of voice, and words do not match (e.g., caregiver says, "Mommy loves you," with scary-looking facial expression)
	Caregiver laughs when child is hurt or looks angry when child is behaving appropriately
	Child smiles and reaches for caregiver; caregiver looks upset, pushes child away
Lack of attunement	Caregiver is intrusive (e.g., keeps trying to get infant eye contact and interaction when baby is distressed, overstimulated, or tired)
	Caregiver teases child by showing but not giving toy or bottle
	Caregiver rejects child request for comfort (e.g., pushes child away when child is hurt or afraid)
	Caregiver has trouble thinking about or talking about what the child's experience might be like

Source: Zeanah, Berlin, and Boris (2011).

our version of these strategies, the PAUSE framework, which providers can use to systematically pause, reflect, and form helpful responses to a variety of situations in home visiting. The steps in PAUSE are Perceive, Ask, Understand, Strategize, and Evaluate. We intend PAUSE to provide a broad framework that can be used alongside other tools, adapted to your needs, and modified to fit a range of communities. Feel free to use these steps individually, as a full sequence, or as anything in between! Using the PAUSE framework, home visitors can integrate relationship and reflective practices with knowledge of child development and behavior. In Chapters 5 through 10, we explore how the PAUSE framework can be applied to a variety of child and family situations that occur in home visiting. We hope you will find this framework flexible for a variety of families and their circumstances and welcome and encourage your personal modifications of our ideas to better fit the communities that you serve.

Good or bad, early experiences require the home visitor's attention because they have the potential for lifelong consequences. A good deal of important brain development occurs after an infant is born. Researchers have learned that social experiences are a key factor in how babies' brains will develop and work (Shonkoff & Phillips, 2000; Bruer & Greenough, 2001; Bourne et al., 2022). Babies depend on caregivers for protection and for responsive input (Bourne et al., 2022). Simple interactions, including making eye contact, smiling, and talking to a baby, help the brain form pathways that will be used for future learning and functioning. In this way, attachment relationships are integrally important to all aspects of development. Building positive relationships at such a young age may actually help prepare children for later relationships and situations. They develop skills needed for playing with other children, sitting at a desk in school to learn various subjects, working with another person in a job environment, having a relationship with another adult and creating a family, and so forth. Again, experiences that some caregivers have had connected to their own racial or ethnic identities can create differences in how they teach their children to behave in social settings. For example, in one interview study, African American caregivers reported intentionally preparing their toddler sons to respond effectively to negative stereotypes and racism they expected them to encounter in life (Blanchard et al., 2019). Home visitors should be aware of the types of experiences that many families encounter and should be willing to learn from caregivers how these experiences affect their caregiving choices. The Early Relational Health-Conversation (ERH-C) intervention (Condon et al., 2022; Charlot-Swilley et al., 2022) is a video-based intervention model that provides an example of how providers can partner with caregivers in a way that is strength-based, supports nondominant ways of knowing, and centers the family experience. In ERH-C, caregivers and facilitators view videos of caregiver–child interactions, and then use reflective prompts to collaboratively observe, interpret, and make meaning of what they see. The facilitator and the caregiver work together to make decisions that are meaningful to the family within their culture and experiences. The authors note that although the ERH-C model was developed for African American families, it may also have utility for other marginalized communities affected by structural racism.

Strategies for Supporting Early Relationships

Home visitors can take actions to help caregivers more frequently demonstrate caregiver behaviors that support their baby's development (Sama-Miller et al., 2018; Slade et al., 2023). Examples of desired caregiver behaviors include demonstrating interest in their infant, recognizing infant cues, and acting responsively to promote a positive relationship. Home visitors can help caregivers build these skills by carefully observing, offering feedback, and providing encouragement around caregiver–child interactions (Roggman et al., 2019). A simple and direct action that home visiting workers can take is to notice and name the baby's social behavior, such as looking or smiling at the caregiver. Next the worker can make a statement that gives voice to the baby's experience, which is often called "speaking for the

Table 1.2. Strategies for supporting attachment

Strategy	Examples
Show interest and empathy	Body language: use an open posture, lean in, maintain eye contact.
	Ask and wonder about the caregiver's experience (e.g., "How has it been for you with Garrett attending the new child care?").
	Recognize and respond to feelings (e.g., "I can see that you are upset that Carter had that big tantrum at the store. That might have been embarrassing for you.").
Clarify and connect	Rephrase and repeat caregiver's statements to ensure understanding (e.g., "So would you say the biggest problem you have right now is Susan's sleep?").
	Comment on the caregiver's efforts and the baby's responses to ensure recognition (e.g., "Beth is smiling at you. I think she really likes to read with you.").
	Ask for clarification when needed (e.g., "We talked about a lot of ideas today. What do you think is the most important thing for you to work on next?").
Demonstrate consistency and reliability	Follow through with plans and promises (e.g., "I wanted to call and give you the phone number for the housing help that we talked about on Tuesday.").
	Check in about previous events (e.g., "I was remembering last week when we spoke about how worried you are about Promise's weight. Did it work out for you to talk with the doctor?").
	Set and keep boundaries as needed (e.g., "I know you are having a hard time getting out to the store. Our agency won't let me give you a ride. Let's think together about other ways we can get you that help.").

baby." When the home visitor highlights the baby's behavior and connects the behavior to a need, caregivers may be better able to notice and respond more regularly to the behavior in the future (Steele et al., 2015). Table 1.2 provides some examples.

Attention to caregiver strengths is beneficial in promoting relationships and increasing positive caregiver actions (Roggman et al., 2019). A simple but very effective technique is to name a positive caregiver behavior (Dozier & Bernard, 2019). For example, during a home visit Donall's grandfather sees him bump his head when standing up under a table. He says, "Come here buddy" as he picks Donall up and rubs the hurt spot. Donall stops crying quickly, and his grandfather sets him back down to return to play. Home visitor Leon remarks, "You were quick to help Donall when he got hurt. That hug really helped him feel better." This technique of frequent "in-the-moment commenting" is one component of the Attachment and Biobehavioral Catchup (ABC) parenting program developed by Mary Dozier and her colleagues. In the intervention, caregivers are coached to provide nurturance, follow the baby's lead, and avoid interactions that are frightening. The intervention has shown to have long-term benefits to the child, including into middle childhood (Dozier & Bernard, 2019). Ongoing work is in process to determine if the benefits may last into adolescence.

Carolyn is a home visitor working with Deidre, a 15-year-old mother, and her 14-month-old son, Gage. Gage has many delays and has few ways of showing his needs or interests. Deidre is a vivacious young woman who has many friends and receives what seem like constant text and other notifications during the hour-long visits with Carolyn. She often laughs out loud and frequently asks Carolyn if she would like to see a funny video or message. Carolyn notices that Gage watches his mother and sometimes smiles when she smiles or laughs. The next time this happens, Carolyn says, "Deidre, look how Gage is smiling when you laugh. He really likes to see your smile. Maybe he wants you to talk to him too." Deidre looks surprised. She looks at Gage and smiles. He smiles back and Deidre says, "Well, hello!"

This example illustrates the role of the home visitor as a voice for the baby. In a gentle way, the home visitor states what the baby can't say. In the case of Deidre and Gage, Carolyn simply noticed how Gage responded to his mother. Carolyn's quiet observation helps Deidre see her son in a way that supports a feeling of connection. Over time, these small moments can be significant in their relationship.

It's important to note that human beings' need for supportive relationships continues throughout their lives and is one of the ways that people can learn new ideas and behaviors even in adulthood. Research on the relationship needs of adults is vast, spanning every possible relationship, including those with romantic partners, friends, co-workers, and even spiritual beings (Thompson et al., 2022). The next section addresses relationships that can form between caregivers and home visitors.

CAREGIVER AND PROVIDER RELATIONSHIPS: THE WORKING ALLIANCE

Caring for young children is hard work. Home visitors know that the ability to respond to a baby in supportive ways does not come naturally to all caregivers all of the time. For many reasons, even the best caregivers may sometimes struggle to give their babies the emotional support they need. It's important to recognize that just as young children learn best when supported by positive relationships, adult caregivers need supportive relationships themselves to be their best with their babies (Edelman, 2004; Slade et al., 2023). As a result, for all professionals who support families with young children, the work includes the responsibility to develop a positive relationship with the caregivers in addition to a relationship with the child (Gomby et al., 1993; Roggman et al., 2019). The term *working alliance* (Bordin, 1979) describes the kind of relationship that home visitors hope to form with caregivers: a collaborative partnership. When providers use themselves and their relationship with families to effect change, it is called *relationship-based practice*. Learning through positive relationships is now a pillar of the work of home visitors and other early intervention providers and is considered the best way to achieve changes in both caregivers and children (Guralnick, 2001; Norman-Murch, 1996; Watson et al., 2014). At times this responsibility to form a positive working relationship is an explicit goal of the home visiting program or practice approach or model. This is often the case for home visitors who work with highly vulnerable families, including those in underserved and under-resourced communities and those at risk for child abuse and neglect. However, even when an intervention is focused on infant development, the caregiver–parent relationship is frequently a central piece of the work.

In early intervention practice, it has been established that caregivers who trust and feel supported by the interventionist are more likely to become engaged and continue in the work that is needed to make changes for their children (Daro & Harding, 1999). Home visitors who act in ways that are described as empathetic, warm, understanding, and responsive toward caregivers facilitate positive changes in both parent and child behaviors (Popp & Wilcox, 2012). Furthermore, "the way that expertise is delivered becomes an essential aspect of the work" (Edelman, 2004, p. 5). This point has been succinctly stated by Jeree Pawl as "how you are is more important than who you are" (Pawl & St. John, 1998).

The COVID-19 emergency resulted in a unique set of challenges for most human service fields, including home visiting. Overnight, agencies had to make decisions about how to continue to offer services, or even whether to continue them at all. Many programs that serve young families, including a significant number of early care and education programs, closed their doors and have yet to reopen, creating a range of problems (Jessen-Howard & Workman, 2020; Mongeau, 2020). In home visiting, workers attempted "social distancing," carried on with protective equipment in place or they shifted their work to the family's porches and yards. Others converted to a virtual service delivery model, often with little warning and less experience. Challenges to virtual home visiting range from issues such as family access to Wi-Fi and appropriate devices to the reality of trying to get an infant or toddler to participate with a provider on screen. In many virtual formats, the provider's role becomes more that of a coach to the caregiver, who will deliver the intervention to the child. Forming and maintaining relationships under these strange circumstances was new to both families and workers.

In one study, home visitors and supervisors in a large urban area reported on their experiences with transitioning to virtual home visiting (Traube et al., 2022). Both home visitors and supervisors reported needs for funding, technology, supervision, and guidance, including from funders and program leadership, in this transition. Supervisors viewed home visitors as having more issues with the transition than did the home visitors themselves, who reported concerns about family engagement. In other studies, home visitors sought practical help for how to conduct virtual assessments and self-care (Marshall et al., 2020). Lessons learned from the pandemic experience continue to be used, as virtual means for connecting have become an important way that some families access our services.

Strategies to Support the Caregiver–Professional Relationship

What home visitor actions help caregivers feel supported? How do these actions build good relationships with caregivers? It is helpful to think about the caregiver behaviors that help a baby feel safe and supported:

Showing interest and attention

Accurately reading signals about needs

Responding to needs in a timely and sensitive way

Consider how these kinds of behaviors can be applied to caregiver–parent relationships. Paralleling the parent's actions toward babies, home visitors build relationships with caregivers when they demonstrate an active interest in the caregiver and their needs. Next, home visitors will need to work to accurately understand what caregivers are saying and showing what they need from the relationship. Extra time and effort may be needed when the home visitor and the family do not share cultural or other similarities that inform child-rearing beliefs and practices. Language differences that require interpreters can add another layer of complexity. Open discussion and exploration about these issues can be helpful. Finally, home visitors make efforts to respond in consistent and reliable ways to meet those needs. In this way, the home visitor's relationship with the caregiver can become part of the caregiver's own attachment network (Thompson, 2022). See Table 1.3 for some examples of how a home visitor might respond to child actions.

At the next visit, Deidre comments that since Gage has started to walk, he can now get into everything. She shares that he got into her purse and scattered her things all around the house; now she can't find her phone charger. Carolyn considers explaining that curiosity is a good thing and suggesting that Deidre make a plan to keep her purse out of Gage's reach. If Carolyn wanted to show interest in Deidre's experience, what could she say instead?

Table 1.3. Child action and home visitor response

When the child...	The home visitor might say...
Lights up when the caregiver enters the room by looking toward the caregiver, smiling, and cooing	"Your baby really notices you when you come into the room. Look how he smiles and watches for you. He wants to be with you."
Hands the toy over to the caregiver	"She gave you the toy. How nice that she is learning from you to share and take turns."
Looks away from the caregiver while sitting in the car seat	"He seems to look away from you now. I wonder if he is telling us he needs a little break from the action. See how he looks back at you after a little while?"
Imitates the facial expressions and sounds of the caregiver during a simple interaction	"Look how she tries to copy what you say and how you look. You two are so expressive with each other. She likes to play with you."

Home visitors may wonder about this emphasis on forming a relationship with the family members and our concern about their experiences. After all, we are infant and toddler specialists, so doesn't that mean we need to keep our focus on the babies? The term *parallel process* can help us understand what happens when we support caregivers and why these caregiver–provider relationships are an important part of the work. Parallel process conveys the concept that one relationship affects other relationships. Events and experiences in one relationship may affect another relationship, either in the present or at a later time. This can occur in many ways. Any time you have a hard workday and then are irritable at home with your family, parallel process may be at work. On the other hand, you could feel your mood lightened after talking with a close friend over dinner and then find yourself giving your server a big tip! Table 1.4 provides a couple of examples of parallel process in action. The concept of parallel process helps home visitors understand how their actions that support caregivers will in turn help caregivers act in more supportive ways toward their young children.

Table 1.4. Parallel process in action

Situation	Relationship A	Relationship B	Parallel process
Caregiver is concerned that child is very hard to manage in public situations.	Lulu cries when she explains how active and aggressive her toddler Isabel is. She tells the home visitor, Sandra, "I am embarrassed all the time. She just runs and grabs things when we go to the store. I really don't know what to do." Sandra says with sympathy, "Wow that's tough! I am sorry that things are so hard for you."	Lulu's shoulders relax when Sandra expresses concern for her. When Isabel comes close, Lulu reaches out to her daughter and rubs her back. She says, "I know it's hard for her when I am yelling all the time."	Sandra addressed Lulu's feelings. Lulu was better able to think about how the situation was for her daughter once her own feelings were addressed.
Home visitor is frustrated when family does not follow through with suggestions.	Desiree arrives for her supervision with Karl. She is visibly upset and immediately starts telling Karl about a phone call she just had with a family. "It's so ridiculous! I have given this family a million ideas for how to get their child signed up for child care. And every time, they just don't do it! I don't know why I even bother." Karl thinks to himself that he and Desiree have had this same conversation several times. He wonders why Desiree has not tried any of his suggestions to address the follow-through problem.	Karl says, "We have talked about this a few times. It can be frustrating to feel that your ideas are not being used." Desiree agrees and seems to calm down. "What can I do?" she asks. Karl says, "Maybe it's not about what you do or don't do. Can we think a little about what might be getting in the way for this family?"	The family did not follow through with the suggestions Desiree gave; similarly, Desiree has not utilized suggestions that she has received from Karl. Karl notices this and wonders about a possible connection. Instead of repeating his suggestions, Karl suggests stepping back to examine what might be getting in the way.

Table 1.5. Filling up the family's emotional tank

At the beginning of a visit	Geneel, the home visitor, began the session by saying, "Emma, I was thinking about you this week. I remembered how excited you were last time with Evelyn's progress and her interest in looking at pictures, pretending to eat the food in the pictures. You were going to practice 'reading' to her again this week. Tell me how it went."
During the visit	Bryan works with Evan's father, William, on interacting more with his baby. During a diaper change, William begins to play a game with Evan to keep him distracted. He flips him over from side to side in between caring for Evan. Evan squeals in delight. Bryan notes afterwards, "Evan really likes to play with you and you found a way to help him learn how to roll over at the same time you did a diaper change. That makes changing a diaper a pretty fun activity. Great idea!"
Summarizing the visit	At the end of the home visit, Susan summarizes what was discussed with Carol by saying, "You asked about finding a different place to live today. We talked about the different options and you decided to talk with your current landlord about changing apartments. We practiced what you might say, and you sounded pretty confident about how to ask for what you need. You really know what's best for your family and how to get that in a respectful way."
In between visits	Samantha sees her home visitor, Rebecca, in the hallway at the agency where the home visiting program is co-located with other agencies. Samantha has come for a WIC appointment and is early. She tells Rebecca in a quiet voice that she realized during the last visit that she could take Anthony to the local library to check out some books, since he seemed to have so much fun with the hard-paged picture books they used in the home visit. She had just gone to the library prior to the WIC appointment; she pulled out a canvas bag to show Rebecca the books they found. Rebecca comments, "What a great idea you had to get more books from the library so you and Anthony can read together!"

The support that caregivers receive from a home visitor can be thought of as energy that can be used to fuel the caregiver's positive actions toward their children (Webster-Stratton, 2019). We encourage caregivers to fill up their emotional fuel tanks so that they have the emotional energy to then respond to their child's needs. See Table 1.5 for some examples of home visitors supporting caregivers in this way.

REFLECT: RECOGNIZING AND REPAIRING MISSTEPS IN HOME VISITING PRACTICE

Carolyn visits Deidre and Gage again after a few missed sessions. She is wondering about what led to the canceled sessions and whether she should mention this during the visit. When Deidre answers the door, she is unusually quiet and appears sad. Carolyn notices that Gage is in need of a new diaper and seems fussy. She is unsure if she should start by addressing Deidre's apparent distress, alert her to Gage's immediate need, or ask about the canceled visits.

Despite best efforts, home visitors and other early intervention professionals may find it very difficult to establish a positive and productive relationship with some families. The block to forming a good relationship can come from the caregiver, the home visitor, or a combination of both.

Barriers for caregivers might include a mental health problem or just having so many competing demands that make this particular relationship not a priority. Sometimes caregivers' own backgrounds and histories include so many relationship challenges that they are unfamiliar with the kind of relationship that the home visitor is seeking to form. Box 1.1 lists some examples of experiences that could block relationships between caregivers and home visitors. In fact, some people may never have experienced the kind of support home visitors offer and cannot understand or even recognize what is being offered. For these families, the home visitor's persistence and consistency can help. It may take a very long time for the caregiver to have enough experiences with the home visitor to begin to trust and listen to the home visitor's guidance.

When establishing trust is an issue, a home visitor may want to create opportunities for the caregiver to learn that the home visitor can be counted on. For example, the home visitor can make plans to bring information or

---

Box 1.1. Caregiver and Family Experiences That May Block Relationships With Home Visitors

- Home visitor reminds caregiver of someone in the caregiver's life who was difficult
- Losses in early childhood (e.g., caregiver's own parent died or left the family)
- Separation, divorce (e.g., of child's caregivers, grandparents)
- Domestic violence or other trauma
- Medical illness or disability
- Mental illness, including depression, personality disorder, or bipolar disorder
- Incarceration of parent or other family members
- Past or current alcohol and/or drug use or abuse
- Past experience with systems such as child welfare and other social programs
- Current worries about housing, food, health care, education, and other basic life needs
- Challenging immigration experiences or difficulties in acculturation
- Current and/or historical experiences of discrimination based on race, ethnicity, religion, and language

activities to the next session so that the caregiver experiences the home visitor as someone who follows through. The home visitor can make a point of bringing up something that happened during previous sessions to demonstrate their attention and memory about the family. Statements that indicate that the home visitor is thinking about the child and family outside of sessions can be powerful indicators that the home visitor is holding the caregiver in mind, even when not with the family. In Chapters 5 through 10, we explore these concepts more specifically using the PAUSE framework to think about caregiver experiences that may get in the way of forming positive relationships with home visitors, and we suggest practical responses and actions.

Carolyn brings a recipe for modeling dough to her visit with Deidre and Gage. She says, "I found this recipe for you. I remembered that you and Gage had a lot of fun with the play doh I brought last week, so I thought you might like to make some yourself." Deidre smiles and says, "Thanks! I bet my mom will like this. We used to make modeling dough when I was little." She puts the recipe in a folder on the table and sits with Carolyn to start the session.

Home visitors can also experience blocks in their own ability to see or do what the caregiver needs. These blocks may come from unconscious biases and have the potential to lead to behaviors that contribute to disparities or to do other harm (Parker, 2021). Home visitors may find the caregiver reminds them of another client who was hard to work with or perhaps someone else from their own past. The caregiver may display behaviors that the home visitor has trouble understanding (e.g., discipline or housekeeping practices that make the home visitor feel uncomfortable). The home visitor may find it difficult to maintain a balance between attending to the caregiver's needs and those of the baby. At other times, a home visitor may simply feel worn out from all the needs that families have. In some cases, the caregiver and the home visitor may just not be a good match. For whatever reason, the practitioner won't always get it right. When mistakes or mismatches occur, the practitioner should acknowledge them and take steps to repair the relationship as needed. (These issues are discussed in more detail in Chapter 10.)

Carolyn is aware that Deidre once again canceled two sessions in a row and that she has not returned several phone calls. She sends a text to ask if they can meet the following week and Deidre agrees to the appointment. However, when Carolyn arrives, the grandmother is at home with Gage and Deidre is not there. Carolyn wonders what could be happening. She decides to keep trying, and the following week Deidre is present for the appointment. Carolyn says, "It's been a while since I saw you. I was wondering if everything is okay with you." Deidre says she is fine, but Carolyn still feels like something is not right. She says, "I am concerned that I might have done something to upset you. Is there anything we should talk about?" Deidre crosses her arms and says, "Well, I am kinda mad at you. You told my mom I am not feeding Gage right." Carolyn is surprised. She doesn't think she said that, but she says, "Wow. I am sorry; I really don't remember saying that. You and I have been talking a lot about how you are enjoying feeding Gage and watching him grow. Maybe we can figure out what happened." Deidre's shoulders relax and she seems calmer. She snuggles a little closer to Gage on the couch and helps him reach for a toy.

SUPPORTS TO HOME VISITORS: MENTORING, COACHING, AND SUPERVISION

One of the best ways for home visitors to gain perspective on their work with families, including their own responses, is to regularly seek support from someone more experienced in the work. This brings us to the third important relationship in home visiting or other early intervention work—the relationship between the home visitor and a supervisor. Whether it is called supervision, mentoring, consultation, facilitation, or coaching, consensus is growing that infant and family workers benefit from ongoing professional development experiences that come from this kind of relationship (Watson et al., 2014; Watson, 2022). Home visitors who regularly receive this kind of guidance feel supported, recognized, and better able to identify their own strengths and needs (Watson & Gatti, 2012). Supervision that includes reflection has been used for years in many settings, but research on the approach is relatively new (Tomlin et al., 2014). There is growing interest in research showing how supporting the workforce will ultimately improve outcomes for parents and children (Huffhines et al., 2023; Watson et al., 2014; Stacks et al., 2021).

There are many types of supervision and styles of supervisors (Heffron & Murch, 2010). Home visitors who have received supervision in the past that did not feel supportive may be skeptical about how reflective supervision might be different and more helpful. Recent work is helping the field understand what is most important to supervisees (Barron et al., 2022a, 2022b). Some preferences include having access to a supervisor who has done the same work, speaks the same language, and is similar in race or ethnicity. These studies are highlighting the challenges of representation in home visiting fields and give impetus to reducing barriers to advancement for historically minoritized members of the workforce. Supervisors should take a lead in discussing any differences such as gender, race, or language between themselves and the supervisee that might present a barrier to forming a collaborative relationship. Good ways to begin are for the supervisor to self-identify and broach discussion of similarities and differences between the supervisor and the supervisee (Hardy, 2016; Stroud, 2010).

Supervision that follows a reflective model has been described as a relationship for learning (Shamoon-Shanok, 2006). Just as consistency and reliability build trust in caregiver–child and caregiver–provider relationships, these attributes are required in the provider–supervisor relationship as well. Therefore, it's important that reflective supervision occurs *regularly*. This allows the home visitor to come to see the supervisor as a consistent source of support.

It is also important in this model that supervisors work to form a relationship with the supervisee that feels more *collaborative* and less hierarchical. This may look different to different people. One way of demonstrating collaboration is avoiding an "expert" stance (i.e., the supervisor should not just tell the supervisee what to do). Using reflective supervision as a method for building skills, the supervisor guides the supervisee to consider many possibilities and to figure out their own solutions. The supervisor will accomplish this goal by using their own reflective skills and by promoting reflection by the supervisee. Use of *reflective* skills that encourage the supervisee to consider their own responses to the work is the third hallmark characteristic of this type of supervision. Such consideration will often include attention to feelings that arise within the work (Alliance for the Advancement of Infant Mental Health, 2018; Fenichel, 1992).

Carolyn keeps thinking about her last few meetings with Deidre and Gage. When she prepares for her supervision time with Toby, she puts talking about this family at the top of her list. During the session, Carolyn shares the story about Deidre canceling sessions and the discussion they had. She tells Toby, "I know I did not say what Deidre thinks I said!" Toby listens carefully and says, "It's pretty upsetting to have someone say something about you that isn't true." "It sure is!" Carolyn replies. "I think I am doing the best I can with them. Deidre is really hard to read. I am never sure if she is really taking in what I say about Gage. Some days I wonder if I am wasting my time." Toby says, "It's hard to feel successful when you don't get a response or the response you get is negative." They continue to discuss this issue for several minutes. Then Toby says, "I was remembering that you said that Gage is kind of a quiet baby. You had mentioned that it's been hard for Deidre and Gage to connect. I wonder what it is like for you to see that struggle." Carolyn responds, "It's frustrating. Last month I even tried to get Deidre's mother to help prompt her a little with him. I asked her to praise Deidre whenever she sees her do something well." Carolyn stops suddenly. She looks thoughtful and says, "I guess that could explain why Deidre thinks I told her mom she wasn't feeding Gage right. She does try very hard and I guess that her being upset was really showing that she does listen and try things we talk about. She must feel bad when she tries but Gage doesn't respond right away."

In the past, evidence for reflective supervision came primarily from clinical thinking and practical experiences (Huffhines et al., 2023; Tomlin et al., 2014). More recently, a surge of attention to the practice has been supporting more empirical evidence (see Hause & LeMoine, 2022). It is becoming clearer that reflective supervision or consultation, while not sufficient by itself, provides many benefits to agencies, providers, and families (Barron et al., 2022a, 2022b; Norman-Murch, 2005; Weatherston, Kaplan-Estrin, & Goldberg, 2009). Reflective supervision is increasingly seen as a form of professional development that improves the participant's skill and increases capacities for insightfulness and reflection (Hause & LeMoine, 2022; Watson, 2022). Agencies benefit when providers benefit. For example, when professionals feel supported, they may be more likely to stay on the job, reducing turnover. Less frequent turnover is a benefit for agencies because it reduces hiring and training expenses. Participation in reflective supervision can also result in home visitors who can deliver better services, leading to better attainment of family goals and higher family satisfaction with services (Stacks et al., 2021). For more about reflective supervision and its connection to worker well-being, see this book's supplement, "Reflective Supervision and Consultation: What Is It, Why Do I Need It, and How Can I Use It Most Effectively?"

WHAT'S NEXT?

In Chapter 2 we talk more about reflective skills, why they are important in early childhood work, and how they can be enhanced in ourselves and families.

TIPS FOR PRACTICE

- Attend and respond to caregiver needs to build relationships and increase caregiver sensitivity to their children.

- Monitor your own feelings about children, caregivers, and family situations. Purposefully attend to your own biases. Awareness of your biases and feelings can provide information about what is happening. Plus, when you are aware of feelings, you can better manage them in order to respond more effectively.

- Regularly seek supports such as supervision, consultation, or coaching, which include reflection to build skills and to obtain support for the challenging feelings that home visiting brings.

KEY POINTS TO REMEMBER

- Early experiences have the potential for lifelong consequences, both positive and negative. Evidence for the long reach of these early experiences includes changes to brain structure and functioning.

- Effective home visitation services attend to the formation of positive relationships between caregivers and their young children (attachments), caregivers and home visitors (working alliance), and home visitors and supervisor/consultants (reflective supervision/consultation relationships).
- Current and past relationships and experiences within relationships are interconnected and have reciprocal effects through parallel process.

SUGGESTED FURTHER READING

Ensher, G. L., & Clark, D. A. (2016). *Foundations for best practice with special children and their families.* ZERO TO THREE Press.

To stay up to date about important home visiting models such as Healthy Families America and others, bookmark the National Home Visiting Resource Center at https://nhvrc.org/

2

Looking Inside

Reflective Practice and
Relationships for Learning

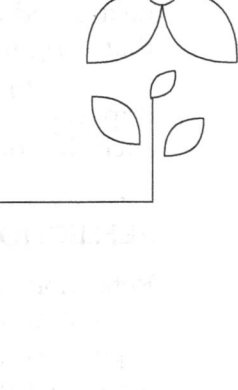

Families face multiple challenges—big and small—every day. Family life is incredibly complex, from making small choices such as what to have for dinner to facing major decisions such as what to do when an infant is born prematurely, a military parent is deployed overseas, or an eviction is looming. For many families, additional challenges can come with being a cultural, racial, or ethnic minority. Home visitors and other early intervention workers often have as part of their duties a responsibility to support families in their coping and decision making. Every day, home visitors too face many decisions. Whose needs are most important right now? What and who can wait? What action would be most helpful? Furthermore, home visitors, like anyone else, may have personal concerns in addition to those related to the work. It can be hard to figure out how to find balance between these competing needs.

At 4:00 p.m. on Friday, Theresa is struggling to complete paperwork due first thing Monday. She is scheduled for a volunteer shift at the high school concession stand at 6:00 p.m. Her phone rings, and she recognizes that the number belongs to a new family she started working with this week. Theresa realizes that this family is just beginning to trust her, and so she recognizes that taking the call is a chance to build the relationship. Theresa feels her shoulders tense as she is aware of being pulled three ways: paperwork, volunteer responsibility, and the needs of a client.

For each person reading this scenario, the best answer to Theresa's dilemma may be different. Some may think that Theresa should absolutely take the call and figure out the rest later. Others would let the call go to voicemail, continue to complete the paperwork, and then try to get to the high school as scheduled, leaving the needs of the caregiver to the next scheduled visit. Although it is not possible to identify one solution that is right or perfect for every person and every situation, home visitors can develop skills that improve thinking and enhance best practices. One important way to develop the kinds of skills that help us feel competent in such situations is to encourage reflection.

REFLECTION AND MINDFULNESS

Reflection is one of many mindfulness skills that allow us to focus on the present and to be truly aware of our own experiences and responses to experiences, as well as those of other people. *Mindfulness* most often refers to giving full attention to what is happening in the moment, including being aware of thoughts, feelings, and sensations. Think about how it would feel to talk with someone who is practicing mindfulness by giving you their full attention; now contrast that with how it might feel to talk with someone who is checking their phone, creating a grocery list, or just answering you automatically without thinking. Mindfulness is seen as a pathway to wellness; the benefits of being more mindful have been noted for health, relationship, and overall well-being (Siegel, 2013).

Taking time to reflect about the pressures of competing demands can offer many practical benefits to the quality of the work, including better decision making, increased confidence or feelings of effectiveness, and enhanced ability to take in and use new information. In this way, skills in mindfulness benefit the practitioner and those with whom they partner. Taking time to reflect may be the most helpful when situations are most complex; paradoxically, this is also often the time when we feel most pressed to act. Home visiting must be counted among the fields in which complex situations are the norm (Frosch et al., 2019). Each family brings its own set of novel situations, and home visitors must learn to adapt to a high level of uncertainty. Reflective skills can help the home visitor find ways to learn to make sense of the situations that face many families (Weston, 2005; Slade et al., 2023). This practice can help the home visitor to better integrate and make good use of the often competing emotional and cognitive processes inherent when addressing complex situations (Mann et al., 2009).

Theresa lets the phone go to voicemail while she organizes her thoughts. She recognizes that she is being pulled in several directions and that the resulting emotions are causing her to have trouble completing any task at all because she cannot concentrate. Theresa considers how her boss, fellow volunteers, and the new family may respond to any decisions that she makes to prioritize these tasks. "I would never call someone this late on Friday unless it was an emergency," she thinks worriedly. Suddenly, Theresa realizes that she does not actually know the reason that the family called. The family is so new to her that she has not yet learned their patterns. Theresa decides to text back to acknowledge that she got the call and to ask if calling in a few hours would be okay. A few minutes later, Theresa's phone pings with a response. The mother replies that she had a quick question and adds that it can wait for their meeting next week. Feeling relieved, Theresa continues with her original plan, glad that she did not let her own assumptions get in the way.

Use of reflection to increase self-awareness, improve self-regulation, and promote learning about self and others is not new. For example, from ancient times, many of the world's major religions have promoted forms of reflection, including meditation and prayer. Reflection is also used as a way of improving work in many professional fields, including education, business, health, and mental health (DiStefano et al., 2014; Mann et al., 2009; Watson et al., 2014). Among modern authors, Donald Schön (1983, 1987) is often credited with bringing the concept of reflection to the forefront for practitioners.

To be effective, home visitors need content knowledge (knowing) and practical skills (doing) (Schön, 1987). Reflective skills help bridge the gap between knowing and doing, making information that we learn in school or continuing education activities concrete and usable (Wesley & Buysse, 2001). We can use reflective skills in the moment when working with families or later when we look back and try to make sense of what happened (Schön, 1987). For example, we use reflection in action when we slow down, observe what is happening, and make purposeful decisions about what to do or say in each situation during our work. We also use reflection on action when we think carefully about our past experiences and consider multiple aspects of that experience when we are outside of the situation, including during supervision/consultation or when processing a situation informally, alone or with colleagues.

Reflection helps us begin to understand the "why" behind behaviors, thoughts, and feelings of ourselves and others (Steele et al., 2015). When done with others (colleagues or supervisors), reflection reduces provider isolation and increases felt support (Wesley & Buysse, 2001). Reflection supports movement between discussion, which involves presenting and defending one's own viewpoint, and dialogue, in which individuals make an effort to suspend their own views in order to listen more deeply and learn more about how others think (Wesley & Buysee, 2001). Reflection as a practice contains the idea of reflection as a skill that can be taught, practiced, and honed (Mann et al., 2009). We must reflect regularly to become comfortable with the practice. Just as practice improves our skills in other areas (e.g., in music or athletics), so will time and repetition enhance our ability to reflect. In addition, an appropriate learning environment is necessary, including mentors or supervisors with specific skill sets (Mann et al., 2009). In the next section of this chapter, we consider how the capacity for reflection develops, its benefits, its role in home visiting fields, and how it can be enhanced.

REFLECTIVE FUNCTION OR CAPACITY

Reflection can be thought of as a skill and also as an innate capacity or function of human beings (Slade, 2005; Slade et al., 2023). As a social skill, reflection is understood to underlie many behaviors that are critical for smooth social interactions. As explained by Peter Fonagy and colleagues (Fonagy et al., 2002; Fonagy & Target, 1998), reflective functioning is complex and involves many components:

1. The capacity to consider many different kinds of mental experiences in oneself and others
2. Appreciation that these mental states are connected to behaviors
3. Recognition that people can have mental states that are different from one's own
4. Awareness that even if a person shares one's mental state, the behavior that results may or may not be the same. (Fonagy et al., 1995)

The interconnected skills that make up reflective functioning allow us to better regulate our own emotions, understand what might be behind our own actions, and make decisions or choices about our future actions. For example, a person who is aware of a bias or attitude that they hold may set aside that bias and think about a situation more critically.

One component of reflective capacity is the awareness that one person's responses—including attitudes, beliefs, thoughts, feelings, and behaviors—in a specific situation are not necessarily the same as those of the next person. Awareness that other people have internal states can help us make sense of another person's behaviors. Recognition that others' behaviors, thoughts, feelings, and other internal states are sometimes different from ours may also provide information about how others may view and respond to us. We may make decisions about how to present ourselves based on our predictions about how the person may respond. Overall, being able to think about the mental states and behaviors of others increases understanding and informs decisions about potential action (Slade, 2005).

Candy is a home visitor in an early intervention program for infants and toddlers with developmental delays. She is preparing for a first visit with Tony, a 30-month-old with delays in speech and social behavior, and his mother, Sierra. As she drives up to the home, she sees a sign in the yard for a candidate for state senator. Candy knows this candidate is advocating some policies and viewpoints that are different from her own. She wonders what this sign means about the family's beliefs and how this might affect their work together.

Reflective capacity can also help us have better understanding about the experiences of other people, making it one of the factors that allow us to form and keep relationships (Slade, 2005). For someone on the receiving end, the experience of having another person show awareness of one's internal state can be powerful. Consider how it would feel to hear statements like these:

I was thinking about you today.

I got you a copy of this book because I know you like this author.

You must be so proud of your daughter.

I imagine this is a very hard time for you.

The connection between attending to someone's experience and the formation of a relationship may sound familiar. As we discussed in Chapter 1, a big part of how a baby's attachment forms is the caregiver's ability to be aware of and attend to the infant's experience and needs. A special case of reflective function is parental reflective functioning (PRF; Slade, 2005, 2006), which refers to a caregiver's ability to understand that their mental states and behaviors and those of their child are connected. PRF underpins the parent's ability to attend to the child's experience, which in turn is part of the prerequisites for forming a healthy attachment. PRF also has a role in the child's growth toward self-regulation of emotions and behaviors. Parents with more developed PRF may be better able to recognize that a child's mental states are connected to behavior, resulting in more sensitive responding to and scaffolding of positive child behaviors. Parents who act in ways that show recognition and understanding of a child's internal states help the child gain self-awareness. This can be done with actions and with words. Here are some examples:

Pamela wakes when she hears her 3-month-old daughter crying. Glancing at the clock, she realizes that the baby is probably hungry. As she picks up her daughter and prepares to feed her, she says, "Hello, little one. Mommy is here. Are you ready to eat?"

Gabby, an 18-month-old toddler, is running in the backyard while her father weeds the flower beds. She stumbles, falls, and begins crying loudly. Her father, Gino, sees that she has a skinned knee but is not seriously hurt. "Uh oh! That was scary. You hurt your knee but you will be okay," he says.

At the playground, 30-month-old Danny watches his friend Donita play with a light-up wand. After a couple of minutes, Danny grabs the wand, pulling it away from her. When Donita tries to take it back, Danny hits her. The children's mothers intervene, comforting both children. Danny's mother says, "You really wanted that wand, so you took it from Donita and you hit her." She goes on to explain to Danny that he hurt Donita and talks to him about taking turns.

Reflective skills fall along a continuum (Slade, 2005). For example, caregivers may have a range of responses when hearing the results of early intervention screening that indicate serious delays. One caregiver might look upset but ask no questions and insist that she is perfectly fine. This caregiver could be having difficulty recognizing her own feelings. Another caregiver might yell at the provider, then apologize, saying, "I am sorry. What you said made me afraid and I took it out on you." This caregiver can recognize her own feelings and connect them with behaviors. Another caregiver may immediately begin to wonder about how to share this news with her partner. This caregiver can think not only about her own responses to difficult news, but also about how another person might respond.

When people have higher levels of reflective functioning, they are often able to blend and connect thinking and feeling, which can lead to more functional and adaptive behavior overall (Mann et al., 2009; Slade, 2005). When people are aware of and able to manage their own thoughts, feelings, beliefs, and behavior, they are better able to think about what might be happening for another person, including their children. Some home visiting programs view increasing the reflective skills of caregivers as a way to improve child development and behavior. Often, a caregiver who has the ability to think about their own experience just needs a little help to apply that skill to their baby's experience. For these caregivers, home visitors can help by supporting them to notice and more accurately recognize the child's experience and needs. Use of comments and questions that draw the caregiver's attention to the baby may be enough.

See Table 2.1 for some examples of the reflective functioning continuum. Some caregivers with underdeveloped reflective skills might benefit from personal therapy to improve recognition of their own internal states and ability to connect these internal states to behaviors. However, even families with high needs and caregivers with significant risk factors may benefit from non-mental-health providers who adopt methods to support the development of reflective skills (Slade, 2005).

Providers can draw on their own reflective skills to respond to families in ways that support emotion and behavior regulation. To work with caregivers in this way, the home visitor is encouraged to make an effort to

Table 2.1. Reflective functioning continuum examples

Little reflective functioning	Some reflective functioning	Skilled reflective functioning
"Susie just turns off that TV to make me mad!"	"When Susie goes to the TV to turn it off, she looks at me first and grins."	"I noticed Susie turned off the TV to get my attention. She wants me to read a book with her."
"Jose is mean to other kids. He hits them hard."	"Jose hits other kids when he doesn't get his way or to get what he wants."	"Jose seems to use hitting as a form of communicating, but the other kids don't understand him. When I see him getting ready to hit, I ask him what he is feeling and if he needs help."

Source: Slade (2007).

recognize the caregiver's general level of reflective skill. This does not mean that the home visitor will be doing psychotherapy. Rather, the home visitor can informally gauge how often the caregiver shows reflective behaviors, such as recognizing feelings and other internal states in others, demonstrating an understanding of the links between their own mental states and behavior, and, especially, taking an interest in and trying to act in accordance with their child's experiences.

Getting a handle on the caregiver's general skill level can help the home visitor zone in on the best port of entry for a caregiver, select interventions that are most effective, and avoid beginning at a level that a caregiver cannot understand or tolerate (Slade, 2005; 2007). For example, Mary is a home visitor who assumes that all the caregivers she serves have high levels of reflective skills and are able to easily consider their babies' feelings and needs. She prides herself on putting the needs of babies ahead of those of adults. Some of Mary's families do well with this approach, but others struggle. One grandparent caregiver, Melissa, finds Mary's talk about babies' emotional needs confusing. Melissa thinks Mary is making things too complicated; she doesn't believe that babies need much more than regular feedings and dry diapers. Another caregiver, Marcus, starts feeling uncomfortable when Mary talks about what is happening inside his baby. It feels like too much to have to think about! Eventually, Mary may find that caregivers like Melissa and Marcus become disengaged or even drop out of the program because they are not relating to Mary's methods (Barak et al., 2014). If Mary can more accurately assess Melissa's and Marcus's abilities to be reflective and modify her ways of supporting them, everyone may experience increased success and satisfaction. In fact, by better understanding their abilities to be reflective and starting where they are, there is greater opportunity for Mary to help Melissa and Marcus increase their reflective capacities, which may ultimately enhance their caregiving skills. Box 2.1 summarizes the points

---

Box 2.1. Caregiver Reflective Functioning Capacity

- Recognize the caregiver level of reflective functioning.
- Work from that level.
- Model or demonstrate reflective skills.
- Make comments or ask questions that encourage caregivers to wonder about the child's experiences.
- Make good use of feelings that happen in a real-life situation.
- Demonstrate in concrete ways that the provider is holding the caregiver in mind.

Source: Slade (2007).

a home visitor might consider when thinking about a caregiver's reflective functioning capacity.

We have discussed how the home visitor can model a supportive relationship by attending to the caregiver's experience first and gradually shifting to supporting the caregiver to attend to the baby's experience. Frequent statements that connect feelings and other mental states with behaviors are helpful (Slade, 2005). For example, the home visitor could say, "She's reaching for your phone. I wonder if she wants to see what you are doing." When a caregiver has little or very limited reflective skill, the home visitor can often help by modeling or demonstrating reflective behaviors. This can include statements that describe one's own inner states or a statement that shows interest in the caregiver's inner state. For example, the home visitor might say, "So the baby is not sleeping well. You must be so tired."

The beginning levels of reflective skill may include some recognition that internal states (i.e., thoughts, feelings, attitudes) are connected to behavior. Often, however, the person still needs help to accurately recognize their own or others' internal state. Home visitors could capitalize on feelings as they occur normally in the course of family life to build caregiver skills. Many routine caregiving activities could lead to negative feelings, such as anger or frustration. Many caregivers are able to manage those feelings and may even be able to use coping strategies such as humor to attenuate them. For example, virtually every caregiver has had the experience of changing a baby only to have the baby immediately need changing again; and sometimes the caregiver then needs changing as well! A caregiver with well-developed reflective skills is likely to take this in stride, recognizing that it is the sort of thing that a baby cannot help and viewing it as a minor nuisance. In contrast, those with less developed reflective skills might view this as the baby doing something on purpose to upset them. A caregiver with a low level of awareness of their own inner state might handle the baby roughly without recognizing their own feelings of frustration. A home visitor could name the caregiver's possible feelings, help set them into context as normal, and support them to cope. In this example, the home visitor could say, "Oh dear, after you just got her cleaned up, she spit up on the new outfit! That can be so frustrating." Statements like these not only support reflection but may also lead to a deeper conversation between the caregiver and home visitor. At times, these discussions can illuminate important differences between the experiences and perspectives of the caregiver and the home visitor that affect the meaning of the situation and that require attention. For example, for some families a baby needing more diapers than expected or having to do extra laundry might be a minor hassle. But for other families, using more diapers than expected could be a financial concern; similarly, having to go to the laundromat an extra time might add a significant time or expense burden. Showing empathy and concern for the caregiver's experience may open space to have these types of discussions leading to greater understanding.

WHAT'S NEXT?

In Chapter 3, we describe the PAUSE approach, which uses both relationship-based practice and other reflective methods to build a foundation of skills that can be used to address the common difficult challenges in home visiting and other early intervention work with families with very young children.

TIPS FOR PRACTICE

- Learn to pay attention to inner experiences such as beliefs, attitudes, and emotions—the baby's, the caregiver's, and your own.

- When you feel strong emotions, such as anger or worry, give yourself time, slow down, and take a breath. Try to avoid pushing for a solution or forcing an action.

- Be an example of how to recognize and respond to emotions. Talk about your response to what a caregiver said and what you imagine the caregiver or baby might be experiencing.

KEY POINTS TO REMEMBER

- Reflective capacity or functioning is the ability to think about mental states or inner experiences in oneself and others, including one's children, and about how those mental states are connected to behaviors.

- Reflection is a mindfulness skill that allows one to pause, slow down, and consider situations from many angles before acting; integrate thinking and feeling in a way that is regulating; develop new insights and ideas; and evaluate actions once taken.

- Both reflective capacity or functioning and reflection can be developed and enhanced through supportive relationships and practice.

SUGGESTED FURTHER READING

Siegel, D., & Hartzell, M. (2014). *Parenting from the inside out: How a deeper self-understanding can help you raise children who thrive* (10th anniversary ed.). Penguin.

Slade, A., Sadler, L. S., Eaves, T., & Webb, D. L. (2023). *Enhancing attachment and reflective parenting in clinical practice: A Minding the Baby Approach.* Guildford.

3

PAUSE– A Problem-Solving Framework

Blending Relationship and Reflective Skills

Carmen arrives for a scheduled home visit with Charley, a 15-month-old girl with developmental delays and multiple medical issues connected to prematurity. Charley's mother, Frances, is near tears. She tells Carmen that Charley has been "cranky" and no one is getting any sleep. Furthermore, Charley is so irritable that she has started hitting her mother when she tries to do anything with her. On cue, Charley smacks Frances and they both burst into tears.

Working with families of young children is complex and can be messy. Every family and child is different, and methods that worked perfectly with one family may be ineffective or even an utter disaster with the next. Furthermore, every home visit, even with a family that one knows well, is different from the last. Many families struggle with serious issues, including poverty, domestic violence, and the serious health needs of their children. These challenges disproportionately affect minoritized groups, who also must contend with issues including racism or marginalization due to their identities related to language, religion, or sexual orientation (Luke, 2020; Walsh & Mortensen, 2020). These concerns can and may draw home visitors' attention away from what feels like our primary role or purpose with a family (Bernstein & Edwards, 2012). Situations like these can feel like distractions, but they are better recognized as realities in family life. Furthermore, acknowledging a sensitive topic, while uncomfortable, can be powerful and affirming, leading to fruitful discussions, and can help identify family strengths as well as struggles (Hardy, 2016; Walsh & Mortensen, 2020).

How do we stay focused on our work when families come with so many challenges? Although there are no "tried and true" recipes guaranteed to work in all situations, there are some ways of thinking and acting that set the stage for flexible partnering and effective problem solving. In the first two chapters, we have separately discussed the benefits of using relationship-based and reflective practice approaches when working with very young children and their families. Next, we discuss how these two methods can be integrated. In this chapter, we explain the PAUSE method to explore a way of thinking about work with families that is grounded in relationships and that encourages reflection on the part of both provider and parents. *PAUSE* is an acronym for a cycle of five steps: Perceive, Ask, Understand, Strategize, and Evaluate (see Figure 3.1). These steps can be used flexibly. Sometimes they may be implemented as a complete sequence or a cycle that repeats. Other times individual steps in the model may be selected to support reflective practice based on identified needs and situations.

As discussed in previous chapters, relationship-based practices and reflective skills complement each other and are critical to forming and maintaining all kinds of relationships. Reflective and relationship-based skills are also used in a specific type of professional development called *reflective supervision* (Watson, 2022; Watson et al., 2014). Use of reflective practice methods within a supportive supervisory relationship can help home visitors avoid getting lost in the weeds of complicated family life, increasing the home visitor's ability to stay focused on the real work of building the parent–child relationship (Bernstein & Edwards, 2012; Frosch et al., 2019; Harrison, 2016). This chapter discusses how to blend these approaches through

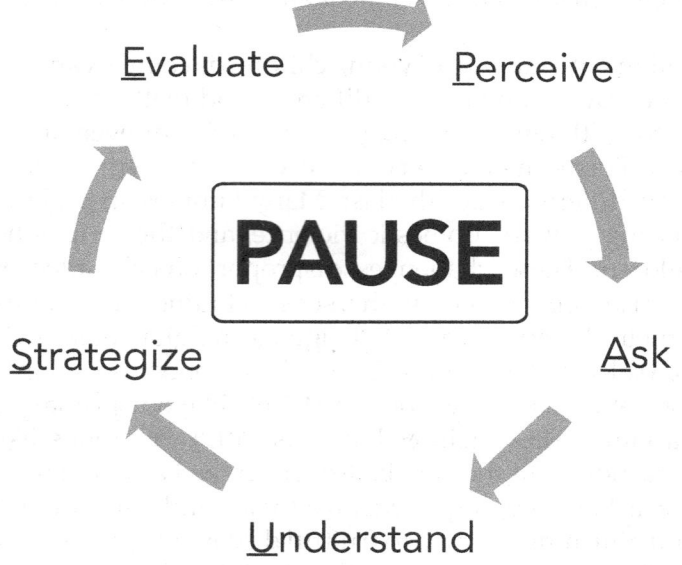

Figure 3.1. The PAUSE framework overview.

a process that providers can use to think together with families about their concerns. The process is a way to organize thinking about the behavior or issue, help providers respond appropriately and effectively, and use reflection to assess the experience. The five main components of the PAUSE process are as follows:

1. *Perceive:* observe and listen.
2. *Ask* questions to learn more about what is happening.
3. *Understand* each participant's experience or viewpoint.
4. *Strategize:* select and take actions.
5. *Evaluate* the outcomes using reflective processes.

The PAUSE Worksheet provides a way for the home visitor to document their thoughts about the child and family in order to work through challenging situations and discuss them with a supervisor. A blank copy of the PAUSE Worksheet can be found in Appendix 3A. This chapter and the following chapters include vignettes and sample completed PAUSE Worksheets. These materials illustrate how to use the PAUSE Worksheet to consider a variety of situations that home visitors may face. Providers can use the full sequence of steps or can select pieces that are relevant in a specific situation. Decisions about what parts of the PAUSE to use at different times may relate to many things. For example, when a relationship is new, the provider may be doing a lot of observing and listening as they get to know the child, caregiver, and overall family context. As the relationship develops and trust is built, caregivers may share more information, and providers may wish to ask more questions. It is also recognized that sessions with families can be very busy as providers connect with caregivers to implement a specific curriculum. There can be a real tension between having to complete agency or program expectations and meeting the family's significant needs. As such, it may not be possible or necessary to complete every step at every session with a family. Next, we will explore each of the PAUSE components in more detail.

PERCEIVE: OBSERVE AND LISTEN

Carmen can see that Frances is nearly overwhelmed with Charley's difficult behavior. She is aware that these issues have been happening for a while, and she has already formed some ideas about what might help. Carmen thinks how easy it would be to just take Charley herself and model how to do an age-appropriate time-out. After that, she could sit down with Frances and teach her how to implement a better sleep schedule.

The PAUSE process begins with learning more about the situation by observing, listening, and asking questions. As home visitors slow down and learn more, we may see that things are not as they appear at first. Observing and listening are not passive behaviors, and they are not as easy as they may seem. Giving full attention is a skill that takes practice and time to develop. Consider how the response "I'm fine" could sound in these two situations:

Situation 1: *Betty slightly trips when going upstairs to work. When her co-worker walking behind her asks if she is okay, Betty laughs and says, "I'm fine, it's just Monday."*

Situation 2: *Shallon comes home from work later than expected; she wasn't able to call because her phone died. As she apologizes for not being home to help get their children to bed, her wife, Kayla, interrupts her, saying, "I'm fine."*

Clearly, the person in the first situation actually seems to be just fine, but the person in the second scenario may not be. The appropriate response to each situation is likely to be very different. For example, in the first scenario, joining Betty in laughing about the situation would be acceptable. Laughing in the second situation, however, is most likely unwise. Listening includes attention to what is said and how it is said (Weatherston, 2000). Slowing down and listening with care also lets us notice and wonder about what is *not* said. For example, in some cases, the speaker may avoid a seemingly critical topic. The home visitor may be left to wonder about the absence of that topic from the conversation. Consider the following two examples:

Kara, a developmental specialist in an early intervention program, meets with a family for an evaluation. The other team members described their concerns for the child's "behavior," and the child's mother describes him as "anxious." Kara notices immediately that the child has very repetitive speech, makes brief eye contact, and walks on his toes. She knows these are characteristics of autism, but because that wasn't in her paperwork, she is not sure if she should mention this.

Beatrice arrives for a home visit with Juliette and her infant son, Alexander. She notices that Juliette has a cast and asks, "Are you okay?" Juliette says she is okay and begins to tell Beatrice a story about Alexander taking steps. Beatrice is concerned but does not feel comfortable pressing for more information.

Observation is a great partner to listening. Much can be learned by what is seen. For example, eye contact, facial expressions, and body language may add a good deal of information about the emotional state of the speaker. Incongruence between body language and words should prompt the observer to wonder. Consider how the home visitor might respond to this mother if she listened only to her words rather than attending to both the words and how they were said:

Katarina held her newborn baby, Heidi, loosely across her lap. The home visitor expressed excitement about seeing the baby for the first time and asked how Katarina was enjoying being a mother. Katarina looked away and sighed. After a long moment, she said, "It's pretty great, I guess."

ASK QUESTIONS TO LEARN MORE ABOUT WHAT IS HAPPENING

In addition to careful listening and observation, information gathering includes asking the right questions (Heffron & Murch, 2010). Different questions are useful at different times. It is often productive to begin with open questions that are conveyed in a simple and supportive manner. Once the provider has the big picture or a general direction, more specific questions can be asked to clarify the situation. It takes practice, but providers can learn to respond and ask questions that open up a discussion instead of narrowing it too soon. Examples of these types of questions or statements include those that express interest or concern, encourage the responder to think about their own or another's experiences, and include an offer to explore an issue together. Here are a few examples of responses that both acknowledge how a person might be feeling and invite more discussion:

I imagine that was difficult for you.

Wow, that must have been an amazing experience!

How is it for you when Jan has trouble sleeping?

I wonder what it was like for your daughter when your family moved.

Questions that start a discussion can be paired with more specific follow-up questions (Green & Palfrey, 2000). Using an answer as a springboard is a great way to continue to expand the conversation while encouraging the person to give additional information or to think about the issue in more detail. In addition, by repeating all or part of the conversational partner's comment, you can confirm understanding and demonstrate your interest:

I was a little confused about the therapy Clara is receiving. How often is that happening?

Could you tell me more about your work schedule?

You mentioned that you have been concerned about Jon's coughing. What things have been tried so far to help him?

I was thinking about how tired you said you feel. It made me wonder if you had been to see your doctor.

Questions that curtail discussion should be used sparingly or avoided (Heffron & Murch, 2010; Sattler, 1998). Often, these types of questions are not really questions at all! For example, a forced-choice question limits the answers that a person can give. The options offered may not be an answer the parent wants to give. Questions that can be answered with "yes" or "no" can be useful for gathering specific information, but they may feel judgmental and leave out the opportunity for expanded information. Some statements can also shut off discussion or indicate that the provider has made an assumption that the family member may not feel comfortable correcting. Examples of questions or responses to avoid include the following:

Forced Choice

- Do you think the problem with Emmanuel's sleep is your work schedule or the bedtime routine?
- Are you using time-out or redirection for discipline?

Yes or No Questions

- Are you giving Abdul enough sleep time? (Compare: How has Abdul been sleeping?)
- Are you following the recommendations you got from the physical therapist (PT)? (Compare: What suggestions has the PT offered that you think could help?)

Presumptive Statements

- I am sure that you are getting Cassidy's shots on schedule.
- No one is playing violent video games when the children are around, right?

UNDERSTAND EACH PARTICIPANT'S EXPERIENCE OR VIEWPOINT

We have emphasized the importance of relationships as a core underpinning of work with families. In order for relationships to function smoothly, each person's experience or perspective should be considered. It is important to recognize that the caregiver, the baby, and the home visitor may each view the situation in a different way. Therefore, one responsibility of a provider taking this approach is to monitor and ensure that all voices are represented (Pawl, 2000), including the baby, the caregivers, and the provider him- or herself. The home visitor should encourage the caregiver to tell the story from their perspective, gently prompt attention to the baby's experience, and share their own observations with care. The skills reviewed earlier, including observing, listening, and asking helpful questions, can be applied to the quest to learn about the perspectives of all the participants, including the babies. Spending this time gathering information assists the home visitor to better understand not only the situation at hand, but also how that situation is being received or experienced by each participant. This additional information, in turn, leads to a decision about the most effective port of entry, or the best starting point, for intervention at that moment. In the following examples, we briefly consider each participant.

Home Visitor: Thinking about one's own perspective may seem redundant or even out of place in this discussion. However, because each of us brings our own biases, beliefs, attitudes, and preferences to every situation, it is necessary to consider the provider's perspective along with those of family members. The home visitor should recognize that their own past experiences and perspectives affect each new experience, what is seen and heard, how the behaviors of others are interpreted, and what choices are made about how to respond. It is not possible or even desirable to have no personal history or to never have opinions! It is possible and highly desirable to recognize that you have your own set of attitudes or beliefs and to attend to their effect on your work with families (Heffron et al., 2005).

Caregiver: A central facet of home visiting work is attending to the caregiver's needs as a way of developing their skills (Bernstein & Edwards, 2012; Watson et al., 2014). Even when the focus of the home visit is the baby's safety or development, gaining the caregiver's buy-in is needed; therefore, a good deal of home visiting involves forming a relationship with caregivers that opens the door to change (Roggman et al., 2016; Slade et al., 2023; Weatherston, 2005). For example, the home visitor might be tasked with instructing caregivers about child development or how to implement a specific therapy technique, or with supporting the caregivers to complete tasks required by the courts. In order for the home visitor to implement this part of the work effectively, he or she must understand young adult learning and be able to read and respond to the caregiver's reactions to their suggestions and efforts (Walsh & Mortensen, 2020). These efforts on the part of the provider lead to "synchrony" in the caregiver and home visitor relationship, which in turn is connected to caregiver feelings of competence and increased responsiveness to the child (Popp & Wilcox, 2012; Steele et al., 2015).

Baby: Although all three parties are important, it may be most critical to avoid losing sight of the baby's experience. Because babies are unable to speak for themselves, their voices can easily be ignored or drowned out by the needs of adults. Therefore, remembering to ask "what about the baby?" (Watson, 2022; Weatherston, 2001, 2005; Weatherston & Ribaudo, 2020) is an important responsibility of the home visitor and a critical part of making real progress with families. The provider's ability to keep the baby in mind will help in many ways, both directly and indirectly. Babies are helped directly when their needs are seen and attended to. Babies are helped indirectly when the home visitor provides a good model for the caregiver of how to consider the infant's experience.

Poised to gather up Charley and demonstrate a time-out, Carmen suddenly stops. Trusting her observations, she realizes that this might not be a good time for teaching, given that both mother and daughter are tired and upset. Furthermore, as Carmen reflects that Frances identified lack of sleep as a primary problem, she questions her initial impulse to solve the problem with a behavior technique. Instead of springing into action, Carmen starts with sympathy and a demonstration that she is listening, saying, "You poor guys! What a hard time you are both having. What can I do to help?"

Later in the visit, when both Frances and Charley are calmer, Carmen is able to ask a few questions. She discovers that Frances has recently increased her work hours, resulting in a corresponding increase in the amount of time that Charley spends in child care. Carmen wonders if this change is the source of both Charley's difficult behavior and Frances's weariness. At the same time, Carmen knows this is a resilient family, so she is confident that they will adjust in time. When Frances admits that she is tired, Carmen says, "I wonder if Charley is a little tired too." Frances snuggles Charley close and says, "I guess we both need a little more time to adjust to the new schedule." Carmen has been successful in two ways: supporting Frances and Charley directly and helping Frances consider Charley's experience. These two interventions may be enough to help this family in this moment.

STRATEGIZE: SELECT AND TAKE ACTIONS

In the first three steps of the PAUSE method, you will gather information that increases your understanding of the situation or problem. As part of this understanding, you will consider multiple perspectives. As you observe, listen, and ask questions in dialogue with the caregiver, a variety of possible action steps will emerge. Together with the caregiver, you will choose some steps to try. As you and the caregiver negotiate the next steps, consider together what results would be satisfactory. As we revisit Carmen's work with Frances and Charley, we see the PAUSE steps can occur across more than one session, and steps can be used more than once.

Carmen returns to the home of Frances and Charley a week later. Frances is noticeably less tired as she opens the door to welcome Carmen. As they settle into the visit, Carmen says, "Last week you and Charley both seemed pretty frazzled. You look much more rested today. And Charley seems better too!" Frances smiles and offers Charley a toy. She says, "We are doing better. But Charley is not sleeping at the new child care. I've been waiting for our visit to ask you about it." Although Carmen had some ideas about how to help with Charley's sleep, she chooses to be content with listening before moving into strategizing. "I'd like to hear what you see happening and what you would like to change. That should get us in a good place to think about what would make things better," Carmen says. As the discussion continues, Carmen learns that Charley's new child care is very different from the one at her old location and has a different schedule. They identify some ways to help Charley sleep, decide that Frances will share these ideas with the provider, and plan to discuss how it went at the next visit. As Carmen prepares to leave, Frances says, "Thanks for helping me with this today. I feel like it will really work!"

Now let's explore the PAUSE Worksheet, which you can use to pull together thoughts, feelings, and actions as you reflect on interactions (Appendix 3A). The PAUSE Worksheet is intended to allow the home visitor to organize the information that has been gathered and to capture what is happening from both the caregiver and the home visitor perspective. In the first section of the worksheet, the home visitor reflects on the caregiver's question or issue and considers how both the caregiver and the home visitor him- or herself view the identified concern. Next, the home visitor is encouraged to clarify what is happening. In this second section, the home visitor reflects on questions he or she could ask to gather more information. In the third section, the home visitor considers possible reasons why the behavior or situation is occurring, again from the caregiver's and home visitor's perspectives, but also from the child's perspective. This encourages the home visitor to reflect on all of the potential relationship dynamics we have discussed. Finally, the home visitor is encouraged to identify some possible responses or solutions with criteria to evaluate progress and success.

A second form, the Provider Reflection Worksheet (Appendix 3B), is intended for use in reflection on action or after the interaction with the family is complete. The goal of this set of questions is to help the home visitor consider actions to improve skills as well as to identify potential issues to discuss in reflective supervision. This is a key part of the process, as the home visitor will gain great insights, both from the self-reflection component of completing this process and from a discussion of it with a supervisor, consultant, or mentor.

Consider how Carmen could use the PAUSE Worksheet format to capture her experience with Charley and her mother, Frances. For example, as Carmen later uses this information in reflective supervision, she may notice her own reactions and her urges to "fix" the problem. She may also note any changes in the behaviors of Frances and Charley when she was more reflective and patient, compared to when she was acting more directively. This information can help Carmen to have a better understanding of the needs that Frances and Charley each present. Carmen would be able to use the PAUSE worksheet to document any plans that she and Frances co-create to address the issues as they have identified them. Similarly, the worksheet can help Carmen and Frances discuss the effectiveness of the strategies they tried. How might you use this worksheet and process in your work with children and families? A sample completed PAUSE Worksheet that illustrates Carmen's experience with this family can be found in Figure 3.2.

EVALUATE THE OUTCOMES USING REFLECTIVE PROCESSES

Because family life is often complex and sometimes stressful, it is not unusual for workers who support families to feel the stress themselves. Reflecting on the choices made in the work provides a way for the home visitor to gain support, evaluate efforts, and engage in continuous learning and growth.

APPENDIX 3A　　　　　　　　　　　　　　　　　　　　　　　　　(page 1 of 2)

PAUSE WORKSHEET　　　　　　　　　　　pause

Child: **Charley**　　　　　　　　　　　　　　　　Date: **1/20/24**

Caregiver: **Frances**　　　　　　　Provider: **Carmen**

PERCEIVE—Explore what is happening.

Caregiver perspective:	Provider perspective:
Charley is misbehaving/hitting. Frances is frustrated with Charley's behavior. No one is getting sleep.	Charley is tired, probably overtired. Frances is struggling with what action to take. Maybe a time-out is needed? Develop a sleep schedule?

ASK—Clarify what is happening.

Starting with the caregiver's priorities and concerns, ask more detailed/specific questions to clarify what is happening.

Ask Frances about changes in family's routine.
Ask when behavior changed and what was happening with Charley.
What strategies have been tried to help the family get more sleep?

UNDERSTAND—Explore why it is happening.

With the caregiver, explore explanations for what is happening. Consider possible explanations that include the environment, the child, and the caregiver. Listen and observe closely as you explore the situation in conversation with the family.

Caregiver perspective:	Provider perspective:	Child's perspective:
Frances changed her work schedule to include more hours. Charley is in child care longer hours each day.	I want to support this mom to deal with Charley's behavior. My first instinct is to take over and model a time-out. When I step back a	Charley is likely adjusting to a new schedule. Her sleep patterns have been disrupted. She is trying to tell her mom this through her behavior.

(continued)

Figure 3.2.　Carmen's PAUSE Worksheet for Charley and Frances.

Figure 3.2. *(continued)*

APPENDIX 3A **PAUSE WORKSHEET** *(continued)*

UNDERSTAND *(continued)*		
Caregiver perspective:	Provider perspective:	Child's perspective:
Frances feels frustrated at not having as much time with Charley and certainly does not like this behavior.	moment, I wonder what might be behind this new behavior and ask some questions. Maybe this mom's change in schedule is more disruptive than I realized and they need some time to adjust.	Since she can't say, "I'm tired and I miss you at the end of a long day," she instead is irritable and sometimes hits. She wants some mommy time and to rest.

STRATEGIZE and **EVALUATE**—Identify possible responses/solutions.

1. Solution/action to try:	How will we know if it works?
Hold off on giving problem solving/giving advice. Instead, respond to the caregiver's emotion about the situation.	Frances may seem calm or report feeling less frustrated. Frances may be more attentive to Charley. Charley's behavior will improve.
	When will we evaluate if it works?
	Monitor Frances' attentiveness and Charley's behaviors during the next session.
2. Solution/action to try:	How will we know if it works?
Acknowledge the change in the family schedule and suggest everyone needs some time to adjust. If the situation does not improve, suggest exploring a sleep schedule to help everyone get better rest.	A family report of improved sleep will indicate success.
	When will we evaluate if it works?
	We'll evaluate this at each session.

Being able to step back and reflect on the work is valuable, whether done on one's own or, preferably, within a supervision or consulting relationship. Therefore, part of taking action is reflecting back on that action in an evaluative way. In the vignettes, Carmen provided support and empathy to Frances and Charley. She was later able to successfully direct Frances's attention to Charley's experience of an increase in time away from her while in child care. Figure 3.3 presents a sample Provider Reflection Worksheet related to Carmen's work with the family.

However, things could have gone differently. Imagine the following variation in the vignette:

Frances responds to Carmen's question about her new work schedule by snapping, "It's fine. I have to do it." Undeterred, Carmen pursues her concern for the child by asking, "I wonder how it's been for Charley to be at child care longer hours?" Frances, now clearly irritated, replies, "Well, we are both stuck, aren't we?" The visit ends shortly after this exchange.

In this version, Carmen missed Frances's tone and pursued her own agenda of highlighting Charley's experience. Later, Carmen may reflect and wonder about the shift that happened during the session. She may note that the sympathy and empathy offered at the beginning were more effective, and she may consider if she could have jumped too quickly from that strategy, resulting in an ineffective and unsatisfying end to the session. She may plan to stay longer with Frances's perspective next time.

So far, we have discussed how a provider can form an initial or on-the-spot response and then evaluate the effectiveness of that effort in reflection later. Sometimes that simple strategy will be enough to resolve the issue. In some cases, the provider may realize that a longer-term solution is needed to resolve the problem. This could mean many things, ranging from helping the family to obtain additional concrete resources to identifying others who can help. In the vignettes, Carmen's strategy of supporting Frances to consider Charley's perspective may be enough. Other simple solutions could include problem solving with Frances to identify someone who can watch Charley while she gets some rest or checking with the child care provider to look for solutions to improve Charley's adjustment.

Considering the scenario with Carmen and all the possible variations, it seems clear that home visitors will benefit from taking time to wonder and reflect about what might be happening with a family. Regardless of practitioners' best intentions and efforts, we will encounter some situations or events that are beyond our scope of practice. Part of our reflection may need to include reframing our understanding of the child, family, or situation. In the vignette, Carmen knows that Frances has increased her work hours and assumes that this was Frances's choice. However, suppose that she does not know that Frances needed more income because her partner,

APPENDIX 3B

PROVIDER REFLECTION WORKSHEET

Provider Reflection Worksheet

Child: _Charley_   Date: _January 20, 2024_

Caregiver: _Frances_   Provider: _Carmen_

1. How did I follow the caregiver's lead to learn what is most pressing or important to them?	I wanted to step in and take over, but I could see it was hard for Frances. I'm glad I was able to pause in the moment and better understand that her main concern was getting back to "normal" and getting some much-needed rest.
2. How did I ask clarifying questions that help me to understand the problem better? How did I inquire about the caregiver's values and beliefs related to the issue?	I did not ask clarifying questions. I only asked how I could help. I wonder what questions I could have asked to learn more.
3. How did I reflect on and offer to discuss similarities and differences between me and the caregiver? These might include race, ethnicity, language, gender, sexual orientation, religious and other beliefs, values, experiences, etc.	I realize I grew up in a household where my parents were employed at the same jobs throughout my childhood. I don't know what it's like to be a single parent trying to make enough money to support my family. I wonder how I can connect to her experience and be supportive without seeming judgmental. I need some help with this.

(continued)

Figure 3.3. Carmen's Provider Reflection Worksheet for Charley and Frances.

Figure 3.3. *(continued)*

APPENDIX 3B **PROVIDER REFLECTION WORKSHEET** *(continued)*

4.	How did I provide information that may help the caregiver better understand the child's behavior?	When we were able to see that the change in the family schedule might be impacting everyone, I was able to offer some ideas and we came up with a plan that might give them some time to adjust. We wondered if Charley's behavior might be a reflection of the stress the family is experiencing.
5.	How did I engage the caregiver to develop a response that may include a strategy to try, a resource to use, or more information to increase understanding?	I decided to wait to offer strategies about sleep schedules or behavior management, in order to see whether, with a little time, they might adjust to the new schedule.
6.	How did I provide support and emotional containment if needed?	I think my action to acknowledge how hard this is helped Frances to see that the issue was about being tired and not something more serious. I noticed that they both snuggled together a bit when Frances calmed down.
7.	How do I plan to follow up on promised actions to maintain trust?	I will explore some sleep schedule resources in case they are still struggling, and I have some behavior management techniques in mind if needed.
8.	What do I want to discuss in reflective supervision to improve my practice and outcomes with this child and caregiver?	I am curious why I was so quick to want to just take control and model a time out instead of really listening to this mother. How can I slow myself down in these situations?

Thomas, has left her and Charley and the family are on the verge of being evicted. If she had this additional information, Carmen might have a very different perspective and response. The questions she asks, the information she needs to gather, and other helpers and resources that may be needed may change dramatically. Furthermore, the home visitor might have reactions or responses to what is learned when working with families. As we will discuss, these personal responses are worth recognizing and reflecting on as they can either advance or hinder the work that must be done.

COMMON CHALLENGING ISSUES

Next, we address a few of the more common but challenging issues that home visitors might encounter with families and we provide some suggestions for helpful responses. In all of the scenarios presented so far, the home visitor and the family have a relationship that includes willingness to engage and work together. However, within any relationship, ruptures can occur, and there will be times when things do not go smoothly. For example, there may be times when a caregiver does not respond or seems unwilling to participate in the dialogue. The range of explanations is virtually infinite but might include the possibility that it's too soon in the relationship for the discussion, the caregiver is preoccupied with something else, or the caregiver does not think the home visitor will be able to help. No matter the reason, resist the urge to keep pushing your perspective! Stay patient, remain available but not intrusive, and continue to build the relationship (Beeber & Canuso, 2012).

Other times, the home visitor may find that their sympathetic ear has unleashed a torrent of emotions or words. Although a caregiver may benefit from venting emotions, the home visitor may find this reaction to be overwhelming and may worry that it is unproductive. It would be understandable for the home visitor to try to set limits, including ignoring the emotional flood and trying to turn the conversation to a more concrete level. However, setting a limit alone is unlikely to have the desired response. If this is an infrequent occurrence, it may be fine to allow the venting to proceed. However, if the emotional flood continues, the home visitor may need to address it directly. Ask the caregiver if it would be okay to step back and revisit the home visitor's role and function with the family. Directly discuss the caregiver's apparent need to vent emotions and ask who else is able to provide this role and support. Help the caregiver to seek out and access appropriate supports as needed.

Another common problem for home visitors is a caregiver who does not follow through with any plan that has been made. Sometimes this is obvious from the beginning, as the caregiver greets every suggestion with "yes, but" or informs the provider that their ideas will not work. Other caregivers may appear to agree with all suggestions but never actually try them. Again, the issue may be timing, so trying again at a later time, when the caregiver is ready, may work. At times, a direct approach may be effective.

The home visitor can identify what he or she observes and ask the caregiver to talk about what is happening. Presenting the issue as something to be discussed and better understood can prevent the caregiver from feeling that they are being accused. Instead, the home visitor conveys the sense of interest and collaborative problem solving.

We have discussed the importance of trying to understand how the family sees various issues or concerns. Understanding a caregiver's perspective is useful because it informs strategies that may be helpful. Also, from a parallel process perspective, the provider's efforts to understand the caregiver's experience are likely to help the caregiver's ability to take their child's perspective. There are likely to be times when it is extremely difficult to come to a shared understanding of the situation, however. Some caregivers may have very strong beliefs about children in general or about a specific child. Acknowledging the difference of opinion and asking the caregiver to share more about their views can be useful and set the stage for gently challenging the caregiver's view. By asking the caregiver to explain their views and ideas, the home visitor can better understand the source of the beliefs and then carefully offer to share other perspectives. Helping the caregiver to name their own beliefs and begin to understand how they connect to behavior is an important reflective skill that allows perspective taking. Consider how Bob, a physical therapist, uses this strategy in a home visit.

Bob, a physical therapist in an early intervention home program, is completing paperwork at the end of a session with Tom and his daughter, Cristy. Suddenly, Cristy pulls over a large plant, spilling dirt everywhere. Tom begins shouting, grabs Cristy, and threatens to spank her. Bob is aware that Tom believes in spanking, but he has never witnessed him doing it and they have never spoken about it in detail. Bob freezes and considers his options: gather his things quickly and leave or address what is happening. Tom, noticing Bob's expression, says, "I know you all think I should not spank her. But just look what she does!" Bob answers carefully, "I see this is a big mess and that you are pretty upset. And it's true I am not in favor of spanking. But I would be willing to hear how you think spanking would help."

There is a long pause. Finally, Tom says, "My dad spanked me and I turned out just fine. I want Cristy to learn that there are some things that aren't allowed, like making a big mess." Bob says, "Yes, I agree that kids need some limits and they need parents to teach them what they should and should not do. I wonder what Cristy learns from spankings?"

In this example, the PT showed respect by asking to learn more about the father's beliefs and parenting practices. This strategy provided an opportunity for the father to think about his ideas about parenting and created a chance for dialogue. The next steps in this discussion could include talking about what Cristy might have been trying to do with the plant and what other ways there could be to teach her not to make a mess.

When working with any family, reflection may be most effective when the overall family context is considered (Bronfenbrenner, 2005; Walsh & Mortensen, 2020). Both strengths and needs are aspects of context to be considered. Home visitors should make intentional efforts to learn about and be able to consider the family's cultural identities within this lens of strengths and needs (Walsh & Mortensen, 2020). At times, a home visitor may learn that program information does not fit within a given family's cultural context. In the previous example, Bob's stance against spanking could be just unfamiliar to Tom or could be highly culturally incongruent for him. Perhaps Tom's views about spanking relate to his religious practices, for example. For some families, certain disciplinary practices are deemed necessary to prepare a child for expected experiences of discrimination or prejudice to come (Blanchard et al., 2019). Taking the time to intentionally wonder about the role of these sources of caregiver beliefs, attitudes, and practices can lead to dialogue and greater understanding, even when caregivers do not choose to change their practices.

REFLECTING ON REFLECTION

When faced with a family that is struggling, a provider may often feel a "press" (pressure) to offer a solution or fix the problem quickly (Heffron et al., 2005). It is hard to maintain the discipline needed to think broadly when the situation seems to call for action. Although it may not be appropriate or possible to solve every problem or alleviate every difficult situation, we often can provide some relief through listening, offering empathy, or asking a question that opens up discussion.

In Chapter 2, we discussed a variety of concepts related to reflective practice. Using reflection in our partnerships with young children and families sounds simple, but it takes a good deal of practice to be able to apply these skills in the moment. Performing skills such as observing, listening, and asking questions also takes time; it can be hard to remain patient and refrain from taking what may feel like needed steps to solve a problem. This may be especially likely for early childhood professionals who are often action-oriented people: those who are more comfortable with doing than talking about doing. We may feel proud of our ability to "get 'er done" or we may have been praised for a "take-charge" attitude. Caregivers, used to professionals working from other frameworks, may seem to want us to take over. At other times, a situation may seem so concerning that the home visitor feels strong internal pressure to take action based on their perception of the family's needs or their own need to resolve a situation that feels intolerable (Heffron et al., 2005). This "press," though normal to feel, can be extremely hard to resist!

Although there are times when being able to solve problems and "just do it" is called for, there are many other times when a different approach may be more effective in the long run. One important outcome of taking time to slow down and deepen our thinking is that it may prevent us from jumping to conclusions that may lead to actions that don't help and may hurt. When we take a wondering stance, we allow for many possible explanations for what is happening and we allow time for many possibilities to emerge. We can consider these multiple alternatives, feeling free to suspend judgment until more information has been gathered. As Jeree Pawl once said, "Don't just do something, stand there and pay attention!" (Pawl & St. Johns, 1998, p. 7). Because the action needed may be different than how it originally appeared, slowing down and asking questions can result in a more accurate picture, leading to better solutions.

In some situations, there is no action that is appropriate for the home visitor to take, regardless of how much information is collected. Perhaps the appropriate action may be to seek help from professionals other than the home visitor, such as a mental health or child welfare worker. At other times, instead of taking direct action or enlisting action from others, the home visitor may be most helpful when providing support for the caregiver to explore and understand the situation him- or herself. Sensitive supports such as this allow caregivers to develop better problem-solving skills of their own that they can use when the home visitor is not there. This support may or may not lead to a decision or action by the caregiver. Finally, it is important to recognize that in some situations there is no adequate solution; it may be that accepting the situation "as is" is really all that can be done. Examples might include sudden tragic situations such as the loss of a family member or chronic problems such as living in extreme poverty. In all of these situations, the message is that the most appropriate step is to better understand the issue before considering any action.

WHAT'S NEXT?

Next, it is time to translate the relationship-based and reflective skills we have reviewed into practice. We will begin by thinking about behavior challenges and how to gather information to help us partner with families to address these concerns. Then we will explore some common issues home visitors encounter in their daily work in the following several chapters. These chapters are intended to serve as reference material for you when you are discussing similar problems with families. The chapters will not give you simple answers for every family, but they will provide context for starting the conversation and problem-solving process.

TIPS FOR PRACTICE

- Be prepared for sessions as planned, and be open and flexible for unexpected changes to the plan.

- Remember to PAUSE—slow down, wonder, and consider multiple perspectives—before taking any action steps.

- At times, an action is not necessary. Simply sitting with a caregiver, hearing their concerns, and connecting to emotions may be best. This strategy can help a parent calm down and allow him or her to have better thinking, leading to the chance that a solution might emerge.

KEY POINTS TO REMEMBER

- Combining relationship-based and reflective practice strategies—including observing, listening, and asking questions—can result in better understanding of situations in home visiting work and thus lead to more effective responses.
- It is important to consider the perspective of all participants (i.e., child, caregiver, and home visitor) when working to understand what may be happening and what will be helpful.
- Recognition of role boundaries is necessary. There may be times when the home visitor should not take action or responsibility; rather, the home visitor would be most helpful when supporting the caregiver to reflect or by encouraging the caregiver to seek help from others.
- PAUSE stands for Perceive, Ask, Understand, Strategize, and Evaluate (see Figure 3.4).

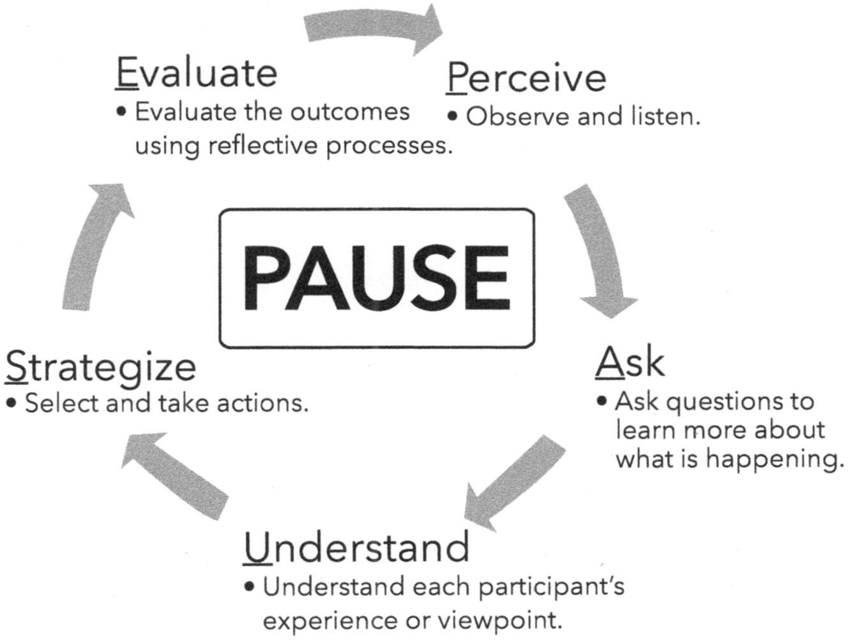

PAUSE

- **E**valuate
  - Evaluate the outcomes using reflective processes.
- **P**erceive
  - Observe and listen.
- **A**sk
  - Ask questions to learn more about what is happening.
- **U**nderstand
  - Understand each participant's experience or viewpoint.
- **S**trategize
  - Select and take actions.

Figure 3.4. The PAUSE framework in detail.

SUGGESTED FURTHER READINGS

Foley, G., & Hochman, J. (Eds.). (2006). *Mental health in early intervention: A unity of principles and practice.* Jossey-Bass.

Weatherson, D., & Tableman, B. (2015). *Infant mental health home visiting: Supporting competencies/reducing risks* (3rd ed.). Michigan Association for Infant Mental Health.

APPENDIX 3A (page 1 of 2)

PAUSE WORKSHEET

pause

Child: _____ Date: _____

Caregiver: _____ Provider: _____

PERCEIVE—Explore what is happening.

Caregiver perspective:	Provider perspective:

ASK—Clarify what is happening.

Starting with the caregiver's priorities and concerns, ask more detailed/specific questions to clarify what is happening.

UNDERSTAND—Explore why it is happening.

With the caregiver, explore explanations for what is happening. Consider possible explanations that include the environment, the child, and the caregiver. Listen and observe closely as you explore the situation in conversation with the family.

Caregiver perspective:	Provider perspective:	Child's perspective:

(continued)

Tackling the Tough Stuff: A Home Visitor's Guide to Supporting Families at Risk, Second Edition, by Angela M. Tomlin and Stephan A. Viehweg. Copyright © 2025 by Paul H. Brookes Publishing Co., Inc. All rights reserved.

APPENDIX 3A **PAUSE WORKSHEET** (continued)

UNDERSTAND (continued)

Caregiver perspective:	Provider perspective:	Child's perspective:

STRATEGIZE and **EVALUATE**—Identify possible responses/solutions.

1. Solution/action to try:	How will we know if it works? When will we evaluate if it works?
2. Solution/action to try:	How will we know if it works? When will we evaluate if it works?

APPENDIX 3B

PROVIDER REFLECTION WORKSHEET

Provider Reflection Worksheet

Child: _____ Date: _____

Caregiver: _____ Provider: _____

1. How did I follow the caregiver's lead to learn what is most pressing or important to them?	
2. How did I ask clarifying questions that help me to understand the problem better? How did I inquire about the caregiver's values and beliefs related to the issue?	
3. How did I reflect on and offer to discuss similarities and differences between me and the caregiver? These might include race, ethnicity, language, gender, sexual orientation, religious and other beliefs, values, experiences, etc.	

(continued)

APPENDIX 3B **PROVIDER REFLECTION WORKSHEET** (continued)

4. How did I provide information that may help the caregiver better understand the child's behavior?	
5. How did I engage the caregiver to develop a response that may include a strategy to try, a resource to use, or more information to increase understanding?	
6. How did I provide support and emotional containment if needed?	
7. How do I plan to follow up on promised actions to maintain trust?	
8. What do I want to discuss in reflective supervision to improve my practice and outcomes with this child and caregiver?	

4

What's Going On in There?

Understanding Causes of Behavior

"Problem behavior" can be counted as one of the primary reasons for which caregivers seek help from any kind of professional because virtually every young child displays challenging behavior at some point. However, the fact that it is a common problem is not likely to be comforting for caregivers, who often just want to know how to stop hard-to-manage behavior. Furthermore, many of the caregivers with whom home visitors work have trouble tolerating even "normal" challenging behaviors, often due to their own vulnerabilities. Primary caregivers are not alone in wanting to eliminate challenging behaviors, such as aggression or noncompliance, however. The home visitor, child-care provider, or other adult working with a family may also have concerns about specific behaviors and may feel highly motivated to reduce or eliminate them. All in all, when challenging behavior is present, the "press" that we discussed in Chapter 3 can seem relentless (Heffron et al., 2005).

Behavioral health or social-emotional issues are now recognized as among the most frequent conditions that cause functional impairment in children (AAP Council on Early Childhood, 2016; Slomski, 2012). The problems are so prevalent that the American Academy of Pediatrics released guidelines in 2015 for routine screening for childhood behavior and emotional concerns, and the following year issued guidelines for addressing social-emotional and behavioral concerns (AAP Council, 2016; Weitzman & Wegner, 2015). Furthermore, there is increasing evidence that early occurring behavior and emotional issues can linger into later childhood and even adulthood (Zhang et al., 2023).

Because they work closely with families, home visitors also commonly observe challenging behaviors directly, either in person or through virtual means. They may hear concerns from all types of caregivers about behavior and social-emotional issues, and so they want to be able to address them. Situations that challenge families are varied, and there are no "one-size-fits-all" solutions to difficult behaviors. For some problems, limited immediate support can be all that is needed to help the family cope. In other cases, a long-term solution may require a good deal more work and, at times, the involvement of other people or systems.

In the previous chapters, we considered the work of a home visitor from a perspective that combines relationship-based and reflective practice strategies in order to gather information, gain a better sense of the concerns, recognize possible cultural factors, and begin to consider the perspective of all participants. In this chapter, we weave in a third piece: knowledge about what leads to and maintains, and what reduces, challenging behaviors. Taken together, relationship, reflective practice skills, and knowledge of behavior form a strong foundation that allows providers to respond effectively to the needs of families with very young children. The reflective stance and questioning methods discussed in Chapters 1 through 3 will be helpful when applied to understanding behavior concerns that caregivers bring to the home visitor.

Let's consider an example. Miranda, 20 months old, often pinches and scratches her mother, Linda, when she tries to stop her from doing something. Linda and the developmental therapist, Jason, have discussed this problem several times in the last couple of months. When Linda brings up the problem again, Jason first considers making more suggestions. Instead, he chooses to slow things down and help Linda *evaluate* what they have been doing so far. Jason says, "I am sorry that this is still happening. I know we have talked about your concerns a few other times. Maybe we can step back and you can let me know what you have been doing." Linda agrees and reports that she has been using time-out. Jason has many questions about what time-out means to Linda. He wonders if Linda has tried other strategies that he has suggested, such as redirection or helping Miranda show frustration in other ways. He also wonders how Linda is implementing time-out, because he knows that in the past she would typically tell Miranda "time-out" but did not actually enforce it.

In this instance, Jason uses several parts of the PAUSE framework to help him make choices about how to proceed in his work with Linda and Miranda. He considers what he knows about Linda and Miranda and reviews their earlier discussions about behavior. Jason will ask questions and problem-solve with Linda as he learns more. Maybe Linda is not implementing a strategy correctly, or maybe she stopped using it before it could start to work. Maybe Miranda has gained some skills and the method is no longer appropriate. From this discussion, Jason and Linda may learn much that guides their next steps. They may retry something discussed in the past, rule out strategies that were ineffective or inappropriate, or develop and try some new ideas. At times, the discussion will need to continue, going deeper in order to achieve better understanding and generate a plan. For example, maybe Linda and Jason will discuss a new stressor that the family encountered and discover that Miranda was reacting to that event. In this case, behavior methods are likely to fall flat, and support to the caregiver might be more appropriate. In the next section, we present some additional frames that the home visitor and the family can use to consider the behaviors of young children from different angles.

SHIFT THE FRAME—THINK ABOUT THE BEHAVIOR DIFFERENTLY

One reflective strategy that can be applied to challenging behavior is to shift the frame, which means thinking about behavior in a different way. This is a key first step as caregiver expectations, beliefs, and perceptions about their child's behavior—many of which have their basis in the parent's culture, personal experiences of being parented, or experiences of marginalization connected to the parent's identity—affect their reactions and intervention decisions (Smith et al., 2020). Many reframes are possible, and understanding the basis of the caregiver's view about the behavior offers an important starting point. For instance, recent work adapting an evidence-based parent training method for culturally diverse families showed that personalizing the method to match caregiver beliefs about behavior resulted in positive changes in child behavior and caregiving practices (Yeh et al., 2022). Some of the more likely and useful reframes in early childhood include the following:

- Considering the behavior as a sign of something intrinsic to the child, such as developmental level or temperament style (e.g., separation problems in a child between 8 and 12 months old at the height of stranger anxiety)

- Recognizing the behavior as a form of communication (e.g., screaming in protest in a child who has not yet learned to use words)

- Identifying the behavior as a response to something in the environment that could be changed (e.g., running off when in large stores as a reaction to the wide spaces; Denno, Carr, & Bell, 2010; Helbig et al., 2019).

Each of these possibilities brings different ways of understanding the meaning of the behavior as well as potential responses on the part of adults. We discuss each of these frames briefly in the following subsections.

Behavior as a Sign of Development or Temperament Style

Knowledge of typical development is useful for helping caregivers have appropriate expectations for young children's behavior. At times, both caregivers and home visitors may need reminders to consider typical development as a source for difficult behavior. Caregivers may feel frustrated that a child "won't" do something, when the truth is that they are not yet able to perform the task independently. Providers who are working to help a child gain skills or meet outcomes can also sometimes lose sight of development as a source of challenging behaviors and should be careful to consider that factor in any planning. When working with a child who is struggling with a skill, for example, a home visitor might think about dropping back to earlier skills to allow the child to regroup and gain confidence. This strategy helps ensure that the child is ready for the skills that will be taught. From this stronger position, the home visitor, caregiver, and child can restart with more success.

Understanding typical development can also help caregivers and home visitors to anticipate challenging behavior that occurs as a result of a new developmental phase that a child has entered. While attainment of new developmental skills is a cause for celebration, the new skill may often result in challenging behavior. This is particularly the case when natural needs for independence arise or frustration results when the child wants to perform a skill that they are not developmentally able to perform. Typical examples include a young child insisting on feeding themselves, even though their fine motor skills are not quite sufficient, or the all-too-common "no" phase has set in. The possibility that a difficult behavior is actually a sign of developmental progress is especially important to consider when a behavior is new (Brazelton & Sparrow, 2006).

When using the frame of development as a driver for challenging behavior, keep in mind that the child's chronological and functioning ages may differ. This situation may often be the case for home visitors who are partnering with families whose young children have or are at risk for developmental delays due to prematurity or other reasons. For young children with delays, a challenging behavior may be out of step with chronological age but perfectly acceptable for the child's developmental age. Furthermore, providers must recognize that there may be some differences between provider and caregiver expectations about child behavior that relate to differences in culture or come from other sources (Lansford, 2022).

A second intrinsic child factor that may result in behavior viewed as difficult by adults is temperament (Denno et al., 2010; Smith et al., 2020; Yavuz-Muren et al., 2022). Although a full discussion of temperament is beyond the scope of this book, we discuss it briefly here and return to it in Chapters 5 through 8. Perspectives on temperament have changed a good deal since the Chess and Thomas (1996) approach familiar to many home visitors. In this pioneering model, temperament is understood as composed of a set of inborn traits that influence behavior and can be organized into three types: easy, difficult, and slow to warm. Current descriptions of temperament retain the idea that it is an inborn tendency but focus on the person's positive and negative emotional reactions along with how those reactions are regulated over time (Rothbart & Bates, 2006; Ursache et al., 2013; Yavuz-Muren et al., 2022). Research suggests that reactivity and regulation work together and that consistent caregiver support is required for babies to develop the ability to manage emotions and behavior in the long term (Ursache et al., 2013). This process, often termed *co-regulation*, occurs over time through repeated interactions between the caregiver and the child. Caregivers who are under stress or who have issues with their own regulation may have more difficulty performing co-regulation effectively (Doiron et al., 2022).

Temperament-related behaviors that most frequently challenge parents include those associated with negative emotions, in combination with tendencies to approach novelty that are too high (impulsivity) or too low (fearfulness). Specific examples of difficult behaviors that have been associated with various temperament styles include high activity, extreme persistence, and resisting changes and transitions. Furthermore, the temperament style or personality of the adult, caregiver, or home visitor may conflict with the style of the child; as can be expected, some fits between adult and child style are better than others. For example, some children with an active or "feisty" temperament may be perceived as very atypical when living with caregivers who are more "laid back," leading to more friction in the family. Other children who are very sensitive and have their feelings hurt easily and who live with caregivers who are risk takers and active might also experience some challenges. Some caregiving preferences for temperament characteristics may be connected to cultural expectations. Examples of differences are cultures that value independence versus those that prefer interdependence. Overall, it is helpful to consider the personality and temperament of both the child and caregiver, as well as preferences related to culture, when gathering information about reported behavior challenges. Some home visitors simply ask the caregiver(s) to share three words to describe the child and then three additional words to describe themselves to both gather information and to begin a discussion about how temperament and personality affect behavior and relationship. Another way to approach this discussion is to ask whether the child reminds the caregiver of someone or whether the child is like anyone in the family. This question can lead to dialogue about how the caregiver views and is affected by child's behavior.

Behavior as Communication

Behavior always has a meaning, purpose, or function. It is useful to realize that very young children have limited ways to communicate needs, feelings, or wishes. Therefore, instead of thinking about difficult behavior as something to get rid of, a more fruitful frame is wondering what the child gets from the behavior or what the behavior is communicating about the child's needs. Often, just figuring out the answer to that question makes the behavior more palatable, if not more understandable. Furthermore, knowing the purpose of the behavior will help later when you make plans to change it.

The communicative functioning of behavior is clearly recognized in very young babies, who use crying to communicate a variety of needs such as hunger, fatigue, and pain. Caregivers can often come to recognize their babies' different cries. Older babies and toddlers have more skills, especially when compared to younger babies. However, their range of skills is still relatively small, and they may not be able to apply their skills in all situations. For example, tantrum behavior is very common in toddlers. Frequent reasons for toddlers' tantrums include frustration from inability to clearly communicate, challenge in performing a task, or an adult preventing the child from doing something. Knowing what is behind the tantrum can help the adult to be more sympathetic and to plan an appropriate and effective response. In the vignette presented in Chapter 3, Charley hit her mother. If Carmen did not recognize the aggression as stemming from fatigue, she might have proceeded to teach time-out. Instead, she provided support that helped Frances to understand the behavior as a result of a family schedule change that was affecting mother and daughter. Getting beyond the surface behavior and acknowledging how hard it was for Frances created additional knowledge that changed how Frances saw Charley's behavior and changed Frances's reactions.

Behavior as a Response to Changes

Another helpful reframe of difficult behavior is to see it as sparked by a change in the child, family, or environment. Remember to consider changes that seem positive as well as those that are not as positive. We have already mentioned developmental changes in the child as a likely source for changes in behaviors. Other common changes for young families include moving, changing jobs, or the addition of a new sibling. Bear in mind that even small changes that might not be troubling to an adult could have an impact on a child. For example, observing a minor change in the caregiver's work schedule, moving to a different bed or sleeping arrangement, or an older sibling adding a sport that shifts the family's dinner time could be the reason for a change in the child's behavior. A caregiver's own history of trauma has also been shown to connect to the child's challenging behavior (Ribaudo et al., 2022).

When the behavioral change is sudden, more intense or extreme, the potential for trauma exposure must be addressed. A good way to introduce this issue is to ask if the child has had any experiences the child thought were frightening, including seeing something scary happen to another person. Give examples, such as medical procedures, weather-related events, car or other accidents, or seeing or hearing serious arguments between adults. Again, consider the interaction between the child's current development and the child's experience of an event or situation. Something that has never bothered a child in the past may be troublesome when experienced at an older age. A common nontraumatic example is a toddler who suddenly becomes fearful of the bath.

Trauma events experienced by the family as a whole or the caregiver can also affect the child (Ribaudo et al., 2022). For example, the worldwide COVID-19 pandemic affected most people's daily routines, creating fear and uncertainty for years and resulting in symptoms in caregivers and children (Egan et al., 2021) as well as in the workers who served them (Swigonski et al., 2021). Families may experience discrimination or marginalization related to identities, including race, ethnicity, gender orientation, and religion. Increasingly, providers may encounter families who have had experiences related to immigration that may have been challenging (Kim et al., 2018; Roggman et al., 2019). These experiences might include trauma related to the family's country of origin, discrimination in the new country, or difficulties with acculturation (Kim et al., 2018), all of which can affect the child directly or indirectly by affecting the caregiver and their caregiving practices. The topic of fears and anxiety is explored in more detail in Chapter 8.

Summary

So far, our problem-solving approach has been extended to consider some of the more likely root sources for challenging behaviors in very young children. These include developmental levels, temperament styles, a need to communicate, the caregiving context, and a response to changes. After thinking about difficult behaviors from these varying perspectives, we may understand them better, but we still may wish to find a way to change them! Next, we review some basics about behavior that can form a foundation for developing a plan to change difficult behaviors.

BEHAVIOR 101

Very young babies enter the world with an extremely limited set of skills. Within a few years, they have learned an amazing amount. Within a few years a typically developing child goes from crying to using sentences, from needing full physical support to running, and from inability to control impulses to being able to follow directions and participate in a group. How does new behavior get started and what makes it keep happening? Basic behavior theory explains that anything that is going on in the environment before a behavior happens and anything that happens after a behavior may each play a role in determining when a behavior might occur and whether it will keep happening (Murphy & Lupfer, 2014; Helbig et al., 2019). Often this is summarized as the ABC model or three-term contingency model. *A* is the antecedent of the behavior. This can be events, situations, and actions of others that occur just prior to the targeted behavior. *B* is the behavior we are interested in changing. It can be a difficult behavior that we want to decrease or a positive behavior that we want to teach or increase. Finally,

C is the consequence, or what happens after the behavior. Although practitioners are often focused on the behavior itself, we must step back and consider all three—A, B, and C—to be successful.

A. Antecedent
- Events, situations, actions of others that happen before the behavior

B. Behavior
- Positive behavior we want to increase, such as cooperation
- Negative behavior we want to decrease, such as aggression

C. Consequence
- What happens immediately after the behavior occurs
- When rewarding, consequences may increase a behavior
  - Praise
  - Getting what you want
- When undesired, consequences may decrease a behavior
  - Ignoring the behavior
  - Loss of something preferred, such as a toy or a privilege

MAKE A CHANGE TO THE ENVIRONMENT, THE OUTCOME, OR THE RESPONSE OF OTHER PEOPLE

When a behavior is followed by something positive, that behavior is said to be reinforced and can be expected to continue to occur. If the behavior does not result in a desired response or event, it is unlikely to keep happening. In a common scenario, a young child asks for a toy or candy in a store. When the caregiver says "no," the child has a tantrum. If the caregiver continues to hold firm and does not purchase the toy or candy, the tantrum behavior is not rewarded and is less likely to occur in the future. On the other hand, if the caregiver does make the purchase, the child may learn that a tantrum is the way to get a treat. This simple example explains how caregivers shape the behaviors of young children by their responses to the children's actions. For very young children, the most powerful type of reinforcement is the response of a caregiving adult. When a very young child hits their caregiver, for example, any strong emotional response (crying, laughing, yelling) may interest the child and actually encourage them to repeat the action. Changing our response following the behavior is one way to stop or increase it. Consider these two similar situations:

Version 1: Braxton went up to the television, stopped, turned, and looked at his father and smiled. He then pushed the off button. William said, "No turning off the TV, Braxton!" Braxton walked away and then a few seconds later repeated the behavior. Again, his father yelled. "No, Braxton! What did I just tell you?"

Version 2: Braxton went up to the television, stopped, turned, and looked at his father and smiled. He then pushed the off button. William said, "Wow! Look at this truck over here. How cool is this!" Braxton immediately turned his attention to the toy truck and made a zooming noise. Without saying a word about the television, William turned it back on and lowered the volume so he could still see the game but help William keep his attention on the toy truck.

In the first example, the "attention" was placed on the errant behavior, which inadvertently had the effect of reinforcing it rather than stopping it. William's telling Braxton not to turn off the television seemed to teach Braxton that he could engage his father by "pushing the button" and turning if off. In the second example, Braxton's father used redirection with positive attention for a different, desirable behavior. Braxton's attention was directed to a toy he liked, and what he learned was that his father will give him attention when he plays with toys. This helped Braxton learn to both leave the television alone and what to do to interact with his father in a positive way. William may also learn something; when he gives his son positive attention, Braxton's behavior improves.

Notice that we have not mentioned use of punishment as a way to reduce a challenging behavior. Although it is true that withdrawal of rewards is a form of punishment, we have chosen to use the term *consequence* because many people think of methods such as spanking when they hear the term *punishment*. Applying a negative, such as spanking, is also a form of punishment. However, this type of punishment is not recommended, as it does not teach alternatives; in addition, it provides an aggressive model and may actually increase challenging behaviors. This topic requires thoughtfulness for some families whose beliefs regarding physical discipline are strong. We talk more about this issue in Chapter 5.

Young children also learn by watching what others do, as described in social learning theory (Bandura, 1977). Children do not automatically know what is expected in all situations and settings. Instead, they learn over time by imitating others. Babies watch the response of their caregivers to decide if interacting with a new person is safe. Similarly, young children copy other children to learn how to play with toys or on playground equipment. Over time, humans learn to do different things with different people and in different places. For example, people may dress, act, and speak differently at home compared to work, school, places of worship, stores, or the gym. Families who are new to a country are likely to encounter a variety of unfamiliar customs and practices that caregivers must sort out when making decisions about raising their children. Providers should think about such differences as representing a variation that is adaptive within the culture, rather than considering if from a deficit model (Roggman et al., 2016).

When looking for the origins of difficult behaviors, it is important to recognize that young children may imitate the full range of behaviors of their caregivers, both desirable and undesirable. Caregiving adults who model good regulation behavior are helping children learn these skills (McClelland & Tominey, 2014). Another aspect of social learning is that people can also learn by attending to what happens after another person acts. If a child sees another person receive a reward after doing something, the child may be more likely to perform that behavior themself later. Caregivers can praise an older child who is demonstrating a skill that they would like to see their toddler develop, such as waiting a turn.

The physical environment itself also can affect our behaviors, often interacting with personal characteristics. Certain types of environments lend themselves to certain responses. For example, wide-open spaces—not only those found in parks, but also in malls and office buildings—invite young children to run. Tempting objects placed at low levels may as well have Lewis-Carroll-like tags stating, "Touch me!" Young children need appropriate environments where they can safely play and be themselves. Home visitors are in a good position to help caregivers consider how well the home environment supports the child to explore and learn safely. They can suggest environmental changes that will reduce friction between parents and young children. Caregivers are typically comfortable with the idea of child-proofing their home for safety reasons; this notion can be expanded to include environmental changes that prevent behavior problems. Some examples of environmental changes might include the following:

- For a young child who has just learned to climb, caregivers might change their furniture around to limit climbing for a time or they can provide safe toys that allow climbing.

- Caregivers can be encouraged to keep special, fragile, or valuable objects out of sight—or at least out of reach—if their child is at an age to explore these objects.

- Caregivers and other extended family members may want to designate special areas for young children and have a small selection of age-appropriate toys and games in that place.

- Child safety locks on doors, cabinets, and drawers as well as on electrical sockets can reduce access to dangerous items and reduce exit from rooms or the home.

Home visitors can also help caregivers plan to be successful when exposing children to environments outside of the home so that they can be supported to develop behaviors that suit these settings. Many families stayed close to home during the COVID-19 pandemic. As a result, many young children may have had fewer chances to gain experience in new environments than they might have had in prior years. In addition, the social skills of many adults might have become a bit rusty too! Home visitors may have to explore what it might be like for families to resume normal activities and to introduce these experiences to their children as part of these discussions.

As part of this discussion, caregivers should be supported to consider the child's typical routine and how it may be affected by the new environment or experience. For example, caregivers may wish to take their child to the home of friends or even out to a family dinner in a restaurant. Encourage the caregiver to reflect on this experience from the child's perspective; so many things are different! The young child may be distracted by all of the new people and things to see and hear, making it hard to settle down and eat. There may be a wait for a table, the meal may take longer than usual, and the food that eventually arrives looks and tastes different, meaning that the child may be hungry or confused when their expectations about eating are violated.

This discussion can naturally lead to planning to prevent potential problems. For example, once the caregiver recognizes how challenging it might be for a child to wait in a noisy, stimulating place, they could bring a favorite book, small toy, crayons and paper, or other items so that the child has something to do while practicing waiting. Alternatively, a caregiver may choose a more child-friendly restaurant or to go out to lunch instead of dinner when the restaurant is likely to be less crowded and the wait might be shorter. The family might also decide to have food delivered or go to a restaurant designed especially for young children and that has activities and child-friendly foods.

TEACH A DIFFERENT BEHAVIOR

Often, home visitors and parents are so focused on getting "rid" of a problem behavior that they don't think about what might take its place. For example, Marsha notices that Betsy cries in her highchair when she is finished eating, to signal that she wants down. Marsha finds this behavior annoying. She remembers that ignoring a behavior is sometimes effective, so she tries to turn away when Betsy cries. As Betsy cries louder, Marsha continues to ignore her. Suddenly, Betsy throws her plate on the floor. Marsha realizes that Betsy has changed her response, but unfortunately Betsy's replacement behavior is worse than the original behavior Marsha sought to eliminate. This undesirable outcome explains why it is important to pair efforts to decrease one behavior with simultaneously teaching a desirable replacement behavior.

The basic information on understanding and framing behavior can help guide how to determine an appropriate replacement behavior. Adults need to know the function the child's behavior serves so they can choose an alternate that serves the same purpose. Some of the more common reasons for a behavior are that it is enjoyable, it results in getting something that is desired, it results in avoiding or escaping something that is not desired, and it fills a sensory need. In the recently described example, Betsy wanted out of the highchair. If Marsha misread the crying as requesting more food, she would likely end up with a bigger mess! Recall that in the first three chapters we talked about attending to the child's inner experiences as part of increasing reflective functioning and building relationship; here we explain the usefulness of thinking about this from a behavioral perspective.

Adults also need to consider the child's developmental level so that they can select a behavior that the child is able to perform or can learn to perform. In the example, Marsha recognized crying as a signal that Betsy was finished eating and would like to get down from her highchair, but she found the crying annoying and wanted it to stop. Marsha might be successful if she chose to teach Betsy that she will be reinforced for doing an alternate behavior that she already can do, such as saying or signing "all done." If Betsy does not have a suitable alternative behavior in her repertoire, then Marsha will need to teach one. Again, considering Betsy's developmental level is necessary for success. Marsha may hope that one day Betsy would ask to get down using a full sentence, but that may be unrealistic at this time. Teaching a single word or sign could be an appropriate next step.

PULLING IT TOGETHER

Sometimes, as we have seen, understanding challenging behavior requires a bit of sleuthing to get the whole picture. We must consider aspects of the child, the environment, and the caregiver when helping families to address challenging behaviors. This kind of dialogue works best within a positive relationship and can benefit from the use of reflective methods.

In the example introduced earlier in this chapter, Jason asked Linda to explain in more detail how she was giving a time-out. Linda explained that she told Miranda to take a time-out, but Miranda never did it. "She knows where her time-out chair is," Linda said, "but she just won't stay." Jason knew that they had talked about the scratching and pinching several times. He felt frustrated that Linda was still not giving a time-out correctly. Linda also mentioned that another provider had shown her how to use a "holding technique," but Jason remembered that restraints have a lot of disadvantages. Jason thought about reteaching time-out but instead decided it would be better to use listening to hear more about what might be happening when Miranda pinched and scratched.

Linda at first said that the behavior happened "all the time." Jason said, "I bet it feels like it is constant! But maybe we can think a little more and figure out exactly when it happens most." With this support, Linda was able to identify that Miranda usually scratched or pinched when Linda tried to stop her from doing something by picking her up. Jason said, "Miranda is getting to be a big girl. She wants to do things on her own. I wonder how she feels when you pick her up like that?" After some discussion, Linda was able to see that picking up Miranda was a trigger, because Miranda did not like to feel confined. In addition, by breaking down the order of what happened when, Jason helped Linda recognize that she would often let Miranda go back to doing what she wanted to do after she pinched or scratched. At this point, Jason and Linda recognized that time-out or a "hold" might have actually made Miranda's behavior worse, and they were able to strategize to come up with other options, such as redirection, that might be more effective.

Figure 4.1 provides examples of questions to ask and perspectives to maintain when addressing behavior challenges using the PAUSE framework. Providers may choose to complete the whole process, or they may select sections that are most helpful for a given situation. See Appendix 4A for a blank reproducible version.

WHAT'S NEXT?

Chapters 5 through 8 explore some specific challenging child behaviors in detail, show how to apply the components of the PAUSE framework through use of scenarios, and review some concrete strategies home visitors can use to support families.

TIPS FOR PRACTICE

- Acknowledge that challenging child behavior is one of the most common issues presented and reassure families that there are steps to take to make things better.
- Encourage caregivers to consider the behaviors from many different frames and perspectives.
- Consider development and temperament, the context of the behavior, and environmental factors such as the family's culture and adult expectations and responses. Invite caregivers to think about how behaviors are started and what makes a behavior stop.

KEY POINTS TO REMEMBER

- Families are increasingly seeking help from all professionals, including home visitors, for difficult behaviors in young children. Home visitors can consider how caregivers' experiences and beliefs affect their caregiving practices. They can assist caregivers to reframe their responses to some behaviors to understand them as a reflection of typical or delayed development, related to temperament style, or as a response to factors in the environment.

APPENDIX 4A

EXPLORING CHALLENGING BEHAVIORS–PULLING IT TOGETHER WORKSHEET

Child: _Miranda_   Date: _7/13/24_

Caregiver: _Linda_   Provider: _Jason_

TARGET BEHAVIOR—Help the parent or caregiver to specifically describe the child's challenging behavior.

Miranda pinches and scratches her mother, Linda, when she tries to stop her from doing something.

Areas to Explore About the Child and Family

What is the child's current developmental level?	_Miranda has some emerging language skills with more understandable words._
What is the child's temperament style?	_Miranda is impulsive and very active. She requires a lot of attention. She also shows a desire to do things on her own._
What is the caregiver's temperament style?	_Linda seems to be pretty laid back, yet she is easily angered by Miranda's behavior._

(continued)

Figure 4.1. Sample Exploring Challenging Behaviors–Pulling It Together Worksheet.

Figure 4.1. *(continued)*

APPENDIX 4A **EXPLORING CHALLENGING BEHAVIORS—PULLING IT TOGETHER WORKSHEET** *(continued)*

Areas to Explore About the Child and Family *(continued)*	
Describe the family culture and environment.	Linda is a single parent who shares that she wants to do the best job she can to help Miranda learn to behave so she is better prepared for preschool next year. The family has stayed in most of the time during COVID and Linda worries about being in public again.
Describe the family's caregiving practices.	Linda is open to trying new ideas. She asks all of the providers for ideas on handling behavior.
Questions to Ask the Caregiver	
How has this situation or behavior been for you?	Linda feels frustrated and like she has already tried many ideas that don't work. Maybe she feels embarrassed that her parenting techniques have not stopped the pinching/scratching.
Who is helping you?	Linda asks for help from all the other providers. Her family has been critical of her parenting. She may be getting some conflicting advice.
Is the concern new or ongoing?	This behavior has been going on for several months.
Have there been any changes in the family?	The family recently moved into a new apartment because Linda got a new job.

(continued)

(continued)

Figure 4.1. *(continued)*

APPENDIX 4A **EXPLORING CHALLENGING BEHAVIORS—PULLING IT TOGETHER WORKSHEET** *(continued)*

Questions to Ask the Caregiver *(continued)*	
How often and how long has this behavior or situation been happening? How long does the behavior last?	It seems the scratching and pinching started a few months ago and has gotten progressively more problematic. It happens most often when Linda tries to pick up Miranda to get her to stop doing something. When Linda puts her down, she calms somewhat.
When, where, and with whom does it happen?	Linda is not aware of Miranda behaving this way with others. It seems to happen most often at home in the evening.
What usually happens after the behavior? What happens before the behavior?	Miranda scratches and pinches as soon as Linda starts to pick her up to stop a behavior. Linda will often put her down when she is pinched or scratched. Miranda often wants to be alone for a few minutes after this happens.
What happens to "end" the behavior (e.g., does the child just give up, does the caregiver give in, does the child get distracted)?	The pinching seems to stop when Linda lets Miranda go. If they have been struggling for a while, sometimes Miranda runs to her room to be alone and sometimes falls asleep.
What might be the purpose of the behavior or what need does it fill for the child? What is the child trying to "tell" you?	When Miranda pinches or scratches, Linda lets her get down, so the behavior results in escape from restraint and sometimes in being able to do something forbidden. I also wonder if part of Miranda's struggle is with communicating her needs and wants. Or maybe she gets tired and less able to regulate herself.
What would you like your child to do instead?	Linda would like Miranda to use words or signs to tell her when she wants something and for her to listen when she tells her to stop doing something.

(continued)

Figure 4.1. *(continued)*

APPENDIX 4A **EXPLORING CHALLENGING BEHAVIORS–PULLING IT TOGETHER WORKSHEET** *(continued)* *(page 4 of 5)*

Questions to Ask the Caregiver *(continued)*	
Does the caregiver know how to perform the new behavior, or will we need to teach it?	Miranda is behind in her communication skills. She may need help with using words to make requests and to follow some commands.
What have you tried already? How did that work?	Linda has tried time-out and holding in addition to telling Miranda to stop whatever behavior is disliked. Miranda "does not stay" in the time-out place. Redirection has been suggested but may not have been tried.
Summarizing the Plan	
What changes to the environment, routine, or adult reactions will we try?	I can encourage Linda to use redirection and to avoid picking up Miranda. Linda may need to moderate her reactions or responses to the pinching and scratching. Miranda might benefit from fewer toys that are out for play. Linda might benefit from creating a more consistent schedule so Miranda gets sufficient sleep.
What steps will we take to teach a new behavior?	We might teach Miranda requesting and refusing skills (words and signs). We can try some games that include following directions. It will be important to stress that this will take some time to change, as Miranda will try her old and currently successful ways to get what she wants before learning the new way.
What would be different if the strategy works?	Miranda will be calmer, will stop doing something when asked, and will use words or signs instead of pinching and scratching.

(continued)

(continued)

Figure 4.1. (continued)

APPENDIX 4A EXPLORING CHALLENGING BEHAVIORS—PULLING IT TOGETHER WORKSHEET (continued)

Summarizing the Plan (continued)	
What does the family need to do in order to stick it out and be consistent with the plan? Are there others in the family who can help?	Linda will need regular affirmation of progress, as she is a single parent. She might benefit from identifying a person to call when she is frustrated, just for some moral support. She has mentioned her mother and sister could also help and might be useful to give her breaks as needed.
How long will we try the strategy before checking in again?	I really would like Linda to try any new behavior method consistently for at least 2 to 3 weeks so Miranda successfully learns a new way.

Self-Reflective Questions	
Is this issue within my scope of practice?	Yes, I can help Linda learn this behavior management approach.
How can I be most helpful in this situation?	Because we are already meeting weekly for therapy, I can make this topic a regular part of our work to help Linda stay consistent with the plan. I can check in to see if Linda has enough support to continue.
What reactions am I having to this behavior or situation?	I feel somewhat frustrated because I feel like we have discussed these strategies before with little success. I'm not sure how to redirect my frustration.

- Developing an effective plan to address challenging behavior in young children requires considering the behavior from multiple frames including family culture and caregiver experiences; having realistic expectations related to child development; gathering detailed information about the meaning, purpose, and overall context of the behavior; and supporting families to develop and implement plans.

SUGGESTED FURTHER READING

Clark, L. (2020). *SOS for parents: A practical guide for handling common everyday behavior problems* (5th ed.). SOS Programs and Parent Press.

APPENDIX 4A

EXPLORING CHALLENGING BEHAVIORS– PULLING IT TOGETHER WORKSHEET

Child: _____ Date: _____

Caregiver: _____ Provider: _____

TARGET BEHAVIOR—Help the parent or caregiver to specifically describe the child's challenging behavior.

_____

Areas to Explore About the Child and Family

What is the child's current developmental level?	
What is the child's temperament style?	
What is the caregiver's temperament style?	

(continued)

Tackling the Tough Stuff: A Home Visitor's Guide to Supporting Families at Risk, Second Edition, by Angela M. Tomlin and Stephan A. Viehweg. Copyright © 2025 by Paul H. Brookes Publishing Co., Inc. All rights reserved.

APPENDIX 4A **EXPLORING CHALLENGING BEHAVIORS—PULLING IT TOGETHER WORKSHEET** (continued)

Areas to Explore About the Child and Family (continued)

Describe the family culture and environment.	
Describe the family's caregiving practices.	

Questions to Ask the Caregiver

How has this situation or behavior been for you?	
Who is helping you?	
Is the concern new or ongoing?	
Have there been any changes in the family?	

(continued)

APPENDIX 4A **EXPLORING CHALLENGING BEHAVIORS–PULLING IT TOGETHER WORKSHEET** (continued)

Questions to Ask the Caregiver (continued)	
How often and how long has this behavior or situation been happening? How long does the behavior last?	
When, where, and with whom does it happen?	
What usually happens after the behavior? What happens before the behavior?	
What happens to "end" the behavior (e.g., does the child just give up, does the caregiver give in, does the child get distracted)?	
What might be the purpose of the behavior or what need does it fill for the child? What is the child trying to "tell" you?	
What would you like your child to do instead?	

(continued)

APPENDIX 4A **EXPLORING CHALLENGING BEHAVIORS—PULLING IT TOGETHER WORKSHEET** (continued)

Questions to Ask the Caregiver (continued)

Does the caregiver know how to perform the new behavior, or will we need to teach it?	
What have you tried already? How did that work?	

Summarizing the Plan

What changes to the environment, routine, or adult reactions will we try?	
What steps will we take to teach a new behavior?	
What would be different if the strategy works?	

(continued)

APPENDIX 4A **EXPLORING CHALLENGING BEHAVIORS—PULLING IT TOGETHER WORKSHEET** (continued)

Summarizing the Plan (continued)

What does the family need to do in order to stick it out and be consistent with the plan? Are there others in the family who can help?	
How long will we try the strategy before checking in again?	

Self-Reflective Questions

Is this issue within my scope of practice?	
How can I be most helpful in this situation?	
What reactions am I having to this behavior or situation?	

5

When Caregivers Say... Calm Down!

Early Regulation: Sleeping, Eating, and Soothing

Darlene arrives for her scheduled early intervention visit with Katarina and Phil, parents of 10-month-old Jasmine. She enjoys working with this family and notices that they have many strengths. However, Darlene finds herself frustrated as she notices that the family seldom seems ready for her visits. Although she has been working with the family for a few months and comes the same afternoon time each week, often the family is not yet dressed, and she frequently arrives in the middle of a meal. On this day, Jasmine is smiling and interactive as usual, although she appears to have just recently woken up. She is sitting with her mother on the couch. Katarina is watching a news program and trying to get Jasmine interested in a bottle with a red-colored liquid. Darlene wonders if it is a soda, as she has often seen Katarina give Jasmine sips from her own beverages.

"Are you ready to start or do you need a minute?" Darlene asks. Katarina says, "You can work with her for a while. Phil went out to get us some lunch 'cause we just got up after going to bed late last night." Just then, Phil arrives bearing bags of fast food. The two sit on the couch and pull out the sandwiches, large bags of fries, "super-sized" drinks, and several desserts. Darlene sits on the floor with Jasmine, unsure of what to do, feeling awkward and a little annoyed that her session is interrupted again. Phil leans down to give Jasmine a fry to chew on, saying, "Look at this! Jasmine is figuring out how to eat by herself." Darlene winces and then smiles as she notices Phil's pride in his daughter's skill. She also remembers that she did discuss how self-feeding promotes fine motor skills and considers this could be Phil's way of showing that he was listening. As Darlene finishes up her paperwork, she reminds Katarina of the next appointment. "I think it would be good to talk about your schedule for bed and eating next time. What do you think?" she asks Katarina. Phil laughs and leaves the room. Katarina says "We can talk about that. It's hard to get a schedule here when things at Phil's work are so crazy. We never know when he will have to go in or stay late. I want him to be able to spend time with us when he can." Thinking back on the whole session, Darlene realizes she may have been jumping to conclusions about the family and wonders if there could be more to this situation than she knew.

Earlier chapters reviewed how important it is for a baby's caregivers to learn to read their young child's cues and respond appropriately to meet their needs. Gradually, as the child gains skills, the caregiver can allow more and more opportunities for the child to do things for themself. In addition to supporting a positive attachment between caregiver and child, this complex set of interactions is one of the ways that the young child gains the self-regulation skills needed to manage behavior and emotions (Brown et al., 2014; Duncan, 2023; Slade et al., 2023).

For all infants, the very beginning of self-regulation can be seen in a triad of skills that develop in the first few months of life: sleeping, eating, and the ability to be calmed or soothed. When these skills are slower to develop or develop atypically, the baby feels bad—and so does everyone else in the house. As infants change to toddlers, these daily behaviors may become battlegrounds related to independence. Throughout the period of early development, caregivers facilitate a baby's growing self-regulation in many ways, including providing a nurturing and supportive relationship, setting up structure through routines, teaching and providing good models for behavior and healthy practices, and talking to babies and toddlers about thoughts and feelings (McClelland & Tominey, 2014; McDermott & Fox, 2019). Caregivers' understanding of the child's developmental levels, their culture and beliefs about caregiving, their sense of self-confidence and efficacy in caregiving, and their personal self-regulation skills are associated with their ability to support their children in these areas (Callejas, Byrne, & Rodrigo, 2021). Problems in these three areas are not unusual in very young children and may or may not rise to a level that is considered clinically significant (ZERO TO THREE Press, 2021). This chapter discusses how a typically developing baby can attain these skills with the support of sensitive caregivers and how home visitors can identify common problems related to learning these skills, and it also suggests ways that home visitors can help families struggling in these areas.

EXECUTIVE FUNCTIONING FOUNDATIONS IN INFANCY

Executive functioning (EF) refers to a set of cognitive skills that allow people to plan and carry out their goals (Duncan, 2023) and are considered key to adapting to the complexities of life (Hughes et al., 2023). Examples of EF skills include those related to attention, memory, and impulse control (Duncan, 2023). *Self-regulation* is an early aspect of EF, with foundations in infancy. Self-regulation describes a person's ability to manage or control their own behavior, emotions, and thinking. Development of skills important in managing thinking, emotions, and behavior is understood as complex and dependent on both neurological readiness and supportive caregiving experiences (Duncan, 2023; Hughes et al., 2023). The foundational EF skills needed to gain self-regulation begin in infancy and continue to be used throughout the lifespan. Consider this situation: You arrive home after working overtime and are looking forward to taking a shower and relaxing for the evening. Instead, you find that family members have dropped in unexpectedly. They have brought food and planned to eat dinner and visit for the evening. What thoughts, feelings, and ultimately actions or behaviors would occur? Whether one is a child, teen, or adult, it is highly adaptive to be able to maintain composure, choose appropriate and effective behavioral responses, and think clearly when in an unexpected, upsetting, or exciting situation. In this example, a person with low self-regulation could blow up, angrily asking why the family members did not call ahead. The person could also break into tears of frustration that their plan was destroyed. Or a person with better self-regulation might be able tell themselves to think about this change in plans as an opportunity to have fun with seldom-seen family members and be able to revise plans to relax for another day. In the long term, self-regulation skills are associated with positive outcomes such as getting along better with others and success in school and work (Duncan, 2023; Hughes et al., 2023). Not surprisingly, poor self-regulation is associated with mental health problems, including depression, anxiety, and behavioral issues such as later attention-deficit/hyperactivity disorder (ADHD) diagnosis (Bridgett et al., 2013; Joseph et al., 2023).

Temperament, a topic briefly introduced in Chapter 4, is a set of inborn tendencies that may relate to EF and to regulation (Joseph et al., 2023; McClelland & Tominey, 2014; Rothbart & Bates, 2006). Frequent negative responses to new experiences, impatience, and being easily frustrated are temperament characteristics associated with problems in regulation. For babies and young children, this could look like difficulty with self-soothing or low ability to accept soothing from caregivers when afraid, hungry, or tired. In some cases, the difficulties are severe enough to be understood as a disorder of sensory processing (ZERO TO THREE Press, 2021). People whose temperament style lets them manage new experiences may also be more skilled in integrating emotional and cognitive regulation efforts. Babies who are less reactive to changes in routine or new people often are also calmer in general. See Table 5.1 for explanations and examples of executive function skills.

It is typical for infants and very young children to need adult support to manage their behavior, emotions, and thoughts. At first, almost all the burden of regulation is on the adult, making the relationship between

Table 5.1. Executive functioning: How we manage or control thinking processes using a specific set of thinking skills

Thinking skills	Description	Examples
Attentional flexibility	Ability to attend to tasks without either becoming too distracted by non-essentials or getting so consumed by the activity that transitions are difficult	Continuing to play with a shape sorter while a big brother is loudly pretending to be "Spectacular Spiderman"
Working memory	Ability to keep information in mind long enough to act on it	Remembering and following a rule or set of directions to go to another room, retrieve a pair of shoes, and come back to the door to leave
Inhibitory control	Refraining from enacting one response or action in favor of a more appropriate one	"Using your words" instead of hitting when things do not go your way

Source: McClelland and Tominey (2014).

caregiver and infant the vehicle through which regulation occurs and is learned (Hughes et al., 2023). Even though it is expected that adult support will continue to be needed throughout the early childhood period, some of the skills that underlie self-regulation begin to appear as early as 12 months (Bridgett et al., 2013); the brain systems required for these skills are present even earlier (McDermott & Fox, 2019). By some time between 18 and 24 months, young children have the beginning skills needed to manage their emotions, such as distracting themselves from upsetting events. Even very tiny babies may break off eye contact and look away to calm down when overexcited. This is one reason that redirection is such an effective behavioral strategy for children this age.

Because very young children are not able to regulate on their own, caregivers need to pay attention to their babies' behavior; make informed guesses about what the child wants, needs, or is reacting to; and then respond in consistent ways. Talking about thoughts, desires, emotions, other internal experiences has been called *mind-mindedness* and may be one of the important ways that caregivers help young children develop EF skills (Bernier et al., 2010). Evidence suggests that these skills are best learned over time through day-to-day interactions (Hughes et al., 2023). The goal is for the caregiver to do just enough so that babies have room to build self-regulation skills gradually without being overwhelmed. Over time, the child begins to practice more and more self-regulation with less adult support. Studies show that self-regulation depends on a combination of the young child's emotional reactivity and caregiving behaviors. In one study, babies who were very emotionally reactive but who had sensitive parents did better at age 4 years in the general executive functioning skills needed for school success (Ursache et al., 2013). In an extreme example, Zeanah and colleagues followed young children raised in Romanian institutions, often in very deprived situations (e.g., see Nelson et al., 2014). Their work showed that children who grow up in these settings had lower EF skills; however, children moved into more responsive foster care environments prior to age 2 years had EF skills more like those who had never been institutionalized when older (Bos et al., 2009; Nelson, Fox, & Zeanah, 2014). Data from this long-term project has helped explain how important it is for babies to receive and accept support from caregivers and demonstrates the urgency of providing this support early in life.

FIRST STEPS IN DISCUSSING ISSUES IN REGULATION WITH FAMILIES

Later in this chapter, we discuss detailed background and recommended supports for specific problem areas in self-regulation. Before we get to those specifics, however, let's start with some important general principles related to sleep, feeding, and self-soothing. Home visitors need to find ways to ask about these three areas of family life and then be prepared to share information about how to develop healthy routines that are meaningful within the family's culture. Fortunately, home visitors are in a great position to observe both successful family practices and potential struggles in all aspects of caregiving and will typically have many good opportunities to ask specifically about sleeping, feeding, and soothing as they are occurring.

Being able to talk about a caregiving practice in the moment is likely to be more meaningful for caregivers. Some caregivers may ask a direct question about how to resolve a perceived problem with sleep, feeding, or soothing. At other times, the home visitor may be the one to initiate the conversation. This means the provider must be alert for opportunities to ask and wonder about a child's behavior when observed and be ready to share recommendations when caregivers ask for help. See Table 5.2 for questions to ask about sleeping, feeding, and soothing.

Table 5.2. Questions to ask regarding sleeping, feeding, and soothing

Sleeping	How is your baby sleeping? What time do they go to bed? What time do they wake up in the morning? Do they sleep through the night?
	How often do they wake at night? What happens when they wake up? What do you do?
	When do they nap? How long do they nap?
	What concerns or questions do you have about your child's sleep?
Feeding	How do you know when your child is hungry?
	How do you know when your child is full?
	What does your child like to eat and drink?
	What does meal time look like? Where do you feed your child? What is happening while they are eating?
Soothing	How would you describe your baby? What three words would you use to describe them?
	What startles or scares them? How do you know when they are scared?
	When they are upset, what do you do to help them calm down? How long does it take for them to get calm?
	Who is able to calm them down when they get upset?
	How do you know when they are going to become upset? What do you do to avoid upsetting situations?

As we have discussed, the first step in helping with a concerning issue is to learn more about it and how the family views the situation. At times, problems with regulation can occur along with a medical concern. Therefore, it is often a good idea to ask if the family has consulted a pediatrician or other primary care provider before giving behavioral suggestions. As always, it is best to ask more about how the family thinks about these areas of child behavior and what their beliefs are around caregiving in general. This step can be very important when a family belongs to a culture that is different from the home visitor's; in this situation, the home visitor may want to specifically inquire about typical practices related to sleeping, eating, and behavior so that suggestions or recommended practices can be a better fit within the family's culture. Finally, finding out who the family can call on for help is smart, particularly when families are struggling with regulation issues. Hungry or overtired children combined with hungry or overtired caregivers may lead to a lot of frustration! Ask if there is anyone who can give the caregiver a break.

PREVENTING PROBLEMS IN REGULATION THROUGH ROUTINES

Putting to sleep, feeding, and calming are activities that caregivers perform multiple times every day with their young children. Preventing problems in these three areas can be effective (American Academy of Sleep Medicine, 2014) and is very important, given that babies who struggle in these areas may develop difficult behaviors by the time they are toddlers.

For example, across many different studies, behavioral interventions have been shown to be effective in improving sleep for young children. There is limited evidence that behavioral interventions are effective in improving sleep for older children, underscoring the importance of developing good sleep patterns early in life (Meltzer & Mindell, 2014). Similarly, caregiving strategies and behavioral and sensory-based interventions can help with feeding concerns (de Brito et al., 2022). For high-risk families, teaching parents the importance of the baby learning to self-soothe may be particularly helpful in avoiding later problems (Sheridan et al., 2013).

One of the more important ways the home visitor can help prevent behavioral problems stemming from self-regulation issues is to help families set up basic routines (St. James-Roberts et al., 2001). In order to set up effective routines, caregivers need information about typical development. Home visitors can share information about typical child development that helps caregivers to view feeding, sleeping, and calming as skills to be developed over time and with adult support. Similarly, the home visitor can assist caregivers to recognize that their children's needs for support related to sleep and skills in feeding and self-regulation will change over time. What works for an infant may not work as the child approaches 3 years. As discussed in Chapter 4, helping caregivers to have appropriate expectations and to anticipate challenges in these areas related to typical development may be beneficial.

As part of these discussions, home visitors should emphasize the effect that caregivers' own behaviors in sleep, eating, and emotional regulation have on their children. Some caregivers may want their children to grow up to have better habits than they themselves have, but they are unaware of how much their children learn from watching them. To help support the general idea that modeling is an important way that children learn, the home visitor can point out times when they observe the child copy something that a caregiver says or does (McClelland & Tominey, 2014). When caregivers bring up concerns about sleep or feeding, the home visitor should ask about the habits of other family members. For example, caregivers may ask about how to get their child to eat more vegetables but will admit that they rarely eat anything green themselves. Asking what the caregivers imagine that the child will learn from watching their routines can be a good way to start them thinking about these issues. For some families, asking about what the caregivers remember about how eating, sleeping, and managing emotions were handled when they were growing up can help them see how modeling works. A list of questions that explore family routines is shown in Box 5.1. The home visitor can document answers to these questions in any format that makes the most sense for the family's daily routines. Some may structure a day by morning, noon, and night. Others might draw a circle to represent a 24-hour period.

> The Centers for Disease Control (CDC) has created the "Learn the Signs. Act Early." materials to learn about and track children's developmental milestones from birth to age 5. The collection of free, easily accessible resources in both English and Spanish is widely available online or in print version. Materials include booklets, checklists, children's story books, a growth chart, a video/photo library, and a free, downloadable app (www.cdc.gov/actearly).

At times, a home visitor, like Darlene in the example, may have a concern about an observed caregiving practice but may be unsure about how to bring up this worry, or even if it would be appropriate to share. The caregivers may be satisfied with their current practices, whereas the home visitor, aware of the potential for problems down the road, is concerned. In this situation, the home visitor could step back from their own perceptions of the caregiving practice to consider the pros and cons of beginning a conversation about it.

Darlene continues to work with Jasmine and her parents but finds herself thinking about the caregiving practices that Phil and Katarina use. In her mind, she checks off the many ways she would like this family to change: get on a sleep schedule, eat healthier foods, and reduce screen time. As she drives to her next visit, Darlene thinks about how to share information about these topics with the family, and she imagines giving Katarina a set of handouts related to these areas. Darlene laughs to herself as she considers how being handed

> **Box 5.1. Exploring Daily Routines**
>
> Tell me about a typical day.
>
> What time do family members wake up?
>
> What happens after waking?
>
> How do you handle meals and snacks?
>
> What happens in between meals and snacks?
>
> Does the child take naps? What time and for how long?
>
> What happens after nap time?
>
> What are the child's activities? What does the child like to do?
>
> When does everyone go to bed?
>
> What happens before bedtime (e.g., bath, reading)?
>
> How does everyone sleep?
>
> Where does everyone sleep?
>
> Do the child's caregivers work outside the home? What is the schedule?
>
> If the caregiver(s) work, who takes care of the child? Where?
>
> Are there other children in the home? What are their schedules?

a bunch of papers about something she is not worried about would seem to Katarina. She wonders how to share ideas in a way that is respectful.

Darlene shares her experience with Jasmine's family with her supervisor. In the discussion, Darlene is helped to recognize that although she might wish the family made some different choices, nothing truly dangerous is happening. With the supervisor's help, Darlene is able to recognize that she missed some opportunities in the last visit to ask what Katarina and Phil see as most important and bring up topics to discuss. For example, when Katarina indicated that Darlene should start the session with Jasmine, Darlene could have said, "You are an important part of this visit too. I'm wondering how you would feel most comfortable participating?" A statement like this could lead to a discussion related to schedules and allow space to talk about the value of regularity in eating and sleeping.

NAVIGATING PROBLEMS IN SELF-REGULATION

Home visitors know that when caregivers use consistent routines and model healthy practices babies and toddlers will benefit both now and down the road. However, many families who use home visiting services may require more help to acquire these skills. In the following subsections, we provide some practical ideas and approaches to help support healthy sleeping, eating, and soothing practices and to address any challenges caregivers or providers identify in these three areas.

Sleep

Many caregivers are unaware of typical infant sleep patterns when they have a new baby, and this lack of knowledge may lead to fatigue and frustration. At first, many newborns do not adhere to the daily sleep cycle that most adults follow. Often, a new caregiver will complain that their baby has the "days and nights mixed up." However, it is routine for typically developing young babies to have fairly short periods of sleep and wakefulness that alternate throughout day and night, spending about half of the time in rapid eye movement (REM) or deep sleep (Krishna et al., 2023). Over the first year of life, caregivers can expect babies to gradually increase the length of their periods of sleep and wakefulness so that there are both longer sleep and wakeful times. This process is often discussed as *sleep consolidation*. In addition to the advantages to the family of longer sleep periods, there is also a benefit of longer periods of wakefulness to allow for more social interactions and learning opportunities.

In order for a baby to be ready to learn to sleep for longer periods, they must be developmentally ready for lengthier sleep times and must know how to fall asleep on their own. This is because longer periods of sleep include very brief times of wakefulness; no one actually stays fully asleep all through the night. We all wake up a little and must use self-soothing to fall back into sleep (Henderson et al., 2010). Sleep is known to contribute to children's psychological and physical health (Bonuck et al., 2011). Conversely, sleep problems can lead to long-term difficulties ranging from behavior problems to increased irritability, delays in cognition, and even slowed growth (Bonuck et al., 2011; Magee et al., 2014; Williamson & Mindell, 2020). Children who continue to sleep shorter amounts of time through age 6 or 7 are more likely to have physical, emotional, and social issues than those whose sleep was typical from infancy or those whose sleep improved over time (Magee et al., 2014). Table 5.3 provides a summary of helpful information about sleep.

Child and caregiver sleep affect each other. Therefore, to understand sleep problems, it is important to consider child factors like temperament and age along with caregiver factors like bedtime interactions. For example, when babies and toddlers have poor sleep, it is likely their caregivers do, too. Both fathers and mothers report feeling more stressed when their young child does not sleep well, and they may have health problems and poorer overall daily functioning as a result (Goodlin-Jones et al., 2008). Similarly, poor caregiver sleep is connected to problems with child sleep, supporting the idea that sleep is a whole family issue.

Table 5.3. Recommended sleep patterns

Age of child	Optimal hours of sleep per 24 hours	Tips and milestones
Newborn	14–17 hours	Watch for signs of sleepiness and put babies to bed drowsy but not asleep so they learn to fall asleep on their own. Many babies can sleep through the night (from midnight to 5 a.m.) by about 2–3 months.
4–11 months	12–15 hours	Use routines for nap and bedtime and a good sleep environment that is quiet and dark with no video or computer screens. More than half of babies sleep between 10 p.m. and 6 a.m. by 6 months, paralleling many parents' sleep patterns.
1–2 years	11–14 hours	Expect to reduce to one nap by 18 months. Encourage a security object to help promote self-soothing.
3–5 years	10–13 hours	Preschool children often still wake during the night, often with night terrors. A relaxing bedtime routine is recommended.
6–13 years	9–10 hours	Continue to avoid video or computer screens near bedtime. Avoid caffeine and begin to teach about good sleep habits.

Sources: Henderson, France, Owens, and Blampied (2010); Hirshkowitz et al. (2015).

Sleep is also connected to family characteristics. Problem sleep is more likely in families with high-risk compared to low-risk characteristics (e.g., psychosocial stressors and low socioeconomic status) (Sheridan et al., 2013), and these risk factors are cumulative (Williamson & Mindell, 2020). Babies from high-risk families start out with similar sleep habits compared with their low-risk peers. By 18 months, however, the babies in the high-risk families already show differences in sleep, including problems settling to sleep, night waking, and inconsistent bedtimes and sleep length, suggesting that family issues rather than infant characteristics lead to the sleep problems (Sheridan et al., 2013). Caregiver depression and low educational attainment, and overall family factors such as a single caregiver and living in a crowded home, predict poor child sleep habits and outcomes, including sleep apnea and insomnia (Williamson & Mindell, 2020). Home visitors in programs that support high-risk families may, therefore, frequently encounter problems with sleep.

Caregiver behaviors can promote or inhibit sleep (Shetty et al., 2022). Consistent with the idea that young children need to learn to self-regulate, it has been shown that children who learn to sleep on their own with little assistance may be the best sleepers. Paradoxically, active maternal strategies intended to help a baby settle to sleep were found in families in which babies were the poorest sleepers. Active settling includes methods such as walking the baby, touching the infant for comfort, and staying with the child to achieve sleep. These strategies were associated with poor sleep, and the families continued to struggle when the child was 5 years old (Sheridan et al., 2013). Helping children learn to self-soothe and fall asleep on their own is needed, as research has shown that children fall asleep more easily, wake less, and sleep longer when a caregiver is not present as they fall asleep (Touchette et al., 2005; Mindell & Williamson, 2018). Caregiving practices reported to relate to poor sleep outcomes include having an inconsistent bedtime routine, use of television or other electronics in the bedroom, setting bedtime later than 9:00 p.m., and allowing the child to have caffeine (Williamson & Mindell, 2020). In this study, over 84% of a diverse group of typically developing children between 2 and 5 years of age had at least one of these poor sleep health habits, suggesting that sleep problems are very common.

Other caregiving behaviors that are not directly part of a sleep routine can also affect child sleep. For example, in one study, both daytime caregiving practices and bedtime routines were associated with sleep problems (Shetty et al., 2022). In another longitudinal study, aggressive caregiver actions, including hitting and slapping, were associated with problems such as staying asleep (sleep continuity) (Kelly et al., 2014). In this study and others, sleep problems were connected to later child emotional and behavioral symptoms. Taken together, these studies suggest that child sleep can be disrupted by myriad issues, including overall caregiving practices, challenges with schedules and routine, family conflict, and caregiving practices that lead to feelings of threat and vigilance, none of which promote good sleep and have the potential to lead to behavior issues in the long term (Williamson & Mindell, 2020; Magee et al., 2014; Sheridan et al., 2013; Kelly et al., 2014).

How Common Are Sleep Problems? Sleep problems are among the most common problems brought to pediatricians and other primary care providers (Goodlin-Jones et al., 2008; Shetty et al., 2022). There are several different ways of categorizing sleep problems, which may include behavioral issues and sleep difficulty related to breathing and other physical problems (Bonuck et al., 2011; American Academy of Sleep Medicine, 2014). The American Academy of Sleep Medicine (2014) groups sleep problems into diagnoses related to sleeping too little, sleeping too much, breathing problems, sleep rhythm problems, disrupted sleep, and movement issues. In early childhood, problems often include delays in falling to sleep, night wakings, partial wakings (night terrors and sleep walking), and nightmares (ZERO TO THREE Press, 2021). Together, these experts help us understand that disorders of sleep can be identified accurately in young children, although usually not until after 4 to 6 months (Paruthi et al., 2016; ZERO TO THREE Press, 2021).

Recent estimates suggest that 25% to 40% of children between 2 and 10 years of age have sleep problems (Shetty et al., 2022; Williamson & Mindell, 2020). Children with neurodevelopmental disorders, including autism and developmental delays, are significantly more likely to have more problems with sleep than their typically developing peers, with estimates between 40% and as high as 93% in those populations (Bonuck et al., 2011; Goodlin-Jones et al., 2008; Wiggs, 2001; Belli et al., 2022); therefore, home visitors who serve these populations should routinely discuss sleep. Although common in young children, sleep problems tend to decline with age. Young children are likely to be more dependent on their caregivers for sleep; therefore, caregivers are more involved with and concerned about sleep problems of young children (Goodlin-Jones et al., 2008). In one longitudinal study, caregivers reported that about 85% of children will have a typical sleep pattern by 4 years, so home visitors can reassure families that sleep will almost always improve.

Co-Sleeping Many caregivers co-sleep with their infants, for many different reasons, including parenting beliefs, reluctance to be apart from the baby, and cultural practices. Some families may co-sleep due to practical reasons, such as not having the money for a separate bed for the infant or young child or enough funds to heat or cool the whole house. In other situations, the child is unable to fall asleep or stay asleep on their own, so one adult stays with the child so that the entire family is able to get some sleep. Most U.S. medical providers caution against co-sleeping in the same bed, citing an association with sudden infant death syndrome (SIDS) and fears about smothering the baby accidentally in sleep (American Academy of Pediatrics [AAP], 2011). The AAP's campaign for Safe Sleep, summarized as ABC, encourages caregivers to put babies to bed Alone, on the Back, and in their own Crib; some home visiting programs may require that providers teach this philosophy (Walsh & Mortensen, 2020). Others have argued vehemently that co-sleeping has an evolutionary basis and that Western concepts of solitary infant sleep and infant sleep training are far from universal (McKenna & McDade, 2005). It is important to note that studies from the United Kingdom and Ireland (Fleming & Blair, 2015) have reported that co-sleeping in chairs or couches is more dangerous than planned co-sleeping in a bed. Other risk factors that increase the risk related to co-sleeping were reported, including parental smoking, use of alcohol or drugs, and infant vulnerability due to younger age (less than 4 months), prematurity, or low birth weight (AAP Council on Early Childhood, 2011; Fleming & Blair, 2015). The AAP and other expert groups note that having an infant sleep in the same room but in a separate bed is not only the safest arrangement but may also enhance breast feeding and provide protective advantages in terms of reduced likelihood of suffocation and SIDS. Of note, other authors suggest that for toddlers and preschoolers co-sharing a sleep space with an adult or older sibling may result in risk factors to good sleep that include electronics in the room, later bedtimes, light and noise interference with sleep onset, and disrupted routines (Williamson & Mindell, 2020). Overall, it is suggested that a more individualized approach that takes into account factors such as poverty, parental smoking and drug use, cultural preferences, and infant and child characteristics (e.g., age, low birth weight, prematurity) is needed when discussing sleeping arrangements (Fleming & Blair, 2015; McKenna & McDade, 2005).

How Is the Whole Family Sleeping? Because sleep is so important and sleep issues are so common, it is critical to ask about overall family sleep, not only when the issue is specifically brought up, but also when caregivers express concern about development and behavior or when caregivers themselves are irritable and fatigued (Bonuck et al., 2011). Providers cannot count on the typical developmental assessment tools used in early childhood programs to gather this information, as most of these measures either do not discuss sleep or may ask only one question (Bonuck et al., 2011). Authors suggest that multiple groups who interact with families with young children, including early care and education providers, home visitors, and primary care providers, take time to ask specifically about sleep (Williamson & Mindell, 2020). Home visitors may find it convenient to ask about sleep in the context of daily routines. Areas to ask about include:

Expectations: Does the child's sleep concern the caregiver? Is the sleep pattern typical for this family and their culture?

Surroundings: Where does the child sleep—room and bed type? What toys or other objects are in the bed with the child? Are there other people in the same bed or in the same room? Are there any noises, lights, or distractions in the room, including screens?

Cycle: How many minutes does it take the child to fall asleep? How often does the child wake at night? What is the total number of hours the child sleeps in a 24-hour period, including nighttime sleep and any naps?

Practices: What is the bedtime routine? How does the caregiver respond if the child wakes?

Disruptions: Are there any night terrors, nightmares, motor disturbances (sleep walking or restless sleep), or breathing issues such as labored breathing or loud snoring?

Responding to Sleep Concerns Once the home visitor has information about how, when, and where the baby or toddler sleeps and about the overall family sleep habits, they can work with the caregiver to identify some strategies to help with identified concerns. Box 5.2 provides a useful checklist for working on improving sleep issues with families.

Feeding

Feeding skills also progress across the first few years of life. Healthy newborn babies with typical development are able to coordinate their sucking, swallowing, and breathing in order to successfully nurse or take formula from a bottle. By about 4 to 6 months of age, a baby should have enough tongue movement to be able to manage soft solid foods, but the ability to bite and chew solids well will not occur until closer to 18 months. Independence in feeding also occurs gradually, beginning with the ability to

> **Box 5.2. Strategies for Responding to Sleep Concerns**
>
> **Observing and Listening**
>
> - Make sure the caregiver's sleep goals make sense from a developmental perspective.
> - Ask the caregiver how sleep typically looks in their family, community, culture.
> - Discuss any potential medical problems that relate to sleep.
> - Identify the child's current skills in self-soothing and needed self-soothing skills.
>
> **Prevention and Intervention Ideas to Discuss, Share, and Try**
>
> - Benefits of a daytime schedule and sleep routine.
> - Offer play time in a well-lit or sunny room to help the child establish a day and night cycle.
> - Encourage caregivers to put the baby down for naps and bedtime when they are sleepy but not asleep so that the baby can learn to fall asleep on their own.
> - Recognize that some babies will prefer to fall asleep on their own and may not like being rocked or held.
> - Discourage hovering or frequent checking in on the baby, as these may disrupt sleep.
> - If the baby or toddler wakes at night, encourage caregivers to wait briefly (e.g., several minutes) to see if the child can fall asleep on their own, but not to wait so long that the child becomes significantly upset or distressed.
> - Encourage caregivers to resettle the child, if needed, while keeping a quiet and calm manner.

hold a bottle around 6 months, some self-feeding as early as 12 months, and demonstration of food preferences or pickiness starting between 18 and 24 months, with as many as half of typical toddlers considered to be picky eaters (Bruns & Thompson, 2010; Borowitz & Borowitz, 2018).

Feeding and eating problems are not unusual in early childhood and can range from typical issues like the finicky eating of many toddlers to a formal feeding disorder (Bryant-Waugh, 2019). Despite the fact that feeding problems are very common, a caregiver whose baby won't eat may find their feelings of competence and confidence eroding (Bruns & Thompson, 2010; Borowitz & Borowitz, 2018). When feeding interactions are not "synchronous and positive" (Bruns & Thompson, 2010), the caregiver and baby may be frustrated, and their relationship can suffer. Problems with feeding directly affect the child on a nutritional basis and may at times have an impact on growth. Finally, sleep and feeding can be related. Young children who have digestive problems such as reflux and those who do not take in enough food can have associated sleep issues, often waking due to discomfort or hunger, for example. Home visitors can help distinguish between normal variations in feeding and eating from concerns that require medical or clinical interventions.

Clinically significant feeding and eating challenges in infants and young children can be roughly summarized as falling into three main types: overeating, undereating, and atypical (e.g., pica) (ZERO TO THREE Press, 2021). Although many feeding problems are behavioral, such as food refusal, clinically significant feeding and eating problems are more likely in children with structural or motor differences or medical conditions. For example, a child with a cleft lip or cleft palate may require special equipment and even surgeries to successfully feed. Infants and young children with developmental issues are also more likely to have feeding concerns, with as many as 80% of these children affected (Borowitz & Borowitz, 2018). Children with autism spectrum and other neurodevelopmental disorders may struggle with the sensory aspects of eating, including how the food looks or feels in the mouth, leading to undereating or atypical patterns. Consulting with the child's physician to make sure there are no medical barriers to feeding is important. Home visitors can share with parents that best practices in treating feeding issues are behavioral and require caregiver involvement (Bryant-Waugh, 2019). Interdisciplinary teams that involve specialists such as psychologists and speech and occupational therapists are often needed (Borowitz & Borowitz, 2018). Be aware that guidance about diets, including vitamins, supplements, and strategies related to food allergies is often updated; for current information, home visitors can refer families to their primary care doctors or to reliable websites such as the American Academy of Pediatrics.

Home visitors will often have a chance to observe feeding early on and can use this opportunity to promote good habits. Because serious feeding problems in typically developing children are unusual, in most cases concerns that are present are transient and developmentally normative (Borowitz & Borowitz, 2018). Therefore, reassurance and simple recommendations are often sufficient (Bryant-Waugh, 2019). For very young children, helpful suggestions include use of supportive positioning and a quiet voice, feeding in a low-traffic area with soft lighting, and gentle patting or caressing. In contrast, behaviors that discourage positive feeding habits might include using loud or harsh voices, using rough touch or strong movements such as rocking, propping the bottle, prodding the baby with the nipple, pushing the baby's chin or cheeks while feeding, and feeding in loud or overly bright environments (Brown et al., 2014). As children get older, attention to the types of foods and drinks offered and a focus on gradually increasing independence with feeding is often appropriate, although family preferences, values, and beliefs around feeding may vary.

Infancy and early childhood are important times for caregiver practices that can influence the child's taste and eating preferences over the lifespan (Riley et al., 2018). As parents fully control the foods available to young children, their own eating preferences must be considered, as they are likely to inform the choices they make for their children. In one study, babies as young as 7 months had diets that were very similar to those of their mothers, the majority of whom were reported to be overweight (Karp & Lutenbacher, 2011). Caregivers' food choices and preferences can start affecting a child's taste preferences and eating habits even before birth. Babies' flavor preferences can be affected by the mother's food choices during pregnancy, for example (Beauchamp & Mennella, 2011). As a result, prenatal home visits are also an opportunity to discuss and encourage good eating habits.

Recent studies indicate that 21% of U.S. children between ages 2 and 18 are obese and a total of 35% are either overweight or obese (Hu & Staiano, 2022), with some differences related to family diversity. For example, low-income Latinx infants and toddlers may experience higher obesity rates than Black and white peers (MacMillan Uribe et al., 2022). Both food choices and feeding practices may connect to later obesity (Borowitz & Borowitz, 2018; Ong et al., 2006). Less preferred feeding practices commonly reported in the first 12 months include overfeeding; providing a diet that includes insufficient fruits and vegetables; substituting water or juice for formula or breast milk; mixing formula incorrectly; being unaware of when to introduce potentially dangerous or allergenic foods such as eggs, peanut butter, or honey; giving young babies foods like french fries; and feeding babies while watching television (Karp & Lutenbacher, 2011).

Home visitors should not assume that families from diverse or those from under-resourced communities will not understand or engage in beneficial feeding practices. For example, in one study, Black, Hispanic, and Hmong families receiving supplemental nutrition supports whose children aged 2 to 5 years had healthier weights reported using commonly recommended feeding practices such as establishing a consistent routine for meals, offering healthy choices and letting the child select from those choices, serving appropriate size portions, trusting the child's hunger cues, encouraging physical activity, and limiting screen time. In another study, Latinx caregivers chose feeding practices for their children less than 2 years based on the perceived benefit to the child, whether traditional within their culture or not (MacMillan Uribe et al., 2022).

Home visitors can encourage caregivers to both offer and model eating healthy foods. They can explain common feeding issues in typical children. For example, it can be helpful to let caregivers know that rejecting a new food is so common that young children may need to see a new food 20 to 30 times before they eat it (Borowitz & Borowitz, 2018; Riley et al., 2018).

Home visitors can share practices to try and explain their potential benefit, such as sharing that encouraging self-feeding in toddlers builds fine motor skills and also helps prevent obesity (Riley et al., 2018). Another helpful strategy to encourage toddlers to try a new food is to pair it with a preferred food (Bryant-Waugh et al., 2019). Home visitors can also share practices to avoid and what to do instead; for example, rather than implement a "clean plate" rule, eating responsibilities can be divided so that adults decide what to serve and children decide how much to eat (Riley et al., 2018). Similarly, when caregivers are unaware of proper portion sizes for young children, they may worry that the child does not eat enough, when in reality the child is eating enough for their age and size.

Home visitors should be aware that maintaining healthy eating habits may be hard for some families who may have limited access to healthy foods in their neighborhoods or who may worry about the costs of wasting food. Caregivers' past experiences, such as childhood food deprivation and a history of disordered eating can impact current choices regarding foods. For some families, concrete supports may be needed to encourage healthy eating practices. For example, families may need referrals to obtain healthy food when needed, including the Special Supplemental Nutrition Program for Women, Infants, and Children (WIC) and food pantries. A summary of expected feeding milestones with strategies for promoting healthy eating habits is given in Table 5.4.

Crying, Calming, and Soothing

Infant crying is considered normal, especially for very young babies. However, crying is also quite common throughout the first year of life (Evanoo, 2007; Gilkerson & Gray, 2014). Across cultures, most babies' crying increases over the first 6 weeks, and most of that crying happens during the night. Over the next couple of months, crying will usually decrease but continue at this lower level until about 1 year (Evanoo, 2007; Gilkerson & Gray, 2014). Although no one knows for sure why babies cry, this pattern has led to guesses that crying is innate or related to maturation. Because the amount and intensity of crying vary widely from baby to baby, may vary each day in individual babies, and likely is influenced by the environment including caregiving practices, there is no "normal" amount of crying. Cross-cultural studies find few differences in infant crying. However, babies in cultures where babies are carried in a sling may have less daytime crying (Keren et al., 2018).

Most people find it hard to tolerate a baby's cry and typically seek to reduce the crying by attempting to soothe the infant. An infant's ability to calm on their own or to be soothed by others may be part of their temperament style and is also considered an early self-regulation skill (McClelland & Tominey, 2014). Babies between 1 and 4 months who cry with greater frequency and cannot be calmed may be said to have colic. Published research

Table 5.4. Encouraging healthy eating habits

Age	Skills and milestones	Reading the baby's independence signs	Strategies and supports	Avoid
Newborn	Baby can coordinate sucking, breathing, and swallowing. Breast-fed babies eat more often than babies who take formula.	Baby turns the head, fidgets, or closes the mouth to signify that he or she has had enough.	Use supportive positioning. Arrange a quiet environment.	Do not try to force the bottle. Do not squeeze the baby's cheeks. Offer only formula or breast milk in the bottle. Babies do not need water or other beverages.
4–6 months	Feeding may begin with solids. Breast-fed babies do not need other foods until 6 months.	Signs of baby's readiness for foods include holding head up and showing interest in foods. Baby opens mouth to take a spoon.	Introduce foods in any order: cereal, fruit, or vegetable. Introduce one food at a time and watch for allergic reactions. Go back to formula or breast milk if the baby does not take food.	Follow the baby's lead. Do not overfeed the baby. Do not prod the baby with the bottle or spoon. Do not prop the bottle.
6–12 months	Baby may learn to drink from a cup. Encourage breast feeding through the first year.	Baby may hold a bottle around 6 months. When the baby can sit well and brings hands to mouth, try soft finger foods that do not require chewing.	Caregiver can let the baby hold a spoon while he or she feeds with another spoon. Mashed-up foods like bananas can be offered.	If parents make their own baby foods, they should avoid food high in nitrates such as spinach or green beans. Juice should be avoided until at least 6–9 months and preferably until toddlerhood. Juice drinks with added sugar should also be avoided.

Table 5.4. (continued)

Age	Skills and milestones	Reading the baby's independence signs	Strategies and supports	Avoid
12–18 months	Baby may eat some table foods. Weaning from the bottle is recommended by 15 months. Weaning from the breast can occur when mother and baby are ready; parents should talk to the baby's doctor.	Continue to encourage self-feeding (finger foods) by offering small pieces of soft foods.	Provide a good model as an adult healthy eater. Encourage family meals.	Avoid processed foods or adult foods with added salt and other unhealthy additives. Do not put the baby to bed with the bottle.
18–24 months	The child can bite and chew. The child eats small amounts at a time, so offer three meals and healthy snacks in between meals.	The child may show food preferences and pickiness. Offer new foods multiple times.	Offer a variety of foods and textures. Provide a good model as an adult healthy eater. Give water or milk to drink.	Do not make feeding a battle. Offer a variety of foods, but do not force the child to eat. Avoid sugary drinks, including juices.

Sources: Brown, Pridham, and Brown (2014); Bruns and Thompson (2010).

on colic goes back nearly 60 years; however, there is still no good agreement about the definition, assessment, etiology, and treatment of colic (Ellwood et al., 2020; García Marqués et al., 2017). The term *colic* typically refers to crying in young babies that is described as having a sudden onset, being intense, and resulting in caregivers feeling that they cannot cope. Perhaps the most frequently used criterion for colic is the "rule of threes"; a baby who cries 3 hours per day, 3 days per week, for 3 weeks (Wessel et al., 1954; Mai et al., 2018). Colic may occur in as many as 40% of babies (Wolke, 2019; García Marqués et al., 2017) and is often associated with other regulation issues of sleep and feeding (Helseth, 2022; Mai et al., 2018). Although common, colic has been associated with undesirable outcomes for babies and for their families (Cook et al., 2019). There is little agreement on the best way to manage colic; fortunately, in most babies it improves on its own by 4 months of age (Ellwood et al., 2020). Children with histories of prolonged crying past 6 months, or beyond the colic period, have been reported to have an increased risk for externalizing disorder at later ages, for example. Other concerns associated with colic include the potential risk it poses for child abuse (specifically, shaking), overall family stressors, and parental depression (Gilkerson & Gray, 2014).

Once caregivers get to know their baby, they can usually identify the need that crying or fussing signifies, such as for food, comfort, sleep, or a diaper change (Evanoo, 2007; Keren et al., 2018). Caregivers will typically learn to guess correctly and, if not, can always go through a process of checking the most likely reasons for tears. Home visitors can encourage caregivers to respond to their infant's needs in a timely manner. A small baby cannot be spoiled, so little is to be gained by making a baby wait. In fact, many caregivers are surprised to hear that research has shown that babies who are attended to quickly actually end up crying less in the long run. Babies who are responded to learn that their needs will be met. When this experience occurs regularly, the pathways in the brain create patterns that help build the ability to self-soothe as the baby develops.

Interventions to help families with crying include helping caregivers to set up daily routines (Keren et al., 2018). For very young babies, those less than 8 weeks, swaddling has often been recommended (Evanoo, 2007). It is helpful to model and suggest that caregivers use a low and calm voice when trying to settle the baby. Higher-register tones may signal play time to babies; unfortunately, some people's voices get higher when they are anxious, which may happen when a tired caregiver feels unsuccessful in soothing an infant. Encourage caregivers to monitor their voices so that their tone matches their goal: drop the voice lower to help downregulate (calm) and raise higher to upregulate (alert). Other simple strategies that may help include making a change in the environment to either provide more or less excitement (e.g., change the light, sounds, activity level), using massage techniques, providing movement by walking or rocking, or offering soothing sounds including music and "white noise." Every baby is different, so home visitors can encourage caregivers to try different types of soothing strategies to figure out what their baby likes. See Appendix 5A for some tips for calming a baby.

There will inevitably be times when the baby does not respond to soothing efforts, and this may be the case for babies with colic or other unexplained crying, which may happen in as many as 20% of infants (Keren et al., 2018). Unfortunately, there is no definitive treatment for these issues, a fact that may lead to even more frustration for caregivers who feel unsure about how to help their babies (Kaley et al., 2011). Although it is unlikely that excessive crying has a medical source, caregivers should be encouraged to check with a physician if physical symptoms such as vomiting or diarrhea are present or if the baby seems to be in pain, indicated by high-pitched cries (Gilkerson & Gray, 2104). Some breastfed babies can be helped by a change in the mother's diet, and some formula-fed babies may benefit from switching to special formula or even probiotics, so consulting the primary care team may be helpful (Ellwood et al., 2020). The occupational therapist can help when sensory concerns are present (Keren et al., 2018). In general, methods for soothing babies with more intense or long-lasting crying are the same as those for babies with lower levels of crying. Home visitors can help by normalizing crying and assuring caregivers that the higher levels of crying are unlikely to last past 4 months. Again, encouraging caregivers to engage in self-care and to have sufficient support is useful when given with sensitivity and support. Some caregivers have suggested that they tire of hearing suggestions about what to do, so make sure that the caregiver wants advice before giving it!

Darlene arrives for a visit with Jasmine and her parents at noon. Phil answers the door with Jasmine, who is crying very loudly. Darlene sees that Jasmine is rubbing her eyes and she immediately wonders if the baby is sleepy. Phil says, "You're here! Please take this grumpy baby." Darlene replies, "She does seem out of sorts. I see her rubbing her eyes. Could she be sleepy?" Phil says, "Well, I'm sleepy! She woke up at 7:00 a.m., so I did not get any sleep." Darlene resists her urge to explain about the sleep schedules of infants. Instead, she empathizes with Phil and then asks more questions about Jasmine's sleep pattern. As they talk, Darlene notices that Phil seems interested in figuring out how everyone can get more sleep. Darlene says, "I have some ideas about how you could all get better sleep. Is that something that we could talk about together?" Phil says he will talk to Katarina about this idea and agrees to let Darlene know what they decide at the next visit.

WHAT TO DO WHEN ROUTINES AND CAREGIVER EDUCATION ARE NOT ENOUGH

Despite their best efforts, some families will experience difficulties in these basic areas, requiring more direct interventions that may include those provided by behavioral or medical professionals. Examples include babies with genetic conditions that affect their eating, babies who have been exposed to drugs in utero and are experiencing withdrawal, young children with exposure to significant trauma leading to difficult-to-manage emotional and behavioral reactions, and caregivers with their own needs that interfere with their relationships with their children.

When the behaviors related to problems in regulation do not resolve, home visitors may determine that the issue is outside of their expertise. In these situations, the home visitor can help support families to gain access to other needed resources, including work with medical or behavioral health professionals. In some locations, specialized programs may be available. For example, the Fussy Baby Network (Gilkerson et al., 2020), a program that provides both practical and emotional support to families, is available in many states. Through this program, parents can receive immediate support by phone within 2 days of the initial contact, followed by additional contacts that are individualized to family needs (Gilkerson & Gray, 2014).

Many health professionals value detailed information about the frequency, duration, and intensity of the concerning behavior and about what has been tried. Therefore, the home visitor should encourage the caregivers to share information with the next provider that the home visitor and the family have gathered together to support their own efforts to address a behavior. When appropriate, the home visitor may need to talk directly with other team members to better serve families. In this way, the home visitor can play an important role in supporting a family while staying within their scope of practice and expertise. More details about coordinating with other professionals can be found in Chapter 10.

Darlene returns to the home of Phil, Katarina, and Jasmine regularly for visits over the next several months. The family is happy with the progress that Jasmine has made with sleep. They now have a simple routine that includes regular bedtimes and naps. Jasmine, at age 17 months, is sleeping better, and her parents also have more rest. However, Darlene notices that Jasmine is making little progress in self-feeding and that she is still primarily taking a bottle with formula or juice. She realizes during one visit that she has not seen anyone offer Jasmine food for a while, even a french fry! She decides to ask about her eating during the next visit.

Darlene says, "Jasmine does really well with the bottle, doesn't she?" Katarina replies, "Yes, she really likes the bottle." Darlene continues, asking, "Does she ever seem interested in trying solid foods?" Katarina explains that the doctor said she could have a few things, like Cheerios, a while ago, but it did not go well so she stopped trying. "She kind of choked when I gave her bites from my plate, so I got scared and quit trying that!" Darlene wonders if Jasmine just needs practice with eating or if there could be another problem. She decides to suggest that Katarina check again with the doctor, because the 18-month check-up should happen soon. She helps Katarina organize what to ask the doctor and offers to help with introducing foods if the doctor still recommends it.

USING THE PAUSE FRAMEWORK

Using the vignette in the previous section, let's see how Darlene thinks through her experiences with Jasmine and her family. See Figures 5.1 and 5.2 for examples of how this might look.

WHAT'S NEXT?

In Chapters 6, 7, 8, and 9, we discuss several specific types of challenging behaviors. Next, in Chapter 6, we apply the PAUSE framework for addressing aggression and tantrums.

TIPS FOR PRACTICE

- Share with caregivers the expected milestones or phases in early regulation to sort out typical challenges from more complicated problems.
- Emphasize prevention methods such as healthy routines and good models for sleep, feeding, and self-soothing. Be sure to discuss how these caregiving routines are typically managed within a family's culture.
- Support and assist families to reach out to health and behavioral health providers in specialized programs, sleep clinics, and feeding teams when basic strategies are insufficient.
- Follow professional groups such as the American Academy of Pediatrics and Centers for Disease Control to stay current on these expectations and practices.

KEY POINTS TO REMEMBER

- Self-regulation is a set of skills that allow a person to consciously control thoughts, feelings, and behaviors so that they can think before acting.
- Although some self-regulation skills are present in infancy, it is best to understand these skills as developing over time as the brain matures in the context of sensitive adult scaffolding and caregiving.
- Home visitors can help families support their young children to develop self-regulation in many ways. These include helping caregivers understand typical development so that they have reasonable expectations and provide good routines that build their child's skills and supporting families to use other resources when needed.

PAUSE WORKSHEET

pause

Child: **Jasmine**   Date: **February 2, 2024**

Caregiver: **Katarina and Phil**   Provider: **Darlene**

PERCEIVE—Explore what is happening.

Caregiver perspective:	Provider perspective:
Jasmine is sleeping better. She has trouble eating solid foods.	We have made progress with the sleep routines, but now I am wondering about Jasmine's feeding habits.

ASK—Clarify what is happening.

Starting with the caregiver's priorities and concerns, ask more detailed/specific questions to clarify what is happening.

Ask more questions about what foods were tried and what happened with Jasmine.

What did the doctor recommend? What questions should the family ask the doctor next time?

What would Katarina like to see Jasmine eat?

What is the family's typical eating practice?

UNDERSTAND—Explore why it is happening.

With the caregiver, explore explanations for what is happening. Consider possible explanations that include the environment, the child, and the caregiver. Listen and observe closely as you explore the situation in conversation with the family.

Caregiver perspective:	Provider perspective:	Child's perspective:
Katarina shares she became scared to try more solid foods when Jasmine "choked" on some table food.	I wonder what ideas Katarina has about the kinds of foods young children eat, where she is getting that information,	It appears Jasmine is eager and ready to try solid foods. She may also need more than milk to grow and develop.

(continued)

Figure 5.1. Darlene's PAUSE Worksheet for Katarina, Phil, and Jasmine.

Figure 5.1. *(continued)*

PAUSE WORKSHEET *(continued)*

UNDERSTAND *(continued)*

Caregiver perspective:	Provider perspective:	Child's perspective:
	and who she might trust to learn more about this.	What ways is she showing Katarina that she is ready for foods?

STRATEGIZE and **EVALUATE**—Identify possible responses/solutions.

1. Solution/action to try:	How will we know if it works?
Ask Katarina to ask Jasmine's doctor about this and share the information with me.	Katarina will share the information she receives from the doctor.
	When will we evaluate if it works?
	When we have our next appointment after the doctor visit.

2. Solution/action to try:	How will we know if it works?
Depending on the doctor visit outcome, we might try some new foods together or pursue other assessment or nutrition information.	We will develop this aspect after the appointment.
	When will we evaluate if it works?

PROVIDER REFLECTION WORKSHEET

Provider Reflection Worksheet

Child: _Jasmine_   Date: _February 2, 2024_

Caregiver: _Katarina and Phil_   Provider: _Darlene_

1. How did I follow the caregiver's lead to learn what is most pressing or important to them?	I have been successful in following this family's lead better. Our success in exploring some sleep practices has helped me with my relationship with both parents. I think I carefully brought up my concern about Jasmine's eating with a good result.
2. How did I ask clarifying questions that help me to understand the problem better? How did I inquire about the caregiver's values and beliefs related to the issue?	I did get some better information by acknowledging Jasmine's success with a bottle and wondering whether she might be ready to try solid foods. From that conversation I found out that Katarina is worried Jasmine might choke. I'm really glad I learned this as I think it could explain a lot of what I'm seeing related to feeding.
3. How did I reflect on and offer to discuss similarities and differences between me and the caregiver? These might include race, ethnicity, language, gender, sexual orientation, religious and other beliefs, values, experiences, etc.	It seems clear to me Jasmine would benefit from a regular eating and sleeping schedule and if the family would have mealtimes together, but I also know that's how I was raised and this might not be possible, or even desirable, for every family. I will ask more questions to better understand this family's situation so we can find solutions that work for them.

(continued)

Figure 5.2. Darlene's Provider Reflection Worksheet for Katarina, Phil, and Jasmine.

Figure 5.2. *(continued)*

PROVIDER REFLECTION WORKSHEET *(continued)*

4. How did I provide information that may help the caregiver better understand the child's behavior?	I shared the idea of connecting to the pediatrician before giving a strategy myself. I helped Katarina come up with some possible questions for the pediatrician and agreed to help implement any ideas they agreed on.
5. How did I engage the caregiver to develop a response that may include a strategy to try, a resource to use, or more information to increase understanding?	Katarina committed to asking Jasmine's pediatrician about trying solid foods.
6. How did I provide support and emotional containment if needed?	I was able to help Katarina name her fear that Jasmine may choke when eating. I recognized that I am worried about Jasmine's eating. I feel good that I was able to slow down and stop myself from just giving reassurance and pushing the family to try food right away. I hope we can come up with another plan if Katarina is not able to bring back ideas from the doctor.
7. How do I plan to follow up on promised actions to maintain trust?	I will ask about the pediatric visit and again offer to help implement any suggestions. I am prepared to find more information or perhaps a referral to a nutrition specialist to help Katarina in any way possible.
8. What do I want to discuss in reflective supervision to improve my practice and outcomes with this child and caregiver?	I am still worried about this family and want to know I am doing everything possible to help Jasmine reach her developmental goals. It's hard for me to follow this family's lead and capitalize on opportunities to address issues when they are ready.

SUGGESTED FURTHER READING

Fernando, N., & Potock, M. (2022). *Raising a happy, healthy eater: A parent's handbook* (2nd ed.). The Experiment.

Lester, B., & Grace, C. O. (2005). *Why is my baby crying? The parent's survival guide for coping with crying problems and colic.* Harper Collins.

Mindell, J. (2021). *Sleeping through the night: How infants, toddlers, and their parents can get a good night's sleep* (Rev. ed.). Tantor and Blackstone Publishing.

TIPS FOR CALMING YOUR BABY

- Respond to your young baby's cry! Your baby will cry less when you do.
- For young babies, try swaddling by wrapping the baby "burrito style" in a blanket.
- Keep your voice low to calm the baby down; remember, a high voice is exciting and tells your baby it is time to play.
- Change something—your location, lights, sounds, or activity level.
- Provide movement—walk or rock.
- Lightly tap or rub the baby's back.
- Add soothing sounds like soft music or "white noise" such as a fan.
- Quietly sing a lullaby or favorite song.
- Remember that sometimes babies need to be alone to calm down and may not want to be held or touched.
- Keep track of what your baby likes and what works to calm him or her down.
- Walk away if you become angry or upset. Call a friend or family member to give you a break.

6

Stop That!

Biting, Hitting, Throwing, and Meltdowns

Laurie and Vince decide to take advantage of a pretty fall day to take their three young children, ages 10 months to 5 years, to a nearby park. Their early intervention provider, Debbie, had suggested they spend more time outside, and the couple feel proud that they are trying to follow her advice. It takes longer than they expected to get ready, so it is almost nap time when they have the stroller loaded up and ready to go. Two-year-old Theresa is rubbing her eyes and fussing, but they decide to go anyway because they are all ready. Once at the park, Vince follows Theresa, who runs and seems to be having a good time. Laurie pushes the oldest in a swing and the baby naps in the stroller. Theresa goes to the sand box, where another toddler is digging with a small shovel. She grabs at the shovel and begins to wail when the other child protests. Vince shouts, "No, no!" but Theresa continues to cry and pull at the shovel. When the child does not let go, Theresa hits him.

Virtually all caregivers have been embarrassed when their young child misbehaves in public settings. Examples of this kind of behavior abound, including hitting or biting another child on the playground or an epic "meltdown" when denied a toy in a store. In some cases, the behavior reaches a level where child care providers or other families complain, leading to worry that the toddler who bites, hits, or has tantrums will have problems getting along with peers or will be "kicked out" of school. In the vast majority of young children, aggressive behaviors are not predictive of serious future problems. Even those with "difficult" temperament styles may eventually learn to modulate these behaviors, given proper supports. However, in some cases, aggressive behaviors in early childhood may be intense and persistent, and they may predict many adverse outcomes into teen and adult years (AAP Council on Early Childhood, 2016; Ramchandani et al., 2013; van den Akker et al., 2022; Xie et al., 2022). Indeed, it is now recognized that serious disruptive behavior disorders are almost always present within the first 5 years (Biedzio & Wakschlag, 2019). Whether a challenging behavior is part of a temperament style, a transient developmental phase, or a sign of serious problems, it must be recognized and addressed.

Although physical aggression is, to a certain extent, part of typical development, or, as discussed in Chapter 5, connected to temperament, it is also one of the most common complaints of caregivers with young children and requires attention. For many reasons, including their own caregiving histories, caregivers may struggle to address these kinds of challenging behaviors. As discussed in previous chapters, caregiver experiences related to racism and bias may increase their worry about how a behavior may be viewed and how a child may subsequently be treated by others (Blanchard et al., 2019). This fear is borne out by studies demonstrating implicit bias in early care and education professionals. For example, preschool teachers were asked to note behavior problems when watching videos of Black and white boys and girls. Although none of the videos actually included any problematic behavior, recordings of eye tracking showed that the teachers spent more time watching Black children and especially Black boys compared to white boys or girls (Gilliam et al., 2016). Studies continue to confirm that everyone carries some implicit bias and that these biases may affect how young children are viewed and treated in early care settings (Garo et al., 2021; Wymer et al., 2022). This chapter discusses family- and child-specific correlates of challenging behavior, explains how to tell when difficult behaviors are typical or age appropriate and when they may signal a bigger problem, and describes how to use the PAUSE problem-solving framework to encourage reflection about caregiver and provider reactions to child behavior and to support families in building skills needed to address aggression and other difficult behavior in effective ways.

WHEN TO WORRY—WHAT IS TOO MUCH AGGRESSION?

When are aggressive behaviors normal and when should caregivers worry? Determining when difficult behavior, such as aggression, tantrums, and noncompliance (addressed in Chapter 7) is a sign of a bigger problem versus an age-appropriate phase can be tricky. Early development often proceeds rapidly, with a wide range of variation, and with much overlap between symptoms that can be part of normal development and those symptoms that signal a long-term problem. Attending to two key parameters—developmental appropriateness and level of dysregulation—helps researchers, providers, and caregivers sort things out (Biedzio & Wakschlag, 2019).

Some behavior challenges are more likely at certain ages and under certain circumstances, such as being tired, sick, or frustrated. Researchers point to signs of dysregulation, including the frequency, intensity, and persistence of difficult behavior as indicators of a larger concern rather than a phase that will pass in time (Ramchandani et al., 2013; Wakschlag et al., 2012; Manning et al., 2019). Recognizing the expected levels of physical aggression in the first 3 years of life can help caregivers and providers to sort out typical difficult behaviors from those that should give them pause. Table 6.1 shows how aggression changes from infancy to preschool age.

In general, both oppositional behaviors and aggression, such as hitting and biting, are fairly frequent between ages 1 and 3 years, and even into early preschool ages. Caregivers can expect to first see aggressive actions around their child's first birthday, with a steep rise into the second year (Alink et al., 2006; Biedzio & Wakschlag, 2019; Manning et al., 2019; Tremblay et al., 2004; van den Akker et al., 2022). It is reassuring to know that most difficult behaviors should reach their maximum at the end of the second year, with much improvement typically seen after age 3 or sometimes 4 years. It is likely that aggression most often occurs as a result of caregiver efforts to limit young children's behavior, clashing with the child's interest in autonomy and independence that is so characteristic of this age range (Alink et al., 2006). At the other end of this process, the reduction in aggression after age 3 years is understood to occur because children have better language and cognitive skills and have internalized some social and moral expectations (Manning et al., 2019). So in both cases, rising and deescalating aggression, much of the changes in behavior are due to changes in developmental skills. As reviewed in Chapter 5, caregiver scaffolding over time provides another source of young children's growing EF skills, self-regulation, and associated reduction in challenging behaviors (Hughes et al., 2023; McDermott & Fox, 2019). Home visitors can use their understanding of these two factors related to challenging behavior when supporting children and families.

Table 6.1. Expected aggressive behavior by child age

	1 Year	2 Years	3 Years
Expected aggression level patterns	Onset of aggression around first birthday	Aggression increases steeply in second year	Aggression should decrease through ages 3 to 4 years as language improves
Common reasons for aggression	Tired or does not feel well Limited language and communication skills	Independence needs High energy; low impulse control	Developmental delays Difficulty matching behavioral expectations to differing situations (e.g., playground versus library) Exposure to aggressive models

Sources: Alink et al. (2006); Ramchandani et al. (2013); Tremblay et al. (2004).

Tantrums or toddler meltdowns are fairly frequent in children between the ages of about 18 months and nearly 4 years, especially when a child is tired, hungry, or distressed (Potegal et al., 2003). Indeed, more than 80% of toddlers have tantrums some of the time, and most children at least a year old have had one or more tantrums (Manning et al., 2019; Wakschlag et al., 2018). A tantrum once or twice per week is not unusual in a child younger than 4 years; 2-year-olds are more likely to have daily tantrums than older children, although this is still relatively rare, occurring in about 12% in community samples (van den Akker et al., 2022). To get a picture of typical tantrums, researchers rely on caregiver reports. In a study that divided responses by child ages, caregivers reported that a typical tantrum for toddlers up to 3 years lasts 1 to 5 minutes with tantrums of 4- and 5-year-olds lasting as long at 10 minutes (Manning et al., 2019). The same study found that tantrums lasting up to 30 minutes were uncommon at any age.

Tantrum behavior often happens when a young child has strong emotions and has not yet learned ways to control these feelings and subsequent behaviors. Adults may most often associate tantrums with anger, but they can also occur when a child is very tired, sad, disappointed, or even scared. In the study by Potegal et al. (2003), if a child showed physical signs of anger early in the tantrum, such as stomping their feet or falling to the floor, the meltdown was likely to be short and caregivers did not report a need to intervene. Showing other angry behaviors such as screaming, kicking, hitting, and stiffening the body was associated with more intense tantrums. Many children moved quickly from angry behavior to distress, indicated by crying or wanting to be comforted. Caregivers in the study described their children as initially angry when they couldn't get what they wanted, and sadness followed when the child began to see that the tantrum would not result in getting their way (Potegal et al., 2003).

Physically aggressive behaviors can be associated with other challenging behaviors. Typical toddlers also have a relatively high activity level, may have problems taking turns, and are likely to have a limited ability to sustain attention (Danis et al., 2009). In one study, caregivers were asked to describe the "hyperactive" behavior of their 17-month-old children by rating the frequency of behaviors such as not being able to sit still, fidgeting, having difficulty waiting turns, and not being able to settle for a task for more than a few minutes (Romano et al., 2013). Almost a third of the toddlers were described as showing frequent hyperactive behavior, and 70% showed hyperactivity at least sometimes (Romano et al., 2013). In the same sample, oppositional and aggressive behaviors frequently co-occurred in children reported to have higher levels of hyperactivity. In a commentary, Schellinger and Talmi (2013) reinterpreted the data from Romano and colleagues as indicating that hyperactivity, but not highly aggressive behaviors, is typical in toddlers.

This discussion may prompt the question, "Can young children have ADHD (attention-deficit/hyperactivity disorder)?" Perhaps the best answer is,

"It's complicated." Diagnosis of ADHD requires that the behaviors be present in two or more settings, last longer than 6 months, and be present prior to age 12 years (American Psychiatric Association, 2022). Although caregivers of many children who later receive a diagnosis of ADHD report noticing emerging behavior problems, including impulsivity, lack of attention, and overactivity when the child is a toddler, the DSM-5 TR acknowledges that these behaviors are harder to distinguish from typical development before preschool age. As a result, it can be hard for young children to receive a diagnosis that describes the caregiver's concerns, makes sense developmentally, and can lead to appropriate treatment. The *Diagnostic Classification of Mental Health and Developmental Disorders of Infancy and Early Childhood, 2* (DC:0-5; ZERO TO THREE Press, 2021) provides a diagnosis to fill this gap: Overactivity Disorder of Toddlerhood (OADT). OADT focuses on distinguishing normal overactive behaviors from those that interfere with development, relationships, and overall family functioning (ZERO TO THREE Press, 2021). When young children present with these behaviors across settings, such as home, child care, and even during early intervention sessions, OADT can be considered and additional support may be sought (Tomlin et al., 2023). We will discuss accessing outside supports later in this chapter.

Earlier, we discussed how normal limitations in language are connected to aggression. For home visitors working with young children with developmental delays, problems with communication may also be a factor in this kind of difficult behavior (Manning et al., 2019). Researchers surveyed nearly 2000 mothers of toddlers in a diverse community sample. They found that children who were delayed in speaking had tantrums that were more frequent and included more dysregulated behavior than peers with typical language. Although boys are often thought to have more acting out behavior than girls, and earlier work suggested that boys who were late talkers had more behavior concerns than girls (see Alink et al., 2006), no gender differences were found in this study. It is likely that a number of factors interact regarding the impact and meaning of a specific behavior a child demonstrates. Home visitors should strive for a nuanced approach that considers a range of child and caregiver characteristics, including gender, ethnicity, and race, when supporting families with challenging behavior.

Although some aggression, noncompliance, and tantrum behaviors are expected in the early years, these types of challenging behaviors should be trending down as the child approaches 3 years of age and language skills improve. Studies of preschool children have suggested that frequent and lengthy tantrums disrupt a child's functioning and are associated with risk for mental health issues and overall family stress (Belden et al., 2008; Wakschlag et al., 2018). More than five tantrums in one day or 10 to 20 tantrums within a month, tantrums that lasted longer than about 25 minutes, and aggression toward caregivers or self, and destroying things during the tantrum were associated with clinical diagnoses of depression and disruptive behaviors in this study (Belden et al., 2008). More recently, in a sample of children ages 1 to 5, more frequent tantrums were associated with acting out behavior problems, whereas longer tantrums were associated with anxious or depressive symptoms (van den Akker et al., 2022). Furthermore, in a 1-year follow-up study of a sample of these children, aggression to self and to others was associated with both internalizing and externalizing problems. The authors suggested that "losing your temper" shown by more frequent tantrums connects to acting out behavior, whereas problems in "finding your temper" or calming back down seem to be connected to emotional or internalizing issues (p. 415). Furthermore, as with other studies, children with tantrums that are both frequent and lengthy tended to have longer lasting behavioral health issues.

One understudied characteristic of challenging behavior that has been receiving more attention is lack of concern for others, often called callousness (Biedzio & Wakschlag, 2019). Lack of concern for others is considered highly unusual even for young children, and it is almost always a red flag. Callousness is not normative: Toddlers can show empathy, prosocial actions, and some understanding of social rules (Kochanska et al., 2010). Even a young baby's distress in response to the distress of others is considered a rudimentary form of compassion. In recognition of the seriousness of this behavior, researchers are creating methods to assess callousness in children as early as 14 months of age (Wakschlag et al., 2018). We will discuss this topic in greater detail in the context of compliance in Chapter 7.

In summary, difficult behavior is not unusual in the first 3 years and may even continue, to an extent, past this age. Home visitors can evaluate how problematic a behavior is by considering how much impairment it causes, how far the behavior falls outside of expectations for the child's age and the situation, and how much dysregulation is present (Biedzio & Wakschlag, 2019). If the behavior usually has a clear trigger, the child can be calmed, and the child seems to be gaining skills in self-regulation overall, caregivers and providers do not likely have to worry about long-term problems (Wakschlag et al., 2018). In contrast, tantrums that are frequent, longer, intense, and seem to happen "out of the blue" can signal a more long-term concern (Biedzio & Wakschlag, 2019; van den Akker et al., 2022). Table 6.2 provides an overview of tantrum behavior.

Table 6.2. Toddler tantrum behaviors

Typical pattern	Possible problem
One to two tantrums per week	Five or more tantrums per day or 10-20 in a week
Tantrum lasts up to 5 minutes	Tantrum lasts longer than 25-30 minutes
Reason for tantrum is clear (e.g., being told no or prevented from doing something; overtired or hungry)	Child cannot be calmed or self-soothe
	Child hurts self, others, or destroys things
Child can calm relatively quickly	Child unaware of feelings of others

Sources: Belden, Thompson, and Luby (2008); Potegal, Kosorok, and Davidson (2003).

FAMILY RISK FACTORS AND MAINTENANCE OF AGGRESSION

So far, we have discussed how most difficult behavior is a common part of early childhood. In fact, the prevalence of emotional, behavioral, and relationship problems in children less than 6 years (7%–10%) is not only very consistent with rates for older children but is also known to persist when not addressed (AAP, 2016; Zhang et al., 2023). Sadly, most children with these behavioral health needs receive no intervention (AAP, 2016).

When home visitors see aggressive child behavior, they may feel a press to suggest and teach behavior management methods. However, it is often more valuable to slow down and to consider the broader factors that may have led to or that maintain both positive and less desired child behaviors. Young children's behavior develops over time and within the context of their family, community, and culture. Factors that support and those that create vulnerabilities include those related to the child, the caregiver, and the overall family culture and neighborhood/community context. Risk and resilience factors can affect a child directly, through the caregiving relationship, or through a combination of both pathways. For example, a traumatic event that happened to the caregiver and was witnessed by a child can impact the child directly, lead to caregiving reactions that disrupt or mute positive caregiving behaviors, and cause challenging caregiver–child interactions and relationship.

Because young children's development is understood to be fully reliant on the caregiver, much attention has been given to risk factors related to caregiver status or caregiving skill (e.g., caregiver is younger, has less education, has their own behavioral health challenges, and lacks caregiving skill) and overall family risks (e.g., crowded housing, unsafe or less resourced neighborhoods, low income, and trauma exposures, including experiences of discrimination) (Carbonneau et al., 2022; Ramchandani et al., 2013; Weitzman et al., 2014). The availability and quality of supports that a caregiver receives from a co-parent or within the community have also been considered.

It is interesting to note that both harsh, overreactive caregiving and inconsistent or lax discipline have been connected to early-onset behavior problems, including developmentally unexpected levels of defiance and aggression (Mence et al., 2014). Home visitors may notice caregivers who seem to be struggling to manage their own responses to stressful situations, including challenging child behaviors. These caregivers may be so overstressed that they have limited resources to respond appropriately to difficult child behavior. These caregivers could range from those who appear to do nothing to help reduce challenging behavior to those who use harsh punishments, frightening their children and providing an aggressive model (Dozier & Bernard, 2019). It is important to engage caregivers in dialogue about discipline methods that are observed, to understand their cultural relevance and to avoid making assumptions based solely on the home visitor's own experience and cultural background. When home visitors take the time to have these constructive conversations, they are better able to help the caregiver find a balanced and effective approach to difficult toddler behavior that is culturally congruent.

A good amount of research has considered the effects of harsh and overreactive caregiving in contrast to caregiving that combines firmness with a level of warmth. We have already discussed how common "negative" behavior is in early childhood. Caregivers who use a lot of verbal or physical force are more likely to notice this kind of difficult child behavior and are less likely to see positive behavior (Mence et al., 2014; Patterson, 1982). These caregivers may believe that the child is displaying the undesirable behavior on purpose or even to hurt them (Keren et al., 2018). As a result, these caregiver–child interactions are predominantly negative, and there are relatively few times that caregivers and children enjoy fun or even neutral interactions. Pioneering researcher Gerard Patterson (1982) explained that both caregivers and children in these families have learned to use "aversive control tactics," described as escalating cycles of behaviors such as whining, nagging, shouting, and hitting. Because both parties are inconsistent, both caregivers and children are sometimes rewarded for their responses, maintaining the patterns of behavior. These negative interaction patterns are in place by age 2 years but escalate over time, with the caregiver hostile behavior getting more frequent and intense as the child gets older. Even within each episode, the negative behavior on both sides escalates until the episode is ended by the caregiver doing something like hitting or yelling. Table 6.3 provides examples of common aggressive patterns in families, with suggested responses.

Table 6.3. Helpful responses to common aggressive patterns in families

What you might see	How you might respond
The caregiver has trouble seeing positive child behavior.	Point out positive behaviors the child displays. Help the caregiver provide simple commands the child can follow to give experiences of competence.
The caregiver thinks the child is displaying negative behavior to annoy them.	Sympathize with the caregiver that it often feels that the child is doing things on purpose. Encourage wondering about what a child might get from their behavior to promote a more realistic view.
Caregiver and child interactions involve escalating cycles of negative behaviors by both parties.	Encourage the caregiver to use a low voice and calm expression. Encourage plans for both the caregiver and child to take breaks to avoid escalation that includes physical aggression.
The caregiver and child are inconsistent, leading to rewards for poor behavior by both.	Help the caregiver learn to pick their battles. Help the caregiver consistently enforce limits they choose to set.
Caregiver-child interactions are almost always negative. There is little room for shared positive experiences.	Ask the caregiver to think of times when they had fun or experienced any positive emotion with the child. Encourage the caregiver to think about how that was for the child, too. Set up some simple, age-appropriate activities and coach the caregiver through them, ending on a positive note.

Sources: Mence et al. (2014); Patterson (1982).

Many home visiting programs, such as those that include families involved in child welfare, support caregivers who are at high risk for negative caregiving practices due to their own low self-regulation and reflective skill (Slade et al., 2023). It is helpful to recognize that often these families include caregivers who received and may be replicating the hostile, harsh, or overreactive caregiving that they received in their own childhoods. Caregivers who did not have a chance to develop effective self-regulation may experience difficulty tolerating their child's negative emotions. These caregivers may perceive their child's angry, scared, or other negative emotions as unexpected and unprovoked. As a result, they may subsequently feel "emotionally flooded," which can be described as feeling overwhelmed and disorganized (Gottman, 1991). In this overwhelmed state, the caregiver has trouble thinking in a way that allows them to read the child's intentions and needs accurately. Furthermore, the caregiver's dysregulated emotions and disorganized thinking may result in choosing discipline strategies that rely on aggression and coercion and decrease the likelihood that the caregiver will use a strategy that helps the child calm down and feel soothed (Dozier & Bernard, 2019; Mence et al., 2014). Additional information about supporting families with very serious challenges, such as trauma experiences, caregiver depression, developmental disorder, or substance use is presented in Chapter 10.

The home visitor can initiate a dialogue by asking caregivers what it is like for them when their child demonstrates challenging behaviors. As discussed earlier, some caregivers of color may see a strong response to challenging behavior as necessary to protect the child from the stereotyped and even dangerous reactions of others (Blanchard et al., 2019). Through discussion, the home visitor can help the caregiver notice and describe feelings in order to make connections between their own feelings and their responses to challenging child behavior. For example, a caregiver may realize that they feel embarrassment when the child hits another person, prompting use of rough discipline methods in the hope of stopping the behavior quickly. Other caregivers may not even recognize their own behavior as potentially frightening to the child (Dozier & Bernard, 2019). Over time, these caregivers might come to understand that seeing their child feel afraid brings on their own feelings of fear, and soon they are both paralyzed. Home visitors may help a caregiver learn some self-regulation methods, such as reframing the difficult behavior as part of typical development, taking breaks when needed, and being able to ask for help. As the caregiver gets better at identifying their own feelings and learns more methods to manage upset feelings, they will be better able to consider the child's perspective.

Vince says, "That's not our shovel. You can't just take things!" Theresa ignores Vince and keeps crying. He feels embarrassed and wonders what the other families think. Frustrated, he picks up Theresa and gives her a swat on the diaper. She yells louder and Vince feels worse. He carries her back to the stroller and digs around in the diaper bag for a toy, but Theresa keeps crying. Laurie is angry at Vince for hitting Theresa. "We said we weren't going to use hitting anymore," she reminds him. "No, you said that. I got whipped as a kid and I turned out fine," Vince retorts. After some time, Laurie finally calms Theresa by letting her play with a cell phone. They leave the park feeling discouraged.

Although less studied, a detached caregiving style is also associated with child behavior concerns. Detached caregiving (Ryan et al., 2006) is characterized by inconsistent discipline and low involvement with the child. Caregivers with a detached style may rarely interact with their child, often due to preoccupation with their own interests and activities (e.g., the caregiver is often observed looking at their phone while the child plays alone). In addition, caregivers with a detached style may fail to respond to their children's bids for interaction or requests for help with frustrating situations. Failure to attend to child needs and support in upsetting or frustrating situations means many missed opportunities to provide regulation or to scaffold the child's self-regulation (Jones Harden et al., 2014). Detached caregiving, like harsh parenting, is associated with caregiver stress, which has been directly associated with child behavior problems in children under age 3 years (Jones Harden et al., 2014). Strategies that help the caregiver notice the child's bids for attention, such as speaking for the baby, may be helpful. For example, speaking in the baby's voice, the home visitor could say "I see what you are eating and want to try some" to encourage a caregiver to notice their baby's interest in solid foods. Home visitors can coach parents through interactions, narrating out loud the positive responses that the child is demonstrating. For example, sitting together with the infant and caregiver, the home visitor could say "He is smiling at you. I wonder if he is telling you he is ready to play." At times, the home visitor may find that some caregivers are hard to engage with this strategy. In these situations, consider dropping back to spend time noticing and responding to caregiver needs, sometimes referred to as filling up the caregiver's "emotional fuel tank."

Home visitors observe and hear about a wide variety of difficult behaviors in young children. Although caregivers often expect home visitors to have ideas and suggestions to immediately fix unwanted behaviors in children, this may be impossible, as things may not be as they seem. Let's use the PAUSE framework to help you consider examples of challenging behaviors provided in the following short vignettes. As a reminder, the PAUSE steps are Perceive, Ask, Understand, Strategize, and Evaluate. For this activity, we will highlight the Understand section from the PAUSE framework to reflect on possible child, caregiver, and provider perspectives. As you think about each vignette, take time to imagine families and the home visitors as being of the same or different socioeconomic, ethnic, racial, and cultural backgrounds. Notice any similarities and differences in your reactions and responses.

Child Perspective

How might child behavior relate to caregiving practices? What is it like for the baby/toddler in this relationship?

Caregiver Perspective

What beliefs, attitudes, or experiences might connect to the behaviors of the caregivers in these examples? How might these beliefs, attitudes, or experiences influence the way the caregiver sees and responds to the baby/toddler?

Provider/Home Visitor Perspective

How would it feel for you to witness these events as a home visitor? What methods can you imagine to manage your own feelings and to address the needs of the caregiver and the child?

Dylan (age 20 months) was playing with his blocks on the floor at the end of the session with Mary, the home visitor. His father, Robert, joined the play, making a tall tower of blocks and then knocking it down with a big punch. As Dylan squealed in laughter, Robert scattered the blocks again, making a "kaboom" sound. He grabbed Dylan and tickled him while throwing him in the air, yelling "kaboom." After a few minutes, Robert noticed the time and realized they needed to say goodbye to Mary and then get ready to go pick up Dylan's brother at kindergarten. He quickly put Dylan down and started to pick up the blocks. Dylan tried to continue the play, laughing and squealing. Robert shouted to Dylan that play time was over, but Dylan ran around throwing blocks and yelling "kaboom." Robert grabbed Dylan roughly and said, "Hey, no throwing blocks! You can hurt someone!" As Dylan quieted and looked a little scared, Mary looked at Robert questioningly. Robert said, "You understand I have to teach him to act right. He can get in big trouble if people think he is a problem."

Elizabeth was talking with the home visitor about the next virtual appointment. During the interaction, her daughter, Lydia (age 2 years), repeatedly came on screen and tried to ask her for a snack. Elizabeth ignored Lydia's attempts to get her attention. Finally, Lydia kicked her mother in the leg and yelled, "I hungry!" Elizabeth responded angrily by hitting Lydia's leg and saying, "I am talking. You are a bad girl for interrupting me!"

Abby and her son, Carson (age 30 months), are meeting with Jill, a home visitor in a prevention program. Carson is driving his toy cars on a mat on the floor while they talk. When Jill asks how things are going, Abby explains that her ex-boyfriend had contacted her over the weekend, even though a restraining order is in place. He wanted to come over to see Carson; Abby did not want to allow it, but she was afraid to refuse. As Abby explained that the visit escalated into an argument, she began to cry. Carson continued to play with his cars, but began throwing them against the walls. Abby shouted at him to stop, and Carson ran over and hit her in the stomach. Abby looked shocked and pulled back from Carson, who then cried and tried to get in her lap. Abby pushed him away while Jill tried to figure out a way to help everyone calm down.

The home visitor brought some different toys with her to the session to see how Billy (age 35 months) might respond. She let him choose a toy from her bag. He pulled out a baby doll and grabbed it by the throat and said, "Shut up. I told you shut up." He then punched the doll on the face and threw it on the floor. Next, he picked up a toy truck and started driving it, making horn sounds. The home visitor looked to Billy's grandmother; she seemed unconcerned.

Susanna (age 15 months) was just learning to sit at the table. She struggled to reach her drink. When she reached, she made a squished-up face and made a grunting sound. Her grandmother laughed at this face. Susanna grinned and made the face again while her grandmother laughed. This little fun game continued for several minutes. After snack time, Susanna was playing with her mother on the floor and made the face and noise. Her mother corrected her, saying she should not make a rude face because she might get in trouble at preschool. Susanna appeared confused that her mother didn't know the game she had played with her grandmother.

After a long morning and no nap in the afternoon, Ryan (age 27 months) played in the family living room while his mother, Gloria, folded laundry and watched television. Ryan moved from activity to activity quickly. Finding a pile of toys in the corner, Ryan tossed some stuffed animals in the air briefly before he found a toy truck and drove it around in circles, making a honking sound. When he drove over some crayons, Ryan picked one up and started drawing on the truck. His mother yelled at him to stop coloring on the truck and to calm down. He looked at her, turned, and jumped into the pile of toys and hit his head on the corner of the toy box. "That's what happens when you act wild!" Gloria yelled.

Nancy was sitting on the floor getting ready to start the home visiting session with Natalie (age 14 months). She was talking with Natalie's mother, Grace, about the past week. As the women talked, Natalie grabbed Nancy's glasses from her face and bent the frame before letting go of them. Grace looked embarrassed and apologized multiple times for the "shameful" behavior. The visit was eventually cut short despite Nancy's efforts to reassure Grace.

These narratives and other examples of difficult child behaviors and unskilled caregiver responses to such behavior may be very familiar to home visitors. Caregivers may describe a behavior that occurred, seeking sympathy and help. Other times, a home visitor may witness the difficult exchange between caregiver and child. Still other times, the child may display difficult behavior toward the home visitor. In any case, the home visitor is often in a position to wonder about the best response to challenging behaviors. What strategies could be considered when supporting caregivers to respond effectively to challenging child behaviors? How might the home visitor attend to context, including the family's culture or past experiences when discussing behaviors with caregivers? Similarly, how can the home visitor become aware of their own biases that can impact how they see and respond to children and families? We first discuss prevention methods, followed by helpful immediate responses when difficult behavior is witnessed and strategies to cover later when everyone is calmer.

To begin, it is helpful to consider ways to prevent behavior problems before they happen. Because children's behaviors are often predictable, preventing misbehavior is actually possible. Helping caregivers to plan ahead, consider development, and make use of their knowledge of their child's rhythms related to sleep and routines can help avoid putting children into situations where problem behavior is likely to occur. Let's revisit the vignette to see how the home visitor begins to help Vince and Laurie consider these factors.

A week later, Vince and Laurie talk to the early intervention provider, Debbie, about their experience at the park. Vince is angry that the outing went so poorly. He tells Debbie, "Theresa was so bad. She does that stuff on purpose to make me mad. I know she knows better." Laurie adds, "I can tell you we won't be trying to take all of them out any time soon. It is just not worth it." Debbie thinks about the many things she would like to address, including the use of spanking, trying the trip when the kids were tired, Vince's lack of understanding of Theresa's perspective, and explaining the behavior from a developmental perspective. She feels disappointed as she realizes that she had been encouraging Vince and Theresa to try to new things for weeks and now when they finally did, it was a disaster. As she takes a breath to slow herself down, Debbie becomes aware that she is nearly as discouraged as Vince and Laurie seem to be. With this self-awareness, she decides to start with the sad feelings that both she and the caregivers share.

Debbie says, "I am feeling so badly that the trip did not work out as we planned and hoped. Let's see if we can figure out what happened. Was there any part that did go okay?" Vince and Laurie agree that it was nice at the beginning. Debbie asks them to think about what happened before Theresa hit the other child. As they discuss the events, Debbie is able to gently direct their attention to how Theresa might have been feeling: perhaps tired, frustrated because she wanted the toy, and then upset when Vince spanked her. She asks Vince and Laurie to talk about what they might do differently if they tried this again. "Maybe we could leave earlier so Theresa doesn't miss her nap," Laurie suggests.

Prevention through planning ahead will not always work. Caregivers will still need to have some strategies to address difficult behaviors that are a normal part of child development and responses to strong emotions. Home visitors can help caregivers learn how to identify triggers for difficult behaviors and to understand how their own reactions and other outcomes might increase difficult behaviors, as discussed in Chapter 4. Use of distraction techniques, such as redirecting the child to another activity, can be helpful if done prior to a tantrum. For this to work, caregivers must become good observers and notice the lead-up to their child's difficult responses.

Remember that the redirection will be most successful if it matches the child's interest and need. If the child is playing in a way that is too active or too loud for the setting, trying to redirect to a quiet activity right away may not work. Instead, having them go to a place where active play is allowed or modifying what they are doing to fit where you are will probably work better. In another example, Suzy is busily emptying out her drawers and tossing clothing everywhere. Her mother sees that she is interested in taking things out of containers, so she provides her with some plastic containers and small toys. She shows her how to put the toys in and dumps them back out. Suzy is delighted and plays with the containers and toys while her mother puts the clothing away. Other strategies that may fend off a tantrum include offers of help, subtle scaffolding, and encouraging a child to take a break from a frustrating activity.

When children are already upset and are having a meltdown, a calm adult is a must. Encourage the caregivers to stay calm, speak in a low voice, and remain available to the upset young child. Use of simple language to explain what is happening at the child's level, especially when paired with feeling words, may be helpful (McClelland & Tominey, 2014). Remember, many tantrums start as anger when the child is not able to have what they want, but sadness may frequently follow. Trying to redirect, explain, or teach will probably not work at that moment. Caregivers may have to set limits when aggressive or oppositional behavior occurs. Letting the child know with simple words that you will not let them hurt you, others, or themselves can be effective when done with closeness and redirection.

Many caregivers believe that retribution for aggression, such as hitting a child or "biting them back," is an effective form of punishment. However, this method or any corporal punishment is typically ineffective. One concern is that physical punishment provides an aggressive model (Durrant & Ensom, 2012). In addition, corporal punishment does not help the child understand what behavior is expected. It is also important to note that holding children against their will in an effort to help them calm down is not recommended for very young children. This method also sends the message that using force is the way to solve problems and may actually frighten a young child (Dunlap et al., 2011). Similarly, restraining an upset child in a car seat or other device is also not recommended. Car seats are not designed to be used in this way, and there have been instances of young children being severely injured when this method was used (Bull, 2014).

As Debbie and Laurie finish making plans to try another outing when Theresa is not tired, Vince suddenly says, "I still think I was right to spank her." The home visitor, Debbie, thanks Vince for letting her know his view. She asks what Vince is hoping that Theresa will learn from spanking. Vince says "To be nice and share." Debbie agrees that these are important things to learn. She tells Vince she is interested in hearing more about his thoughts and asks if he would also hear her ideas. Vince, with Laurie's urging, agrees that they can talk more about this. "Nobody else ever said they would listen to my side. I guess I can at least listen to yours," Vince says.

SUPPORTING POSITIVE BEHAVIORS THROUGH TEACHING AND REFLECTION

There are several other strategies that home visitors can share with caregivers to help when young children show aggression. As discussed in Chapter 4, the parents can identify a behavior that they would like the child to display instead of the aggressive behavior and provide reinforcement for that behavior. The behavior might be one the child already knows how to do or one that is taught. The home visitor can support the caregivers to think of an appropriate substitute behavior and help them understand the best ways to reinforce it. Chapter 7 describes how to use praise effectively as part of this method.

It can be helpful to encourage caregivers to recognize how they are responding to their child's behavior. A nice starting point is to ask, "How is it for you when your child is hitting?", for example. This type of question demonstrates interest in the caregiver's experience and perspective and provides an opening to discuss the caregiver's reactions. Often, caregivers are having a hard time tolerating their children's upset feelings or behaviors but are not aware of their own experience. This may be related to their own childhood experiences or simply a result of current stresses. Caregiver responses can also connect to their concerns for potentially serious outcomes when others view their child's behavior through biases. Home visitors who have not personally experienced these types of bias and stereotyping may be unaware that this experience is common for others. Some caregivers may feel mildly stressed by their child's behavior, whereas others may be totally overwhelmed. Regardless, the home visitor may support caregivers to think about ways they can calm themselves at these times. Some quick ways caregivers can feel calmer include reminding themselves that their child will not be this age forever, taking three long breaths, and using humor to lift their own mood.

When the caregiver stays calm, they will be better able to think about an effective response to their child's distress. If caregivers are too stressed on a routine basis, asking them to identify who else can help, so that they can take a break, may also be helpful (Mence et al., 2014). When there is no one who can help quickly, caregivers can be coached to give the child an age-appropriate time-out or to give themselves a time-out. Either of these "breaks" can help stop escalating high emotions of the parent and child (Mence et al., 2014).

Overall, providers should encourage caregivers to engage with their young children in warm and supportive ways. This may be even more important to emphasize when young children are exhibiting challenging behavior than at other times. Warm and engaged caregiving is related to children learning how to self-regulate emotions and manage their behavior in difficult situations (Dosman & Gallagher, 2022). When home visitors show warmth and develop positive relationships with caregivers, it is more likely that caregivers will develop and demonstrate similar skills with their young children. For a summary of timely tips for tolerating challenging behaviors, see Appendix 6A.

EXPLORING THE PROVIDER'S FEELINGS AND REACTIONS

As discussed in earlier chapters, it is not unusual or wrong for home visitors to have many feelings, both positive and negative, related to their work with families. Furthermore, just like caregivers, home visitors can have personal responses to challenging child behaviors, such as aggression, or to the choices they see caregivers make regarding discipline methods. Some reactions might relate to the home visitor's beliefs about families, how caregivers and children should be with each other, or caregiving or other household practices. At times, these responses may even relate to the home visitor's previous experiences with families and their own personal history with relationships, including being cared for or as they provide care to their own children. The ways that family members respond to a home visitor personally and their recommendations or ideas may lead to positive or negative feelings. Home visitors might find it hard to accept if a child acts aggressively toward them, for example. They may really enjoy working with some families and feel frustrated when other families are angry, disengaged, or not receptive to their recommendations. We talk more about the effects of the home visitor's personal experiences on their work in Chapter 10.

When home visitors see practices that evoke negative feelings or reactions, it is helpful to try to learn more about the caregiver's perspective—for example, how the caregiver is seeing the child, what the caregiver is hoping the child will learn from use of a specific caregiving practice, and how the caregiver learned about raising children. As we have discussed, the home visitor is in the best position to learn these pieces of information when they have a positive relationship with the parents. Using the sections of the PAUSE Worksheet (Appendix 3A) related to perceiving, asking, and understanding will be helpful in gathering this kind of information.

Stopping to reflect and connect with one's own personal feelings about the situation can help the home visitor slow down and form some good questions that engage caregivers in a dialogue. Developing reflective skills can also help home visitors be aware of their own biases, beliefs, responses, and reactions and may improve their ability to consider the experiences of caregivers and children. Practicing reflection is always needed and can be particularly useful when the home visitor is unfamiliar with a family's culture and caregiving practices. The Provider Reflection Worksheet (found in Appendix 3B) provides a structured way of thinking about personal responses and reactions. Discussing these types of responses with a supervisor or supportive colleague can be beneficial. When appropriate, the home visitor may also want to discuss their own response with the caregiver as part of their collaborative problem solving.

USING THE PAUSE FRAMEWORK

Using the vignettes in this chapter, let's see how Debbie thinks through her experiences with Theresa and her caregivers, Vince and Laurie. See Figures 6.1 and 6.2 for examples of how this might look.

WHAT'S NEXT?

In Chapter 7, we apply the PAUSE problem-solving approach to look at another type of common but difficult behavior, noncompliance.

TIPS FOR PRACTICE

- Recognize and help caregivers understand that aggression and tantrum behaviors are very common in children between ages 1 and 3 years.

- Be aware that caregiver experiences including experiences such as trauma and racial bias may contribute to caregiving practices.

- Help caregivers connect to their feelings to build their own capacity for self-regulation to more effectively manage challenging child behaviors.

KEY POINTS TO REMEMBER

- Difficult behaviors, including verbal and physical aggression, are fairly common in children between 1 and 3 years of age. With the growth of overall EF skills, and in particular self-regulation and communication skills, improvements should gradually be seen as the child is closer to age 3.

PAUSE WORKSHEET

Child: __Theresa__ Date: __March 17, 2024__

Caregiver: __Laurie and Vince__ Provider: __Debbie__

PERCEIVE—Explore what is happening.

Caregiver perspective:	Provider perspective:
Theresa purposefully behaves in ways to make them mad. My ideas and suggestions failed. They will never be able to go out to the park or to a restaurant.	The parents are struggling with understanding Theresa's needs and the way she communicates. They tried these activities when the children were tired, a set-up for failure. They feel the strategies we discussed won't work.

ASK—Clarify what is happening.

Starting with the caregiver's priorities and concerns, ask more detailed/specific questions to clarify what is happening.

Ask more about what led up to the event they described to try to understand what might have contributed to the problems.

Ask about what went well to build on the successes.

Ask Vince to talk more about how he knows that Theresa is purposefully misbehaving.

UNDERSTAND—Explore why it is happening.

With the caregiver, explore explanations for what is happening. Consider possible explanations that include the environment, the child, and the caregiver. Listen and observe closely as you explore the situation in conversation with the family.

Caregiver perspective:	Provider perspective:	Child's perspective:
What is behind Vince's anger and frustration? How can I help him see this in a different way?	How can I remain calm during this discussion? This raised my own red flags about spanking	Theresa is little, was tired, and just wanted to play with a toy.

(continued)

Figure 6.1. Debbie's PAUSE Worksheet for Laurie, Vince, and Theresa.

Figure 6.1. (continued)

PAUSE WORKSHEET (continued)

UNDERSTAND (continued)

Caregiver perspective:	Provider perspective:	Child's perspective:
	and misunderstanding Theresa's viewpoint. No one stands up for her.	
	How can I build their relationships through activities where they have fun together?	

STRATEGIZE and **EVALUATE**—Identify possible responses/solutions.

1. Solution/action to try:	How will we know if it works?
Discover activities to use at home to help build the relationship between the parents and Theresa.	*Vince and Laurie identify positive aspects of their relationship with Theresa.*
	When will we evaluate if it works?
	Evaluate after 2 months.

2. Solution/action to try:	How will we know if it works?
Practice "going out" by doing it at home, but as a play activity, to simulate what might happen and practice.	*Vince and Laurie can identify the parts of the planning process that might ensure a successful outing.*
	When will we evaluate if it works?
	Evaluate after two trials of a pretend outing.

PROVIDER REFLECTION WORKSHEET

Provider Reflection Worksheet

Child: **Theresa**   Date: **March 17, 2024**

Caregiver: **Laurie and Vince**   Provider: **Debbie**

1. How did I follow the caregiver's lead to learn what is most pressing or important to them?	I thought the family was ready to try an outing, but I missed something, as they didn't seem to plan well and then felt like they failed. How can I find the positive in what happened? What could I do differently next time?
2. How did I ask clarifying questions that help me to understand the problem better? How did I inquire about the caregiver's values and beliefs related to the issue?	I did not ask these types of questions. Thinking back, I could have explored several things such as . . . What was the preparation phase like? How did it feel when Theresa acted out? How did the other parents react? The other children? What would it take to try this again?
3. How did I reflect on and offer to discuss similarities and differences between me and the caregiver? These might include race, ethnicity, language, gender, sexual orientation, religious and other beliefs, values, experiences, etc.	I know I have some different ideas about spanking than Vince. I wonder what might be behind his strong views? I asked him what he wanted Theresa to learn from being spanked and he said to be nice and share. Should I talk more openly with the family about the different ways people view spanking or do I need to learn more about his values and experiences first?

(continued)

Figure 6.2. Debbie's Provider Reflection Worksheet for Laurie, Vince, and Theresa.

Figure 6.2. *(continued)*

PROVIDER REFLECTION WORKSHEET *(continued)*

4. How did I provide information that may help the caregiver better understand the child's behavior?	I wonder if there is a way to discuss this from Theresa's perspective. She was tired, so she was not at her best to try something that we knew is hard. Theresa is also learning about sharing and how to be with other children her age; how can I help explain this phase of development?
5. How did I engage the caregiver to develop a response that may include a strategy to try, a resource to use, or more information to increase understanding?	I wonder if we might explore everyone's temperament as a way to better understand each person's perspective. How would I do this? How can I make this information meaningful to Vince and Laurie?
6. How did I provide support and emotional containment if needed?	Vince's anger is surprising for me and almost scary. I'm not sure why, or how I can be helpful in containing that, but this feels important in our work. I am glad he is willing to hear my ideas after I offered to understand his viewpoint.
7. How do I plan to follow up on promised actions to maintain trust?	I am worried this family might not trust me with future ideas since this activity seemed to backfire, in their minds. How do I repair this?
8. What do I want to discuss in reflective supervision to improve my practice and outcomes with this child and caregiver?	I want to discuss my strong reaction to the idea of spanking and my worry that this family seems to be missing Theresa's perspective. I want help to be better able to acknowledge the parents' frustration and their worry about Theresa's behaviors. I would like my consultant's help thinking about balancing these perspectives.

- Similarly, short tantrums as often as once or twice per week are not unusual for young children. Tantrums in this age range are frequently related to the child's frustration over not getting what they want. Tantrums may start as anger and shift into sadness. Recognizing the triggers for tantrums can help caregivers prevent them and respond in better ways.

- Caregiving practices and related family characteristics bring both risk and resilience to families. Home visitors should create opportunities for discussion with families about caregiving practices that are common in families' culture and community. They should work to become aware of their own implicit biases and avoid making assumptions when families engage in caregiving practices that are unfamiliar. Using this partnering and reflective stance, a home visitor can effectively address concerns for child behavior in ways that are culturally congruent.

SUGGESTED FURTHER READING

Dunlap, G., Strain, P. S., Lee, J. K., Joseph, J. D., Vatland, C., & Fox, L. (2017). *Prevent-Teach-Reinforce for families*. Paul H. Brookes Publishing Co.

Webster-Stratton, C. (2019). *The incredible years: A trouble-shooting guide for parents of children aged 3–8 years* (3rd ed.). Incredible Years.

TIMELY TIPS FOR TOLERATING CHALLENGING BEHAVIORS

Prevention

- Provide structure and routine.
- Know your child's rhythms and schedules.
- Maintain realistic expectations! Do not take young children places where they might get overwhelmed or take them out when they are feeling bad or tired.

Immediate Adult Responses That Help

- Stay calm, shown by a low voice and neutral facial expression.
- Provide containment and safety, such as removing the child from a situation to calm down.
- Comfort the child and help the child express negative emotions appropriately: stay close, use physical comfort and a soothing voice.

Follow-Up Responses

- Remember to follow up when everyone is calm and well rested.
- Talk about what happened; make a plan to do better next time.
- Teach a substitute behavior to replace a behavior that is undesirable.
- Teach, coach, and reinforce prosocial behaviors.

Caregiver Self-Care

- Take a break or ask for some help.
- Maintain perspective—remember the child will not be this age forever, and look for the humor in the situation.
- Use a calming strategy such as taking three long, deep breaths.

7

Why Won't You Listen?

Cooperating and Following Directions

Colleen arranges to meet Jeanette and 20-month-old Paul, a family on her caseload, at a local library. Paul is an active boy who lives with both parents in a small apartment. He likes to run and be loud, like many boys his age. Jeanette worries that the neighbors will be angry when he is so loud. Colleen has been trying to get Jeanette to bring Paul out more often. She has chosen the library for several reasons, including that it is located on a convenient bus route and has a good children's section. Colleen plans to introduce the young family to the library, help them check out some books, and encourage Jeanette to participate in the library's programs for children.

About 10 minutes past the scheduled meeting time, Colleen hears the family arrive before she can see them. Jeanette can be heard loudly whispering for Paul to stay quiet, while he is happily and loudly singing his version of "Twinkle, Twinkle, Little Star." Jeanette is flustered and rushing along the hallway as she talks nonstop to her son. Jeanette says, "Now, this is the library, so we can't yell or run. If you don't be good and listen to mommy, then we'll have to go home and you won't get to see Colleen." Colleen suppresses a wry smile as she hurries to help out. She thinks that she will once again need to review with Jeanette how to give clear commands. Paul is such an exuberant child, and Colleen wishes that Jeanette could enjoy his happy personality. She sees that Paul is in a stroller; he smiles a wide smile when he sees Colleen and says "up, up" while reaching his arms up to his mother to be taken from the stroller. Jeanette presses her lips together and hesitates. "I don't think this will work out. He is just going to run around and he never listens to me when I try to stop him."

Colleen thinks carefully. She doesn't want to push Jeanette into something she is afraid to try, and she definitely does not want to put Paul in a position of getting into trouble. However, she really thinks that Jeanette and Paul could get a lot out of a library visit. She also feels a little frustrated, as she knows that Paul can manage the library with just a little redirection and planning. "Why does Jeanette continue to give such long instructions when other methods work so much better?" she wonders. Colleen smiles and says, "It's so great that you guys made it all the way here. If you want to wait until a better day, we can. I am happy to help you try if you want, though." Jeanette looks dubious, but she starts to unbuckle Paul from the stroller, resuming her nonstop stream of instructions as she does.

Learning social skills such as how to cooperate and follow directions doesn't happen overnight. Caregivers and home visitors can be frustrated when young children don't comply or refuse to comply in ways that are perceived as "defiant" or "not respectful." Some caregivers may be embarrassed when the child's behavior is out of sync with cultural values and expectations; others may worry that their child will be judged by others or have a hard time in school if they do not become more cooperative. In order for young children to cooperate and follow directions, many skills must be present. These include understanding instructions, being able to perform the behavior asked, and being able to inhibit behaviors the child would rather do. As in physical aggression, delays in development, particularly in communication, may play a role when young children do not follow directions. In addition, a certain degree of refusing to follow adult instruction is to be expected in younger children. As a result, it is important for home visitors to help caregivers know the difference between behaviors that signal a need for independence and those that suggest true problem behavior.

In Chapter 6, we discussed how a child's growing skills and temperament result in a temporary increase in physical aggression around age 2 years. By age 3 or 4, physical aggression and behaviors such as tantrums are gradually shaped into more socially appropriate responses. Similarly, between 2 and 3 years, most young children become less defiant and more cooperative (Xu et al., 2021). In this study, researchers observed children during play activities with their mothers at 3 points between 18 and 42 months. True defiance was rare at all ages; but it decreased over time. By 42 months, more than 80% of the sample did not show any defiant behaviors during the play session. Both improvement of developmental skills (Biedzio & Wakschlag, 2019; Manning et al., 2019; van den Akker et al., 2022) and caregiver scaffolding and supports (Hughes et al., 2023; Keren et al., 2018; McDermott & Fox, 2019) are understood to anchor these changes.

In this chapter, we continue to look at how temperament, developmental skills, and caregiving behaviors interact with and influence executive functioning (EF) and self-regulation capacities related to the performance of positive or prosocial behaviors such as following directions, helping, and cooperating with others. Many factors underlie behavioral and emotion regulation—including genes, brain changes, hormonal controls, cognitive and language development, temperament differences, cultural expectations, and caregiving environment (Kuhns & Cabrera, 2019; Rosenblum et al., 2019; Thompson & Goodvin, 2007; Xu et al., 2021). As refraining from aggression is linked to better outcomes, so too are positive social behaviors. Children who show better early prosocial behaviors are likely to have enhanced longer-range outcomes, including getting along with others and even better school performance (Kochanska et al., 2001; Manning et al., 2019). Therefore, attention to promoting positive behaviors is just as important as preventing and reducing negative behaviors.

DEVELOPING PROSOCIAL BEHAVIORS

Although prosocial behaviors are not unusual in even young children, some may need guidance in these skills. In the following subsections, we discuss the development of the prosocial behaviors of compliance and self-regulation of feelings, as well as of other social and emotional skills, such as helping.

Developing Compliance

The term *compliance* is used to describe a child doing what the parent or other caregiver wants, requests, or commands (Landy, 2009; Leitjen et al., 2019). This can include following directions to complete a specific task ("do tasks") or instructions to stop doing or not do something ("don't tasks"). As any caregiver will attest, convincing a young child to do what the caregiver wants or getting them to stop doing what they want to do can be challenging. Both understanding what the caregiver wants and being willing to do it are involved in compliance.

Although most children are able to share an object when asked by 12 months and understand what a caregiver wants, in most situations, by age 3 years, they may not always perform to their potential ability. In younger children, normal deficits in EF and other self-control skills may contribute to lower compliance. This can confuse caregivers who may hear their 2-year-old correcting their dolls or telling others "no, no" and believe this behavior indicates full understanding of discipline. Being able to repeat a command is not the same as fully understanding it or being able to comply in the moment. In addition, of course, it is not unusual for the caregiver and the child to have different ideas about what the child should be doing. So, at times, a child may just not want to comply in given situations, even though they have the skill. An example might be the caregiver instructing a child to put away toys to get ready for bed. From the child's perspective, playing is fun or perhaps the tower is not finished. Although the child understands the command and is able to perform it, they do not want to because going to bed means missing out on more fun with toys.

Parents and other caregivers generally begin sharing concerns of problems associated with compliance with commands when their child turns 2 years of age. Thus, we have terms like "the terrible twos." However, compliance refusals typically start much earlier. Higher levels of noncompliance are reported between 12 and 24 months (Biedzio & Wakschlag, 2019; Landy, 2009). Once a child becomes more mobile, generally around the end of the first year, compliance becomes very important to caregivers. This is because as infants become toddlers, they are able to have more control over how close or far they are from caregivers, resulting in games of "catch me" and other safety concerns. Children in this age range can run, jump, climb, and explore; therefore, they can also find interesting and often possibly forbidden objects, resulting in the need for caregivers to monitor them closely. Caregivers have been shown to respond to this new skill by talking and gesturing more to their babies, with the content of their communications centered on action (Schneider & Iverson, 2021). They also must increase their prohibitions. Caregivers who feel that they are in near continual conflict with their young children are probably right! From this rocky start between 12 and 24 months, most typically developing 3-year-olds will increasingly show skills such as knowing what behaviors adults expect, following rules, demonstrating self-control, and expressing feelings of pride and shame (Forman, 2007). These skills will continue to improve as the child approaches 4 years.

The combination of toddlers' greater ability to "get into things" and their higher interest in doing things their way results in increasing conflicts. As their infants become toddlers, parents and other caregivers find themselves greatly increasing the number of do and don't commands they must make (Forman, 2007). Caregivers have to give commands repeatedly because young children frequently display behaviors that need correcting and often do not follow instructions. Specifically, children under the age of 2 years follow instructions less than half the time (Kochanska et al., 2001). In addition, young children also do not follow "don't" or "stop" commands very well; parents or other caregivers may have to tell a child in this age range to not do a specific behavior as many as 20 times in a single day (Landy, 2009).

Most of our discussion to this point has involved how young children comply when adults are present and are giving the command. The top commands that caregivers provide in this age range have to do with immediate needs, such as staying safe, instructions related to self-care, or taking care with objects or possessions. Common instructions include statements about here-and-now behaviors, such as "Don't run," "Let's get dressed," or "We don't take toys from friends" (Forman, 2007). However, caregivers and toddlers can experience conflictual interactions outside of discipline. For example, toddlers and caregivers can clash when the caregiver does not do something the toddler wants, such as allowing a piece of candy or letting them play with their phone. Toddlers and caregivers can also disagree over facts. A common example might be a caregiver announcing that the child needs a diaper change and the child insisting they absolutely do not (Laible & Thompson, 2002). This behavior is most likely a form of avoidance and should be distinguished from actual lying.

Whatever the type, conflicts between caregivers and toddlers vary widely in frequency but have been reported to occur as much as 19 times an hour (Laible & Thompson, 2002). These many conflicts are opportunities for caregivers and children to learn how to come to resolution and for young children to begin the process of internalizing family, community, and cultural values and rules. Children who have internalized their caregiver's agenda begin to display committed compliance, described as willingness or even eagerness to cooperate (Kochanska, 2002). This type of compliance is distinguished from situational compliance, in which the child may only comply when the authority figure is present and enforcing the rule (Landy, 2009). Committed compliance is important as children with a lower level of this type of compliance tend to have more externalizing problems and social issues when in school (Xu et al., 2021). See Table 7.1 for a picture of how developmental capacities affect compliance.

Language skills have been connected to emotion regulation and compliance (Curtis et al., 2019). In order to follow a direction, young children have to understand what the caregiver is telling them. Children who have better verbal skills are more able to understand what they are to do and

Table 7.1. Links between development and compliance behaviors

Age	Emerging developmental skills		Parent response
	Physical	Cognitive and language	
<12 months	Child begins to move limbs but is still fairly stationary.	Cause-and-effect skills emerging; may understand more than can communicate	Able to leave child for a moment in a safe place; limited noncompliance
12-24 months	Moving, walking, running, jumping, and climbing skills develop.	Growing curiosity and interest in exploring surroundings; able to verbally refuse (e.g., "no!") and indicate possession (e.g., "mine")	Set new limits; monitor child activity more closely to ensure safety; expect to repeat commands
24-36 months	Becomes more coordinated in movement; use of hands allows exploration of smaller objects and containers.	Can follow some rules and make requests to repeat enjoyable activities; more able to wait when requested, show some self-control, and express emotions	Use of routines; explain and predict activities to help with transitions and compliance

to actually do it (Vallotton & Ayoub, 2011). Language skill is also important in children's ability to internalize caregiver rules as part of their own EF and self-regulation, in both the present and the future. As children gain language comprehension, caregivers are able to talk about rules and expectations in more complex ways. An example might be, "When Nana gives you a present, be sure you say thank you." Early language capacity is also related to later EF and other self-regulation skills. For example, in one study, young children who had better overall language skills at 18 months later demonstrated less anger and better coping when in a frustrating situation at 4 years of age (Roben et al., 2013). When young children have language delays, problems in compliance can stem from lack of understanding and may lead to long-term issues with compliance and emotion regulation.

Although noncompliance in early childhood is expected, not all forms of noncompliance are equal. Normal or expected noncompliance in young children is goal directed, flexible, can be explained in context, and is usually tempered with some interest in pleasing the adult (Biedzio & Wakschlag, 2019). For example, 34-month-old Maddy does not want to change out of her favorite pink bunny slippers to walk to the car, even though it is pouring outside. She first ignores the instruction and then demonstrates how well the slippers match her t-shirt. However, she easily agrees to her grandmother's suggestion that she could carry the slippers in her backpack and cooperatively puts on her boots. Maddy's goal of wearing the slippers made sense from a toddler perspective since they were her favorite. Furthermore, she could be flexible when offered an alternative way to enjoy the slippers. Researchers distinguish between skilled noncompliance, such as that showed by Maddy, and nonskilled forms of noncompliance. Skilled noncompliance, including negotiating with or attempting to redirect a parent, is more sophisticated than unskilled noncompliance, such as simple refusal. Noncompliance that includes unregulated anger and confrontation, such as defiance or aggression, has been associated with later clinical behavior problems (Biedzio & Wakschlag, 2019).

Young children spontaneously talk about emotions in themselves and others by 24 months but may have some sense of feelings earlier (Brownell et al., 2013; Rosenblum et al., 2019; Wittmer, 2008). As with physical aggression and tantrums, adult responses are associated with children's abilities to build better skills, feelings, and emotion regulation. Caregivers' talk about their own feelings or feelings of others can promote sharing and other positive behavior at least by 2 years. Ideally, parents and other caregivers will provide an environment that helps young children to be able to identify and discuss emotions, gain coping skills to tolerate frustration, and manage other negative emotions such as fear, and will set up situations that reward children for compliance and other positive social skills. When these kinds of support are offered, children learn that upset feelings, though real, are not bad or dangerous and can be managed (Thompson & Goodvin, 2007).

Methods to Help Young Children Build Self-Regulation of Feelings

Methods to build self-regulation of strong feelings are varied and can include prevention strategies. Proactive or prevention methods include helping children to stay on a consistent routine that ensures predictability, reduces anxiety, and builds expectations. Caregivers can also avoid putting young children into situations in which they are likely to struggle, such as taking them to places that are not child friendly or scheduling activities when the child is likely to be tired and less cooperative (e.g., avoid taking a young child to a fancy restaurant, especially when dinner starts after bedtime).

It will not be possible for parents and other caregivers to completely avoid upsetting situations, and as discussed, a certain amount of difficult or challenging behavior is age appropriate and to be expected. Although it is not appropriate to expect toddlers to comply quickly or never have a tantrum, caregivers can use many strategies to help young children cope with their feelings and perform more competent social behaviors (Thompson & Goodvin, 2007; Xu et al., 2021). Caregivers can support and coach children to use their highest skills, even when under pressure or stress. For example, caregivers can support the young child to use words to ask for help when frustrated or to give polite refusals, such as "no, thank you" instead of more defiant refusals. Providing additional information to reinterpret a child's view of a situation as threatening can also help (e.g., "It's just a shadow.").

Caregivers can use a range of strategies to try to manage or change their child's behaviors. These methods include prohibitions (e.g., "Stop"), commands (i.e., "Do this"), redirection/distraction, modeling, scaffolding, ignoring inappropriate behavior, time-out, loss of privileges, threats, physical control (e.g., pick up the child, prevent the child from touching something), and corporal punishment (Leitjen et al., 2019; Livas-Dlott et al., 2010; Xu et al., 2021).

Distraction can pull attention away from something that might be scary or away from a tempting but forbidden object, such as great auntie's special glass knick-knacks. Scaffolding and breaking down challenging tasks can help young children with frustration while gradually building skills that help them gain competence. Additional details about methods to help young children build self-regulation are provided in Table 7.2.

The overall emotional climate in a family, including the caregiver's own responses to emotion-provoking situations, impacts child behaviors, as young children will typically use social referencing to determine how to feel about various people, events, and situations. A young child watches adults and older children to learn how to behave in specific situations (e.g.,

Table 7.2. Methods to help young children build self-regulation

Method	Example
Prevention strategies	Providing routines
	Choosing environments where children will be successful
	Avoiding times when the child will be tired
Distraction	Redirecting the child to an activity that is less frightening
	Providing the child with something else to do instead of a forbidden activity or object
Scaffolding	Breaking down tasks into small components (e.g., "First put on your socks. Now let's put on your shoes.")
	Giving help to complete parts of tasks (e.g., "Mommy can pick up the blocks while you pick up your books.")
Coaching	Reminding the child what he or she can say and do when upset
	Giving words to the child's feelings (e.g., "You feel sad because you can't have a new toy.")
Providing information and modeling	"There is no monster. It is a shadow."
	"That lady is mommy's friend. It's okay to say hi to her."

"Should I stay close, or is this a place to run and play?") and to gather information about how people handle emotion-provoking events generally. Home visitors can help caregivers recognize that their models of emotional language and emotional expression are also important. In addition to providing a positive model, adults can coach and help young children practice emotional language to cope with situations. In a study by Brownell et al. (2013), parents were observed sharing picture books about emotions with their toddlers. The researchers found that when parents encouraged labeling and explanations about feelings, their toddlers were more likely to help and share with an adult when the opportunity presented later (Brownell et al., 2013). In the study, caregiver talk about emotions was less important than adult encouragement for the child to think, label, and explain emotions.

As the above discussion may suggest, for the most part, gentler strategies have been associated with less defiance and more cooperation, compared to harsher strategies (threats, physical intervention) (Xu et al., 2021). However, it is acknowledged that much of the literature that supports these findings focused on middle-class and white samples (Bocknek et al., 2020). In many cases, researchers have viewed strategies used by caregivers from minoritized groups from a deficiency model, missing adaptive qualities that reflect family resilience. Increasingly, studies that include more diverse families may find some subtle differences in caregiver choices about discipline related to cultural values and caregiver experiences. For example, a recent study with lower-income Latinx mothers and fathers of toddlers ages 24–35 months found that these caregivers used strategies that were similar to those reported for middle-class samples. Mothers in the sample who endorsed the value of *respeto* (e.g., respect and deference to authority), however, used more direct, but not harsh, commands. Another study considered caregiving strategies used by Black mothers who experienced risk factors, including low income and high potential for stress (Bocknek et al., 2020). In this sample, Black mothers of toddlers were more likely to use scaffolding methods in a low-stress situation and more likely to use commands immediately following a high-stress situation. Toddlers with mothers who used this caregiving pattern had better self-regulation when under stress. Bocknek and colleagues suggested that the mothers were intentionally using "culturally tailored" methods to support their toddler's regulation based on culturally relevant experiences. They proposed that these strategies reflected an *adaptive parenting* style of Black women (after *adaptive culture* previously proposed by Garcia Coll et al., 1996).

Recently, researchers have successfully adapted some behavioral treatments to be more culturally responsive or even personalized to fit caregiver styles (Yeh et al., 2022). Home visitors may also help caregivers learn methods that are most effective for their family and their child within their community and culture. They can also support caregivers to fine-tune the methods that they use most. For example, although young children have limited language, verbal commands are most used by caregivers of toddlers (Livas-Dlott et al., 2010). It therefore becomes important for home visitors to help caregivers learn to give commands that are effective. In most cases, a young child will be more likely to understand commands that are short, direct, and say what to do (McNeil & Hembree-Kigin, 2010; Webster-Stratton, 2019). The command should be neutral in tone and not harsh or threatening. For example, when a child begins to run in the store, the parent or other caregiver can say, "Walk, please." When a child grabs a pet in a rough manner, the adult can say "Easy hands." In addition, when children are just learning language, pairing of words with gestures may increase understanding and compliance (Rader & Zukow-Goldring, 2012). For example, a caregiver can touch or pat a chair while saying, "Sit down."

For younger children, and especially for children who have more challenging temperaments or who are defiant, use of commands that tell what to do is recommended over prohibitions or don't commands (Kohlhoff et al., 2021; Landy, 2009; Webster-Stratton, 2019). A command that is phrased in positive terms is easier for young children to understand than commands that include negative words such as *don't*. Parents and other caregivers should give the command up to two times and then support the child to complete the task if needed (McNeil & Hembree-Kigin, 2010). Long explanations, such as telling why a rule is needed, will be best understood by children over age 5. Talking about and explaining the feelings of others is probably not effective with young children during discipline situations, but is likely to be helpful at other times, as discussed earlier (Landy, 2009; McClelland & Tominey, 2014). Demonstrating or modeling what is expected is sometimes recommended but may not always be effective when children are noncompliant. In one study compared to modeling alone, toddlers were more compliant with a cleanup task when their mothers took a collaborative approach by first helping the toddler to do part of the task, followed by encouraging the child to complete it (Larzele et al., 2023). The collaborative approach also showed a more positive lasting impact on child behavior at follow-up.

Once the child has followed the direction or instruction, the caregiver's job is not done. It is recommended to follow the child's compliance with a reinforcer. This does not mean that adults have to follow their child around and hand out candy after every positive behavior. A more genuine and useful form of reinforcement is praise (Kohlhoff et al., 2021; Webster-Stratton, 2019). Many caregivers have heard that they should "catch the child being good." What they may not know is that global or vague praise is probably not very effective. Statements like "good job" or "way to go," though often appearing on motivational posters, are nice, but they probably will not increase the chances that the child displays the behavior again. A specific praise statement, called *labeled praise,* is more effective. Labeled praise tells the child what they did that you liked and would like to see again. Instead of saying, "good work," encourage the caregiver to try a more specific statement, such as "I like it when you pick up your cars" (Kohlhoff et al., 2021; Webster-Stratton, 2019). See Box 7.1 to learn about giving clear commands. Use these ideas to help caregivers practice giving effective commands.

Box 7.1. Giving Good Commands to Increase Child Compliance

How to Be

- Stay calm.
- Speak in a low voice.
- Keep your facial expression relaxed (neutral).

What to Say

- Use few words (one to three is great).
- Say what to do.
- Follow up by saying what the child did that you liked (labeled praise).

What to Do

- Get at the child's level.
- Gain the child's attention with eye contact and gentle touch.
- When possible, show what to do.

Appendix 7A provides examples of commonly heard commands, with suggestions about how to reframe them. Use this form to help caregivers practice framing clear commands.

Jeanette takes Paul from the stroller and holds him on her hip. He looks excitedly at the children, books, and other interesting things in the library, jabbering and reaching out. Jeanette looks at Colleen doubtfully but puts Paul down on the floor. He immediately starts to run toward a shelf with puzzles. Jeanette runs after him and picks him up again while giving a long explanation about running and the library. Paul's face puckers up and he starts to cry. Jeanette raises her eyebrows as she looks at Colleen and says, "I knew this wouldn't work."

Colleen realizes that Jeanette is easily embarrassed by Paul's behavior, even when it is age appropriate. She says, "I think he was pretty excited to see everything here. Maybe if you hold him while we walk over to the puzzles we can help him play in a calmer way." Jeanette shrugs her shoulders but does it. Colleen coaches her to show Paul one toy at a time and to use one or two simple words to help direct his attention. Jeanette is surprised when Paul watches her, tries to say the words she models, and then is able to play with one toy for about 2 minutes while seated on the floor. "Wow, good boy!" Jeanette says. "Yes, you listened and stayed with mommy," Colleen adds.

Later during a video visit, Colleen and Jeanette talk about their trip. Colleen asks Jeanette to say what she liked and did not like. Jeanette explains that she actually had fun when Paul was able to stay near her and play with a toy for a time. Colleen asked Jeanette to think about what she did to help Paul play in a more organized way. "I guess I did a better job keeping it simple. I showed him what to do with a toy and used fewer words to talk to him," Jeanette said. Colleen smiled and replied, "You did such a great job using easy words and showing Paul how to play."

Supporting Other Social and Emotional Skills

So far, we have focused on how compliance develops and how it can be supported or encouraged in young children, but this is not the whole story. Beginning in infancy, most young children show other positive social behaviors, including participating in social games such as Peekaboo, sharing or giving something to another person, and early empathy shown by crying when another baby cries (Hay & Cook, 2007; Landy, 2009; Rosenblum et al., 2019). More complex social behaviors occur as children get older.

Prosocial behaviors have been divided into three main types: doing something for others (i.e., helping), working and playing with others, and feeling for others (i.e., empathy) (Hay & Cook, 2007). Most babies and toddlers show interest in other people and will play simple games, share food or show objects, and follow simple directions. Between ages 2 and 3 years, young children are increasingly able to demonstrate other social behaviors, such as spontaneously helping another person, that show they have some level of understanding of another person's perspective (Reschke et al., 2023). Examples of these types of behaviors include sharing, cooperating in a game or tasks, trying to help with chores, and attempting to comfort another person (Hay & Cook, 2007). Thinking, language, self-regulation, and understanding about other people's inner experience (i.e., feelings, motivations, beliefs) combine to change very young babies' tendency toward social interest into more deliberate and sophisticated social behavior as they get older (Hay & Cook, 2007; Reschke et al., 2023). Older toddlers are pickier about whom they engage with socially and begin to understand social rules related to their own culture, for example.

It has been commonly understood that toddlers tend toward egocentricity, meaning that toddlers view everything from their own viewpoint and may have difficulty understanding or responding to the needs of others (Gopnik, 2010). A series of studies by Allison Gopnik and her colleagues demonstrated that young children's skills for understanding their own and other people's thinking may have been significantly underestimated (Gopnik, 2010; Gopnik et al., 1994). For example, in one study, children as young as 18 months old used an adult's facial expression to guide what kind of food they offered the adult (Repachouli & Gopnik, 1997). Through this kind of work that examines how babies solve problems, it has been shown that under the right circumstances, young children have a beginning understanding of the difference between real and pretend, that people have wishes that are not always the same as their own, and that things may be different than they appear. Young children's skills in peer relationships are also likely to be better developed than previously thought (Wittmer, 2008). Some of the examples of peer interactions that can be observed include infants and toddlers laughing together, teaching another person with explanations and modeling, and cooperating on a task.

All of these great skills can be developed through adult support and scaffolding (Landy, 2009; Wittmer, 2008). Importantly, the type of adult scaffolding of prosocial behaviors that is most helpful may depend on the toddler's age (Dahl et al., 2017). These researchers showed that toddlers less than 15 months, who were just learning to help, were more likely to help a strange adult when given explicit instruction and praise to do so. In fact, helping rates were double in the group that received scaffolding compared to the group that did not receive scaffolding. Older toddlers who already knew something about helping benefited more from less direct scaffolding, such as being directed to the adult's needs, reasoning, and negotiation. Home visitors can help caregivers build more positive or prosocial skills in early childhood simply by increasing awareness that young children have these capabilities (Wittmer, 2008). Caregivers can then be alert for opportunities to reinforce prosocial behavior when it occurs. Encouraging young children to use words and modeling additional emotion words are also recommended (Wittmer, 2008). Adults can stay near young children to encourage and support their social interactions with others. Adult modeling of positive social interactions can help, including self-talk about emotions and helping children to recognize other people's feelings and responses to their actions. Parents and other caregivers may be surprised by just how much a baby or toddler can do.

Jeanette was feeling a little more confident about taking Paul out to be around other children after the help she got from Colleen. She decided to try a local fast food restaurant that had a play area. Jeanette and Paul arrived at the restaurant about 10:30 in the morning. Paul was excited and bounced in his stroller as they walked in the door. Jeanette was proud that she remembered to come in between breakfast and lunch so that it would not be too crowded and overwhelm Paul. Jeanette saw that there were a few other children in the play area, including a little girl who seemed close to Paul's age. Jeanette stayed near Paul and watched him closely. When Paul approached the little girl, Jeanette felt nervous and started to give him some directions and warnings. She remembered her talk with Colleen and instead tried out narrating what Paul might be thinking, saying, "Oh, here's a little friend to play with!" Paul and the little girl approached each other and smiled. The little girl was holding a small toy; Paul pointed at the toy and said "car." Jeanette felt an urge to remind Paul that the toy was not his, but instead she just said, "Yes, that is a little red car." Paul nodded and found a ball. He held the ball out to the little girl and said "ball." As Jeanette helped the children trade their toys, she thought about how nice it would be to tell Colleen about her success.

USING THE PAUSE FRAMEWORK

In the presented vignette, Colleen uses the Perceive strategy to observe and listen to both Paul and his mother Jeanette. She recognizes that she sees Paul as a happy, active toddler and considers how these same behaviors seem problematic to Jeanette. Colleen also notices that Jeanette tries hard to teach Paul but uses very verbal methods that are not working. Later, Jeanette helps Colleen reflect on the experience to identify what went well. You can see Coleen's full PAUSE worksheet and reflections in Figures 7.1 and 7.2.

WHAT'S NEXT?

In Chapter 8, we apply the PAUSE problem-solving approach to fears and separation issues.

TIPS FOR PRACTICE

- Encourage caregivers to be good models of emotion regulation by staying calm, using appropriate emotion words, and being a supportive presence when children have strong feelings.

PAUSE WORKSHEET

Child: _Paul_ Date: _May 29, 2024_

Caregiver: _Jeanette_ Provider: _Colleen_

PERCEIVE—Explore what is happening.

Caregiver perspective:	Provider perspective:
Jeanette is struggling with how to handle Paul in public places like the library and how to deal with his loud voice and high energy levels.	Jeanette talks too much to Paul, giving him long instructions. He can't understand all of what she is saying.

ASK—Clarify what is happening.

Starting with the caregiver's priorities and concerns, ask more detailed/specific questions to clarify what is happening.

What must Jeanette feel when Paul behaves this way? Is she worried about complaints from the neighbor if Paul is too loud? Is the neighborhood safe? Are there nearby, safe places for Paul to play?

How can we make the visit a success?

UNDERSTAND—Explore why it is happening.

With the caregiver, explore explanations for what is happening. Consider possible explanations that include the environment, the child, and the caregiver. Listen and observe closely as you explore the situation in conversation with the family.

Caregiver perspective:	Provider perspective:	Child's perspective:
Jeanette feels embarrassed about Paul's behaviors. She is overwhelmed and parenting with limited support.	Jeanette is missing out on a lot of fun with Paul. She is worried about how others will perceive her and Paul. She is not sure	Paul is ready to experience the world. He likes activity and has a lot of energy. He needs help regulating his energy and emotions.

(continued)

Figure 7.1. Colleen's PAUSE Worksheet for Jeanette and Paul.

Figure 7.1. (continued)

PAUSE WORKSHEET (continued)

UNDERSTAND (continued)

Caregiver perspective:	Provider perspective:	Child's perspective:
	how to understand Paul and how to regulate his energy.	

STRATEGIZE and **EVALUATE**—Identify possible responses/solutions.

1. Solution/action to try:	How will we know if it works?
Direct Paul to one toy or book at a time, using the positive language and commands we have been practicing.	Paul will remain engaged and interested in one toy at a time.
	When will we evaluate if it works?
	At the next planned outing.

2. Solution/action to try:	How will we know if it works?
Think about different places Jeanette can take Paul where they will be successful, such as a fast-food restaurant with a play area.	Jeanette will share about the experience and we will explore what worked and did not work.
	When will we evaluate if it works?
	At the session after she tries another outing.

PROVIDER REFLECTION WORKSHEET

Provider Reflection Worksheet

Child: _Paul_   Date: _May 31, 2024_

Caregiver: _Jeanette_   Provider: _Colleen_

1. How did I follow the caregiver's lead to learn what is most pressing or important to them?	It was very hard for me to stop myself from instructing Colleen on how to be with Paul. She likes to give so many directions and explanations. When I slowed myself down, I was able to see that Colleen was very worried about not being successful when taking Paul out to different places and how people might look at her. She really wants to see Paul be successful.
2. How did I ask clarifying questions that help me to understand the problem better? How did I inquire about the caregiver's values and beliefs related to the issue?	I practiced the skills I have been working on to hold back and be with Colleen to better understand her perspective and how to see Paul in different ways. I feel I am doing well in asking questions that help Colleen see what is working and how to implement changes.
3. How did I reflect on and offer to discuss similarities and differences between me and the caregiver? These might include race, ethnicity, language, gender, sexual orientation, religious and other beliefs, values, experiences, etc.	Jeanette seemed very concerned about not breaking the rules or causing trouble in the library and keeping her child under control. I saw this location as a place of discovery and opportunity. I wonder what our own past experiences bring to this situation and how I can learn more about her values and beliefs.

(continued)

Figure 7.2. Colleen's Provider Reflection Worksheet for Jeanette and Paul.

Figure 7.2. *(continued)*

PROVIDER REFLECTION WORKSHEET *(continued)*

4. How did I provide information that may help the caregiver better understand the child's behavior?	Colleen has noticed some successes after we tried some basic and simple things. We can build on these successes and help her to better understand Paul's behaviors. I hope she can apply this learning to other situations.
5. How did I engage the caregiver to develop a response that may include a strategy to try, a resource to use, or more information to increase understanding?	We were able to try a technique that worked for Colleen. When she helped Paul direct his excitement to a toy that he liked, he was able to play with it calmly for several minutes.
6. How did I provide support and emotional containment if needed?	I was aware that Colleen was becoming very upset and perhaps embarrassed that day at the library. It was helpful for me to stay calm and help direct her to find a way to help Paul navigate his experience that day. I think that when she found success, she felt good and learned something about how to better handle him in the future. It was so nice to see her having fun with her son.
7. How do I plan to follow up on promised actions to maintain trust?	Colleen was so excited to tell me about her successes when taking Paul to the play area at the restaurant. We talked about what worked well, including her plan to go in the middle of the morning, and how she helped him meet the little girl there. She was so excited that he shared a toy with her!
8. What do I want to discuss in reflective supervision to improve my practice and outcomes with this child and caregiver?	As I completed this form, I noticed that when Jeanette starts to talk a lot to Paul, I feel an urge to talk too much to her! I think this is what my consultant means when they talk about parallel process. I plan to explore this to understand it better.

- Teach caregivers to support young children's positive behavior by avoiding situations that will be difficult for them (e.g., busy restaurants, stores with expensive items, activities scheduled at nap time).

- Teach caregivers to give clear commands and to follow up with specific praise to help children know what they are expected to do. Ensure that caregivers deliver the command in a warm or neutral way, not as a threat.

KEY POINTS TO REMEMBER

- Very young children have better skills in recognizing their own and other people's feelings than was understood in the past. Early prosocial behaviors are present in infants and toddlers and can be expected to increase and expand along with language, cognition, and self-regulation skills.

- Caregivers often focus on teaching their children compliance, or following the commands of others, but many other social skills are also important for smooth interactions with peers and adults. These include sharing, cooperating, and showing empathy.

- Caregivers can scaffold young children's social behavior in many ways. These include joining with and encouraging them to complete activities, providing appropriate models, understanding typical development and applying suitable behavior methods (e.g., clear commands and labeled praise), and providing an environment that supports discussion of feelings and emotions.

SUGGESTED FURTHER READING

Gopnick, A. (2010). *The philosophical baby: What children's minds tell us about truth, love and the meaning of life.* Farrar, Straus & Giroux.

Phelan, T. (2016). *1-2-3 Magic: The new 3-step discipline for calm, effective, and happy parenting.* Sourcebooks.

Siegel, D., & Bryson, T. (2016). *No drama discipline. The whole-brain way to calm the chaos and nurture your child's developing mind.* Random House.

Wittmer, D. (2008). *Focusing on peers: The importance of relationships in the early years.* ZERO TO THREE Press.

PRACTICE REFRAMING COMMANDS

Change these typical commands given by caregivers to commands that might be more easily understood by a toddler. In the blank spaces, add other examples of commands and practice reframing them.

Ineffective commands we have used	Examples of reframed commands that are more effective	Your ideas to reframe the ineffective command
Johnny, stop running! You'll fall down and hurt yourself and we'll have to go to the hospital!	Johnny, walk!	
Don't throw your food! It makes a mess!	Give me your plate. Say "done."	
You can't take that toy from that boy. Give it back and say you are sorry.	You like that toy. That boy does too. Let's take turns.	
No yelling. You are giving me a headache. You are making me crazy.	Use your quiet (or inside) voice.	
Quit jumping on the couch! You'll break it and have to buy me a new one!	Sit on the couch. Jump on the floor.	

(continued)

APPENDIX 7A PRACTICE REFRAMING COMMANDS (continued)

Ineffective commands we have used	Examples of reframed commands that are more effective	Your ideas to reframe the ineffective command

8

Don't Be Such a Baby

Fears and Separation Issues

Grace visits Amanda, a 27-month-old girl who is in the care of her grandmother, Margaret, at her new child care setting. During a virtual visit the previous week, Margaret discussed her frustration with Amanda's clingy behavior and whining. She said, "This girl will not stay off of me for 1 minute. I can't get anything done around here. So, I signed her up for day care starting next week." She hugged Amanda roughly and added, "Maybe being around the other kids will help her. I don't seem to be having any luck."

Grace is concerned about Amanda's ability to adapt to this new situation but does not share this worry with Margaret. Grace has noticed that Amanda is shy and quiet with her. She has seen that she stays close to her grandmother and that she is very hesitant to try toys that Grace brings to share. She wonders if Amanda has always been shy or if this behavior is part of a reaction to the loss of her mother, who was incarcerated several months earlier. Prior to the incarceration, Amanda lived with her mother in a different state. Margaret agreed to take Amanda in order to avoid foster care, even though Margaret had seen her granddaughter only one time before becoming her guardian. She admits being confused that Amanda has not warmed up to her and wonders aloud if she did the right thing in taking her.

In Chapters 5, 6, and 7, we discussed how problems in emotion and behavior self-regulation result in acting-out behaviors. Adults may think of children with acting-out behaviors, including aggression, low attention, oppositional behavior, and defiance, as lacking in self-control. Because it has been shown that challenging behaviors are often connected to a lack of caregiver control or support, it may seem that a solution is to simply crank up the level of emotional and behavior control, on the part of both the parent and the child (Rosenblum et al., 2019). However, when thinking of emotion regulation, home visitors should help caregivers work toward a balanced approach, meaning that both the child and the caregiver should demonstrate balanced or a "just right" level of control and management. Otherwise, the child may demonstrate overcontrol, shown by fears, worry, physical symptoms, anxiety, depression, and withdrawn behaviors (Comer et al., 2019; Malik, 2012).

There are two main ways in which young children may act when they are overcontrolled in emotions: either too dependent or too independent. Clingy or dependent behavior is likely when adults do not allow autonomous behavior, perhaps due to their own fears and anxieties (Bahtiyar-Saygan & Berument, 2022; Comer et al., 2019). Alternatively, the child may seem "independent" or as though they do not need or want adult help. The young child may have learned that adults will not provide help in frightening situations, so the child has given up asking and simply handles things on their own (Keren et al., 2018; Rosenblum et al., 2019). Other young children may lack the skills needed to request help from adults. In either of these situations, the home visitor can help caregivers to teach children how to make requests and support caregivers to recognize and respond to those requests, as reviewed in Chapter 1. Finally, some young children may have had very difficult experiences that led them to shut down feelings that are too hard to tolerate and, ultimately, to show very little emotion. For these children, long-term emotional concerns are possible, including depression, poor social skills, and low self-esteem (Malik, 2012; Sciaraffa et al. 2018). We talk more about trauma later in this chapter and again in Chapter 9.

As we also discussed earlier, there are times when virtually any difficult behavior in a young child might be expected as part of typical developmental phases. This is as likely to be true of fearful behavior as it is of acting-out behaviors. In order to respond effectively, it is important to recognize when fearful behaviors are part of typical development and when they represent something more serious. Therefore, we now consider normal fears and anxieties in infants and young children.

NORMAL FEARS IN YOUNG CHILDREN

Fearful behavior is not unusual in young children and, as with any challenging behavior, the reasons are quite varied (Keren et al., 2018). Infants and toddlers' fearful behaviors may stem from any of the following:

- Typical developmental phases
- Cautious temperament style

- Genetic predisposition
- Exposure to trauma or loss
- Caregiver modeling or example
- Environmental issues, including caregiving styles, that are a poor fit for the child

Over time and with support, most young children learn skills to cope with people, objects, and situations they fear. Feelings of fear or anxiety occur when a person feels threatened or believes that something is dangerous and cannot be controlled or predicted. Many of us experienced increased anxiety during the COVID-19 emergency, for example (Pew Research Center, 2020). Although younger babies may react to many things with apparent fear, serious anxieties or trauma responses are unlikely prior to 9 months of age (Scheeringa, 2004; ZERO TO THREE Press, 2021). Fears and anxieties increase over the early childhood period, peaking at about age 3 years (Keren et al., 2018; Landy, 2009). This pattern shows that both developmental capacities and experience in the world are needed for fear and anxiety to occur. A baby who doesn't realize that they could be hurt or injured is unlikely to fear harmful things or events.

The timing of specific fears makes sense when you consider what is important and what young children are learning to do at different times. For example, fears typical of very young babies reflect their need for almost total physical and emotional support from adults; fears of heights, loss of physical support, separation from caregivers, and strangers are common in babies (Lieberman & Van Horn, 2013). Toddlers, who are able to move around more autonomously, also fear new people and places, as well as water, baths and drains, the toilet, and falling. In addition, toddler fears of being hurt can show up as struggles with haircuts or cutting fingernails (Lieberman & Van Horn, 2013). As children get closer to age 3 and are now even more mobile, they begin to fear things that may have represented danger to our ancestors, including snakes, animals, and bugs, along with people they see infrequently but who may be associated with discomfort, such as doctors and dentists (Landy, 2009). Three-year olds, with their better language and cognitive skills, also fear imaginary creatures such as ghosts or monsters. Table 8.1 provides a summary of typical fears and anxieties in very young children, along with some ideas for caregivers to help children cope.

Starting at about 6 months and gradually increasing through the end of the first year, most babies show an apparent fearful response to new people that is called *stranger anxiety* (Brooker et al., 2013). Stranger anxiety is a good example of a behavior that relies on attainment of new cognitive skills. In this case, the infant has developed a skill called *object permanence,* or the ability to recognize that people and things continue to exist even when they are out of sight. Once this happens, babies begin to demonstrate selective

Table 8.1. Common fears and helpful responses

Age	Common fears	How to help
Infants over 9 months	Heights Loss of physical support Separation from caregivers Strangers	Stay close. Provide physical comfort. Play coming-and-going games (e.g., Peekaboo).
Young toddlers	New people and places Water, baths, and drains; the toilet Falling Being hurt (haircuts or cutting fingernails)	Stay close in new settings until the child is comfortable; follow the child's lead. Let the child watch another person do the new thing first. Read books or tell stories about new or feared things, people, and events.
Older toddler to early preschool	Insects, snakes, animals Doctor or dentist Imaginary beings (ghosts, zombies)	Provide chances to see and learn about feared objects and settings. Take short practice visits to the doctor and dentist. Provide play materials related to fears, such as a doctor kit. When the child is calm, explain about real and pretend.

Sources: Landy (2009); Lieberman and Van Horn (2013).

preferences for specific caregivers and to recognize that some people are not known, or strangers. Being wary of strangers is a protective behavior for infants, who have likely become mobile at this age and could be at risk. However, young children who have higher levels of stranger fear or a sharply escalating level of stranger fear are at increased risk for anxiety (Bahtiyar-Saygan & Berument, 2022; Brooker et al., 2013; Keren et al., 2018). Let's check in with Grace to see how she uses observation to begin to understand Amanda's fearful behaviors.

Grace asks Margaret how she thinks Amanda is responding to the new child care program. Margaret reports that Amanda had a hard time separating from her. She tells Grace, "I usually just have to sneak off or she screams. I just can't take that." Margaret adds that the child care provider has told her that Amanda is quiet and that there are no problems. She expressed relief that the program has worked out so well. "Now if she would just stop following me around at home!"

Curious, Grace visits the child care center, where she is concerned to see that Amanda sits alone and is sucking her thumb. The child care provider reports enthusiastically that Amanda is "sweet and easy to take care of" compared with her other 2-year-olds, who display a good deal of activity and frequently fight over toys. Grace sits near Amanda and shows her some toys. She has chosen ones that Amanda has seen before and likes. Amanda looks at Grace with a somber facial expression and cautiously touches the toys but does not play right away. Other children, seeing the new toys, approach curiously. Amanda hurriedly drops her hand and looks away. Grace wonders again if she should have asked to discuss Margaret's plan to enroll Amanda in child care.

TEMPERAMENT

In Chapter 5, we briefly mentioned temperament, or inborn styles of responding to the world (Joseph et al., 2023). Along with developmental level and previous history, temperament style contributes to the response that infants and young children have to events, people, and experiences. Current discussions of temperament focus on two main issues, reactivity and regulation, that work together to create behavioral styles (Bahtiyar-Saygan & Berument, 2022; Rothbart & Posner, 2006). It is helpful to think about each of these responses as falling on a continuum from high to low. When children's responses are very high or very low, clinical diagnosis might be considered; high reactivity or low inhibition may result in impulsivity and other acting-out behaviors, whereas low reactivity or high inhibition, especially in combination with negative emotionality, may connect to anxiety and other internalizing problems (Bahtiyar-Saygan & Berument, 2022). Table 8.2 illustrates how reactivity and regulation interact.

Inhibited Temperament and Anxiety

Kagan, Reznick, and Gibbons (1989) estimated that between 10% and 20% of typically developing children are classified as behaviorally inhibited (i.e., shy and withdrawing in new social situations, less likely to approach new things, and more anxious with new things). These babies and toddlers have been described in many ways, including slow to warm, fearful, cautious, and shy. Babies who have this temperament pattern may show more intense or persistent stranger fear. As they become toddlers, shy or inhibited children tend to hang back and are less likely to try new things or to interact socially with peers (Grady & Karraker, 2014). As a result, they may have fewer opportunities to learn social interaction skills, such as conversation and cooperation, that are useful later. Home visitors can reassure caregivers that although temperamentally cautious young children may need attention

Table 8.2. Temperament features and child behaviors

Reactivity	Regulation	
	High	Low
High approach: uninhibited; likely to approach, touch, and try new things	Social Extroverted	Impulsive, low attention Aggressive
Low approach: inhibited; likely to hang back, hesitant to try new things, appears cautious	May appear worried but can cope Can self-calm	Withdrawn Has trouble interacting

and adult support, most do not develop anxiety disorder (Buss, 2011). In fact, research indicates that most slow-to-warm infants typically do not continue to show this tendency by first grade. It is helpful to note that children who appear shy at first, but who can warm up and engage over time, are less likely to have later anxiety problems compared to children who have sustained withdrawal (Keren, 2023). We discuss how caregiving behaviors support this turnaround later in this chapter.

Adults often think about shyness as a challenge, and much of the initial research focused on the problems associated with this temperament style, especially when viewed from a Western cultural perspective. However, recently researchers have begun to think about shy behaviors in more positive ways. Home visitors can help caregivers to view cautious behavior as a coping strategy that can help lower the risk for anxiety disorders in children who are inhibited. When the home visitor observes a young child showing shy behaviors such as looking away while smiling or nervously touching their hair, clothes, or body, the home visitor can explain to the caregiver that these actions help the child calm down. These types of behaviors allow the child to stay available to interaction and may also signal to caregivers that some kind of support or help is needed (Colonnesi et al., 2014). Home visitors can also reassure caregivers that these behaviors are fairly common; in one study, slightly more than half of 2-year-olds and more than 80% of 3-year-olds showed this kind of shyness in at least some situations, including seeing themselves in a mirror and when a stranger smiles or complements them (Geppert, 1986).

Finally, it is also important to recognize that shy behavior may have a different meaning in various cultures (Colonnesi et al., 2014). In some cultures, what we may think of as a "shy" appearance may be seen as modesty, a valued trait. When working with families from backgrounds that are different from their own, home visitors should remember to ask about how the family understands the meaning of any behavior. Overall, being able to recognize forms and levels of inhibited behavior may help home visitors to understand and respond to young children who demonstrate different kinds of shyness.

Communication and Cognitive Milestones and Anxiety

In Chapters 6 and 7, we have recognized that children's emerging language and cognitive development gradually improve their ability to manage frustration and other challenging emotions and to gain more socially desirable skills (Biedzio & Wakschlag, 2019; Hughes et al., 2023). Similarly, these developmental milestones also help children get better at managing anxious feelings. The home visitor should recognize the ages when children begin identifying their own and other people's feelings. Children improve their ability to recognize emotions between 2 and 5 years, beginning with happiness and sadness (Denham & Couchoud, 1990; Rosenblum et al., 2019).

By age 5, typically developing children recognize these basic feelings, along with others such as anger and fear. Lack of recognition of basic emotions in preschool children has been associated with the presence of serious behavior problems; furthermore, such children may have some biases toward negative emotions, particularly sadness (Martin et al., 2010). This means that the child may be more likely to incorrectly interpret another person's facial expression and emotion as a negative emotion. As a result, the child's responses do not match with the actual events. Home visitors can encourage caregivers to recognize and respond to children's feelings and teach children to name feelings as part of developing emotion regulation. Box 8.1 provides examples of ways caregivers can help children learn and recognize emotions.

Box 8.1. Helping Support Emotional Development

Examples of caregiver statements that help children learn emotion labels

1. Model emotional statements.
   - "I am happy to see you!"
   - "I am upset because my car is broken."
2. Point out emotional states in other people.
   - "That girl got a present and she is excited."
   - "That boy's mommy had to go in the other room and he was worried about where she was."
3. Name emotional states in the child.
   - "You are frustrated. That puzzle is hard."
   - "You are so excited to go to the park! Tell your feet to be calm so they can go into their shoes so we can leave."

Activities to practice learning emotions

- Read books that label emotions.
- Make "emotion" faces with the child. Say "show me your happy face" or "show me your surprised face."
- Play with dolls or action figures and include emotions in the narrative. Say, "Superman feels sad when the building falls down" or "Sally feels happy when the family works together to dig the garden," for example.

CAREGIVING STYLE AND RESPONSES

Clinging to the parent or caregiver when in new situations or when frightened is very typical of an infant or toddler (Malik, 2012; Keren et al., 2018). A caregiver response style that provides support as the fearful child warms up or comfort when the child is too dysregulated by fear is needed for these children to feel comfortable enough to interact with other people, approach new toys, or explore new situations, for example. Caregivers who try to push the child to interact too soon, insist on interactions with new people, or leave the child too quickly in new situations will find that these methods do not work or may even make things worse. However, caregivers who are overprotective and never challenge the fearful young child are missing an opportunity to help the child learn the skills needed to regulate their anxieties (Bahtiyar-Saygan & Berument, 2022; Comer et al., 2019).

Most research examining the effects of caregiving behaviors on young children's anxiety has focused on caregiver and especially maternal anxious behaviors. Maternal anxiety is connected to increased infant anxiety, from both behavioral and genetic perspectives (Aktar et al., 2014; Brooker et al., 2013; Kerns et al., 2017). Caregivers can transmit tendencies to be anxious through caregiving behaviors such as modeling fearful behaviors, being overprotective including keeping children from trying new things, and excessively accommodating the child's fearful behaviors (Comer et al., 2019; ZERO TO THREE Press, 2021). For example, caregivers may pass on caution through social referencing as babies watch their parents to learn how to feel about new people, places, things, and situations (Aktar et al., 2014). Social referencing is especially important around the age of 12 months, as this is the time when the baby becomes mobile. Anxious parents may send a signal with their facial expressions, postures, and tone of voice that certain people, situations, and places are unsafe (Bahtiyar-Saygan & Berument, 2022). Other fearful caregiver behavior such as frequent expressions of anxiety (e.g., "be careful," "don't get hurt"), use of avoidant coping (i.e., choosing to stay away from certain places or people), and little ability to encourage the child to approach something new are other ways that anxiety can be developed in children. Some forms of caregiver overprotection can result in the child developing overcontrol of emotions and behaviors, leading to child anxiety (Aktar et al., 2014; Comer et al., 2019; Kerns et al., 2017).

A particular form of adult anxiety disorder, called *social anxiety disorder*, may be most involved in toddler anxious behaviors. Social anxiety disorder in both mothers and fathers has been associated with parents and their children both demonstrating more anxiety in a new situation. This may look like avoidance (i.e., hiding or hanging back) or showing fear relating to social and nonsocial events, such as saying hello to a stranger or trying out a new toy that seems scary or unpredictable (Aktar et al., 2014).

Research suggests that anxious behavior often has a developmental or temperament basis, may decrease in time, and may actually be adaptive

(Bahtiyar-Saygan & Berument, 2022). Home visitor strategies discussed earlier that support caregivers to demonstrate sensitive caregiving and avoid providing anxious models are helpful and may be sufficient for this type of anxious behavior. However, some young children may demonstrate anxious behaviors that go beyond these descriptions and that may reach a level that suggests a behavioral health disorder (Keren et al., 2018; ZERO TO THREE Press, 2021). Next, we consider how to recognize when a fear extends beyond what can be explained by development or temperament.

Out of the norm levels of anxiety can be identified as early as 1 to 2 years and may affect as many as 15% of young children (Bahtiyar-Saygan & Berument, 2022; ZERO TO THREE Press, 2021). Young children can show the full range of anxious behavior, including problems with separation, social fears, and fears about specific situations or things (Comer et al., 2019; ZERO TO THREE Press, 2021). As with other challenging types of behaviors, anxieties or fears that are more intense and frequent compared with those of peers occur across situations, or persist after adult intervention may signal a problem. Earlier onset and higher levels of fearful behavior that occur consistently and impact functioning are most likely to reflect risk for anxiety in later years, including into adulthood (Brooker et al., 2013; Buss, 2011; Comer et al., 2019).

Extreme reluctance to engage with new people, experiences, and things has recently been recognized as an early form of anxiety that can be identified in toddlers less than 24 months (ZERO TO THREE Press, 2021). Termed *inhibition to novelty disorder*, the diagnosis grew from research with toddlers who demonstrate fear responses to things or events that most young children would not view as dangerous (Buss, 2011; Keren, 2023; ZERO TO THREE Press, 2021). In one study, overcautious young children reacted similarly to a friendly stranger as they did to a scary spider or robot and they failed to use self-coping strategies or seek out a caregiver for comfort. Children who show the same response to different threat levels may have trouble accurately interpreting threats, or they may lack flexibility in responding. Toddlers who showed undifferentiated fear at 2 years of age were more likely to be rated as having anxious behaviors by parents and teachers when the children were followed up in preschool and kindergarten (Buss, 2011). Finally, negative emotionality shown by more frequent irritable behavior (i.e., being easily frustrated or angered) has been associated with mental health diagnoses, including depression and anxiety, as early as 18 months (Bahtiyar-Saygan & Berument, 2022; Dougherty et al., 2013).

Severe anxiety and avoidant behavior can also interfere with daily activities of the child or of the family as a whole. Examples include anxiety that prevents a child from having an experience that leads to learning or something that the child would actually like to do. At times, the young child's fearful behavior is so debilitating that the entire family schedule is arranged around accommodating the child, interfering with family functioning or

> **Box 8.2. Red Flags for Possible Anxiety Disorder**
>
> - There is a family history of anxiety disorder.
> - Irritability and/or excessive inhibition starts in infancy and continues in early childhood or school age.
> - Compared to peers, the child's fears are more intense and frequent and occur across settings.
> - The child's fears are undifferentiated (i.e., they occur with dangerous and nondangerous things).
> - The child's irritability, anxiety, or avoidant behavior interferes with family functioning (e.g., the family cannot go out due to extreme child reactions to new places and people).
> - The child is so fearful that they are unable to do something they like or want to do.
> - The child displays excessive clinginess with caregivers, refusing to be alone or left with others.
> - The child experiences sleep disturbance due to anxiety about sleeping, dreams, or being alone at night.

even simply the ability to go out to dinner (ZERO TO THREE Press, 2021). At this point, the diagnosis of an anxiety disorder may be considered. Box 8.2 provides some examples of red flags to watch for regarding anxiety in very young children. Referral to a child's physician or a mental health specialist may be indicated when red-flag behaviors are observed.

Let's see how the home visitor, Grace, continues to explore Amanda's slow-to-warm behavior and to share her ideas with Margaret.

Grace visits Amanda at the child care center a few more times and is glad to see that she is slowly starting to seem more comfortable. Grace even sees Amanda protest when another child takes a toy. Grace realizes that she has assumed that all of Amanda's behaviors are connected to her recent experiences, but now she wonders if some of the behavior is connected to temperament. She asks Margaret if she knows much about Amanda's behavior before she came to live with her, but Margaret has little information to share. She remembers that Amanda's mother, Jody, was an active and outgoing little girl, just like most people in their family. "Amanda is kind of different from the rest of us, I guess," Margaret says. "I only met her dad once and he was pretty shy," she adds. "It must be really different for you to have a child that is so quiet," Grace suggests. "I don't mind the quiet, but I can't stand how she just hangs on me," Margaret says. Grace wonders out loud, "You said she might be shy, like her dad. Maybe Amanda needs help to get used to all this new stuff she has to manage." Margaret thinks and then says, "Well, she did have a lot of changes, and we really don't know how long it will go on. I mean, I'd like to know how long she'll be here too." Grace thinks a bit too and adds, "It has been a lot for both of you."

WHAT ABOUT TRAUMA?

New fears that do not seem typical of the child or that do not correspond with a typical developmental phase deserve a closer look, as they may have a trauma component (Malik, 2012; ZERO TO THREE Press, 2021). Growing evidence has led to a consensus among researchers and clinicians that acute and chronic trauma exposure in early childhood is common and has the potential to have lifelong effects on development, behavior, and physical health (Briggs-Gowan et al., 2012; Lieberman et al., 2011). Experiences that may be traumatic are varied but include directly or indirectly experiencing events or circumstances that pose psychological or physical threat. Some examples include the following:

- Abuse
- Severe neglect
- Witnessing domestic and community violence
- Car or other accidents
- Medical procedures
- Natural and humanmade disasters
- Exposure to media violence such as commercial television, cable, and adult-level video games (Osofsky, 2011)

Adverse childhood experiences (referred to as ACEs) are known to relate to many later problems in adulthood, including mental and physical health challenges (Felitti et al., 1998; Guyon-Harris et al., 2021). The unfortunate results of early ACEs begin to appear much sooner than adulthood, however. In fact, adverse experiences are connected to developmental, social, and behavioral concerns even in very young children (Cprek et al., 2019; McKelvey et al., 2018). Infants and younger children, children who live in poverty or who have other risk factors, and children from minority groups are disproportionally affected (Lieberman et al., 2011; McKelvey et al., 2018; Merrick et al., 2019).

Healthy young children can be expected to learn to manage and recover from typical stressful events, including physical, emotional, and relational stressors, when they live in a supportive family and in safe and predictable environments (Lieberman & Van Horn, 2013). For some children, the environment is not safe, and their caregivers do not have the emotional resources to provide the needed support. Difficult child behaviors are common and could include any of the behaviors that we have discussed so far, including sleep and feeding problems, aggression, tantrums, lack of compliance, and anxiety characteristics. Many caregivers may struggle to respond appropriately, often due to their own histories of trauma exposure, either in the past or concurrent with those of their children. Therefore, in addition to being aware of the potential effects of trauma on children, home visitors need to consider the possibility that caregivers are also affected (Keren et al., 2018). In Chapter 9, we talk more about how caregiving can be affected by trauma and how home visitors can help families affected by these issues.

CAREGIVER LOSS AS A FORM OF TRAUMA

A special form of trauma for infants and young children is loss of a parent or other primary caregiver (Keren et al., 2018). Because babies and toddlers are entirely dependent on their caregivers, losing a caregiver, even temporarily, can be very distressing. Young children expect and need a parent to be available, both physically and psychologically, in order to feel safe. Parents and other caregivers may be separated from young children for various reasons that are expected to be temporary, such as military deployment, foster care placement, incarceration, and serious illness. Permanent reasons for caregiver loss include death, abandonment, and placement with other caregivers through court actions. Although from an adult perspective the meaning of these separations may be very different, to infants and toddlers, the core issue may be the same: the primary caregiver is suddenly not available. These types of separations affect hundreds of thousands of American children each year (Child Trends Data Bank, 2019; Creech et al., 2014; Lieberman & Van Horn, 2013; Tomlin et al., 2020).

Children may experience repeated separations and reunions in many of these situations. For example, many families have experienced repeated military deployments, leading to a series of separations and reunions (Lieberman & Van Horn, 2013). For children in foster care, visits can be experienced as a reminder of loss for both child and parent. For those children who have a parent in prison, high rates of recidivism may mean that the parent returns only to leave again. In one survey, 45% of parents in prison reported being under supervision such as probation or parole at the time of the present arrest and 75% had prior arrest histories (Glaze & Maruschak, 2008). Children of color, and especially Black children, disproportionately experience parental incarceration stemming from systemic racism and policies that resulted in significant racial disparities in incarceration (Tomlin et al., 2020). These results suggest that many children and their caregivers endure repeated experiences of little, no, or inconsistent contact as a result of incarceration. For families in which one caregiver is absent for any reason, the remaining caregiver's emotional health is critical to the child's resilience and may be connected to the child's ability to cope with stress related to the separation. Relationships between the absent parent and the current caregivers and reintegration of the absent parent back into the family can be difficult (Creech et al., 2014; Harris et al., 2010; Lieberman & Van Horn, 2013; Poehlmann-Tynan, 2020). Home visits can be an important part of the support that is given to the caregiver who remains, either directly through a positive relationship, provision of resource, or through encouragement to connect to other supports and to use self-care.

Responses to separation may vary based on the child's developmental level, temperament, previous experiences, and other individual factors, as well as overall family risk and resilience (Tomlin et al., 2020). Although many families and children are resilient, leading some children to adapt to frequent separation, others may struggle and even eventually show more generalized anxiety symptoms (Lieberman & Van Horn, 2013). Developmental level can also affect how a child understands a separation and how they respond to reunification. It may be hard for the returning caregiver if the child doesn't seem to recognize them right away, leading to feelings of rejection. Home visitors can help caregivers consider the experiences of young children when a parent or other caregiving adult is away temporarily or will not return.

Margaret tells Grace that she has heard from Amanda's mother, who would like Amanda to visit her in prison. The prison is several hours away, and Margaret is not sure a visit is a good idea. Grace asks, "Do you think that Amanda misses her mom?" Margaret says no and then tells Grace that she has not really said anything to Amanda about her mother because she thought it would be upsetting and did not think Amanda could understand anyway. Grace talks about how young children become connected to their parents, and she explains that they could miss them even if they don't understand everything. Margaret is surprised. She says, "Then wouldn't the visit just make it worse? How would I explain why Jody didn't come back home with us?"

WHAT HELPS ANXIOUS INFANTS AND CHILDREN?

Home visitors can help caregivers to understand typical fearful behavior in young children, use caregiving practices such as positive routines to prevent anxiety, and share what to do when children inevitably show these behaviors. For example, strong reactions to loud noises are common in young babies. Home visitors can coach parents and other caregivers to consider prevention strategies such as avoiding noisy places. When the infant is upset by a loud noise, the home visitor can encourage the caregiver to provide comfort, move away from the noise, and then show the baby where the sound came from later when they are calm. Another developmentally typical but challenging behavior is difficulty with separation. Again, home visitors can share that this is a typical and usually short-lived phase. They can encourage caregivers to play traditional children's games that involve "coming and going," such as Peekaboo, as a way to help infants learn to tolerate separations (Landy, 2009). At child care drop off or when leaving children to go out, encourage caregivers to develop a routine that includes first settling the child with the provider or other caregiver and/or activity and then following three steps: say you are going, say that it is okay to stay with this person, and say that you will be back. Caregivers should be advised not to sneak out and to try to avoid looking afraid or worried, as children will take their lead from their them as to how to feel about the separation.

Home visitors can encourage caregivers to display balanced reactions to people, events, and situations so that children learn to accurately perceive relative danger or risk. They can work with families to teach parents and other caregivers to refrain from making fun of their young children's fears and to sensitively support exploration when appropriate. Also, caregivers can be supported to choose age-appropriate activities, such as shielding young children from scary movies and video games used by adults or older children in the home.

Children who have more significant or longer lasting anxious symptoms for reasons such as inhibited temperament characteristics or history of trauma can also be helped by supportive parents and other caregivers, including a range of early care and education providers (Comer et al., 2019; Rice & Groves, 2005; Tomlin et al., 2020). In general, cautious toddlers will do better with new things when given plenty of time and preparation. Talk to caregivers about the importance of taking a balanced approach with hesitant toddlers: encourage but do not push too hard. Avoid pressuring the child who hangs back or shows fear to do something before they are ready, whether that is speaking to a new adult or trying out an unfamiliar activity. Instead, proactively use books, appropriate videos, or other indirect ways to get a child used to a new object, person, or situation. We can use the example of a visit to the doctor or dentist, which may be anxiety provoking because it involves close contact and touch with a person who is not seen frequently and who may have caused discomfort with an injection in the past. To help a toddler prepare to visit the doctor, read books and watch children's programs about doctors to gain familiarity. Take the child to the office for a visit that does not involve a check-up. It might also help to see an older sibling successfully complete a doctor's visit. Provide a doctor's kit and encourage the child to pretend to give the caregiver, doll, or stuffed animal a check-up.

Home visitors can help caregivers to find the right balance of avoiding overaccommodation and forcing a behavior the child is not ready for. Research has shown that moderate but not too intense levels of caregiver encouragement can help behaviorally inhibited or shy children to engage socially. In particular, encouraging statements have been found to be more helpful for shy children than just warm statements. Examples of encouraging statements include providing a specific suggestion about what to do (e.g., "You can sit and play in the sand box with that little girl.") instead of simply making warm or praise statements (e.g., "You're doing great!") (Grady & Karraker, 2014). Because some types of shy behaviors are perceived more positively (Colonnesi et al., 2014), parents can coach their inhibited toddlers to perform low-contact but appropriate methods of interacting. For example, caregivers can teach toddlers to smile and wave to strange adults when making eye contact or when speaking is too hard. With family members, a child who does not want to give a kiss or hug could give a high five or fist bump instead. See Box 8.3 for tips to share with caregivers.

As we have discussed, child and parent or other caregiver anxieties may interact (Comer et al., 2019). Remember that anxiety runs in families and can be transmitted through both genetic mechanisms and caregiving behavior (Buss, 2011; Comer et al., 2019). When you observe anxious or inhibited behavior in young children, consider if the caregiver is also showing symptoms. It is likely that some of the families that participate in home visiting include caregivers who have clinical diagnoses of anxiety or depression, or who have symptoms that are not well managed. This likelihood increased during the COVID-19 emergency (Pew Research Center,

---

Box 8.3. Tips for Caregivers to Reduce Young Children's Anxiety

- Prevent anxiety by creating a safe and healthy environment.
- Play games that involve coming and going, such as Peekaboo.
- Provide increased structure and routine.
- Recognize and name feelings.
- For the child who hangs back or shows fear, avoid rushing or pressuring to do something before they are ready.
- Avoid noisy places; offer comfort, distraction, or a way to escape if you must be in a noisy place.
- Recognize children's activities and accomplishments.
- Encourage children's curiosity and play and choose age-appropriate activities.
- Remember that anxiety may run in families; explore one's own issues when warranted.
- Work toward the "right balance" when encouraging children to engage socially and when providing discipline (i.e., supportive yet firm).

2020). Encouraging caregivers to participate in evaluations and treatment when warranted is recommended. Some home visiting programs may have a special emphasis on screening for caregiver depression or anxiety; we will discuss this in greater detail in Chapter 9.

Although many children experience trauma, not all develop a traumatic stress response or disorder. Perhaps about 30% have reactions severe enough to lead to a diagnosis and need for treatment (Cohen & Scheeringa, 2009). For these children, reactions to people, experiences, or situations connected to the trauma in some way may lead to responses that can interfere with child and family functioning (ZERO TO THREE Press, 2021). When possible trauma reactions are observed, it is always advisable to ask about any recent situations or activities the child has experienced that could have been frightening. When trauma is known or suspected, in addition to accessing any needed outside care, home visitors can encourage caregivers to seek a safe environment, return to typical routines, and understand a child's reactions as trauma related. It is acknowledged that some families experience long-term anxiety-provoking situations, including living in unsafe communities and experiencing racism as part of their everyday environment. These circumstances have deep roots that home visitors cannot expect to solve. Accessing supervision and consultation may be helpful for home visitors to engage effectively with families about these kinds of experiences without becoming burnt out or overwhelmed themselves.

Separations from primary caregivers, whether temporary or more permanent, are significant stressors for very young children and can result in anxious and other difficult behaviors. In addition, these behaviors can occur when children experience repeated separations and reunions due to circumstances such as shared custody, visitation within a context of foster care, or even as a result of military deployment (Lieberman & Van Horn, 2013). In many of these situations, caregivers may have strong feelings about each other, (e.g., biological and foster parents) or the overall visiting situation. Even when parents and other caregivers have angry, sad, or other negative feelings related to these experiences, the child's needs for support must be addressed. Developing a standard way of talking about the situation can be helpful, even when a child is very little. Lieberman, Ghosh Ippen, and Van Horn (2015) suggest that caregivers explain to their children that a judge or court has decided that it has to be this way, for example. Caregivers can be encouraged to explain that they feel sad about leaving and will miss the child. Keeping the visit schedule consistent will be helpful in the long run, as the child can learn that the caregiver will come back.

Lieberman and Van Horn (2013) offer suggestions about how to help families when parents or other caregivers must be away for military deployment. This information can also help families who are separated for other reasons. First, if the family is aware of the pending separation, some preparation may be helpful. Home visitors can encourage the caregivers to recognize that children attend to and pick up on adult behaviors and conversations, and caregivers should therefore watch for child reactions. Encourage caregivers to build up a cache of positive memories by spending focused time together or taking photos or making recordings for younger children who may need more concrete materials to support their memory. Encourage the caregivers to provide a verbal explanation of what is happening and describe what each person will be doing while apart. Some free and easily accessible examples of how to speak with children about difficult issues, including separation, have been developed by the Public Broadcasting Service (http://www.pbs.org/parents/parenting/). In addition, Sesame Workshop has developed a number of materials for helping children affected by parental incarcerations, a particularly challenging situation due to stigma (https://sesameworkshop.org/topics/incarceration/).

At the beginning of the separation, young children may show increased emotionality, behavior issues, and sleep problems (Barker & Berry, 2009). These reactions are most likely to occur in the first month but may improve somewhat thereafter. As the time apart continues, children will benefit from routine, structure, and visual depictions of time passing, such as a calendar. To keep the absent caregiver in mind, build in time to talk about that person in daily routines, such as during bedtime prayer if that is part of the family traditions (Lieberman & Van Horn, 2013). Contacts with the caregiver through mail or video can be helpful. When a caregiver is in jail or prison, visitation is often not very child friendly, so visits need to be carefully planned and at times may not be indicated at all (Poehlmann-Tynan, 2020). Foster care visits can be stressful too, especially when supervised, as biological parents may feel judged and awkward and may confuse their children by behaving differently than expected.

Parents and other primary caregivers may need help to understand a range of reactions that a child might show during visits. The home visitor should prepare the caregiver that patience is needed, as the child may appear to not recognize them or may look afraid and confused. If a returning military parent is injured and looks different, the young child's age-typical fears of injury are likely to be activated (Lieberman & Van Horn, 2013). Again, young children's egocentric thinking may lead them to believe that they are responsible for the injury in some way. When the injuries are severe, about a third of the time the other caregiver needs to travel to see them or provide caregiving, causing another separation (Cozza et al., 2010). Providing explanations appropriate to the child's developmental level and helping the temporary caregiver to keep the routines the same will help.

Reintegrating a caregiver back into home routines can also be challenging for everyone (Poehlmann-Tynan, 2020). The family has had to adapt while one person was absent. When that person returns, it may take time before they can reclaim specific roles and responsibilities. The returning family members may need time to catch up to the changes at home, including the child's changed development and new abilities (Lieberman & Van Horn, 2013).

Sadly, for some families, the ultimate separation may happen when a parent or other primary caregiver dies. Although it may be very difficult for adults to discuss the death of a loved one, truthfulness is recommended (Lieberman et al., 2003). Family members will need support to explain the loss of the caregiver in clear terms. They will also need to be prepared for the likelihood that children will repeatedly ask questions about what happened and when they will see the person again. These questions can reappear periodically for a long time and can be upsetting for caregivers who are experiencing their own grief. Caregivers often feel confused about how the child is feeling because young children cannot sustain long periods of continual sadness. It can be helpful to share that a young child can appear sad, then seem to play normally, and then suddenly ask if the parent will be home to tuck them in, for example (Lieberman & Van Horn, 2013). The home visitor should take advantage of reflective supervision/consultation when supporting families through these very emotionally hard situations in order to maintain clear perspectives and boundaries while identifying and dealing with any potential reactions they may experience.

USING THE PAUSE FRAMEWORK

Using the scenario presented in the vignettes, let's see how Grace thinks through her experiences with Amanda's grandmother Margaret. See Figures 8.1 and 8.2 for examples of how this might look.

WHAT'S NEXT?

In Chapter 9, we apply the PAUSE problem-solving approach to family challenges and issues that affect the work of home visitors.

TIPS FOR PRACTICE

- Help caregivers recognize when anxious behavior is part of typical development or a child's temperament style. Coach parents and caregivers to provide sensitive supports and to avoid teasing or belittling a child who is anxious. Encourage caregivers to use structure and routine to help children who are anxious for any reason, including a developmental phase, temperament, or a stressor.

- Assist caregivers to recognize that children will notice and may mirror adult anxieties. For those caregivers whose anxiety is significant, encourage personal treatment.

PAUSE WORKSHEET

Child: **Amanda**   Date: **July 14, 2024**

Caregiver: **Margaret (grandmother)**   Provider: **Grace**

PERCEIVE—Explore what is happening.

Caregiver perspective:	Provider perspective:
Amanda's grandmother (temporary guardian) wants her to be less clingy and more outgoing.	Amanda has had a traumatic experience, having lost her mother to incarceration and been moved to a different state to live with a relative she does not know.

ASK—Clarify what is happening.

Starting with the caregiver's priorities and concerns, ask more detailed/specific questions to clarify what is happening.

What information is available about Amanda prior to the move, such as her personality, activities, relationship with her mother, and so forth?

What is Amanda's temperament style? And her mother's? And father's? Other family members'?

Have other family members experienced traumatic events? How did they respond?

UNDERSTAND—Explore why it is happening.

With the caregiver, explore explanations for what is happening. Consider possible explanations that include the environment, the child, and the caregiver. Listen and observe closely as you explore the situation in conversation with the family.

Caregiver perspective:	Provider perspective:	Child's perspective:
Amanda is being needy, which can be annoying and interrupts the family schedule.	Amanda has experienced a trauma and needs some structure/routine and reassurance that all is going to be okay.	Amanda misses her mommy and doesn't understand the loss.

(continued)

(continued)

Figure 8.1. Grace's PAUSE Worksheet for Margaret and Amanda.

Figure 8.1. (continued)

PAUSE WORKSHEET (continued)

UNDERSTAND (continued)

Caregiver perspective:	Provider perspective:	Child's perspective:

STRATEGIZE and **EVALUATE**—Identify possible responses/solutions.

1. Solution/action to try:	How will we know if it works?
Introduce some information about loss so Margaret and the child care provider can see Amanda's behavior in a different way.	Margaret and the child care provider use alternative strategies to support Amanda.
	When will we evaluate if it works?
	In one month.

2. Solution/action to try:	How will we know if it works?
Work with Margaret to set a routine to introduce some structure for Amanda.	Amanda's clinginess decreases at home; separation for child care is less stressful.
	When will we evaluate if it works?
	In about 6 to 8 weeks, after implementing a plan.

PROVIDER REFLECTION WORKSHEET

Provider Reflection Worksheet

Child: _Amanda_ Date: _July 14, 2024_

Caregiver: _Margaret (grandmother)_   Provider: _Grace_

1. How did I follow the caregiver's lead to learn what is most pressing or important to them?	Although it was difficult for me to be patient because of Amanda's needs, I was very mindful to try to fully understand Margaret's concerns.
2. How did I ask clarifying questions that help me to understand the problem better? How did I inquire about the caregiver's values and beliefs related to the issue?	I think I have done well to stay in a place of exploration with this family and child care provider by asking a lot of questions. This seems to help them better understand Amanda's individual experience and situation.
3. How did I reflect on and offer to discuss similarities and differences between me and the caregiver? These might include race, ethnicity, language, gender, sexual orientation, religious and other beliefs, values, experiences, etc.	I don't have children of my own (yet), and I can't imagine what it must be like for Margaret to be raising a grandchild. How do I share what I think are helpful resources to reduce her stress and make things better while I also respect her situation and experience?

(continued)

(continued)

Figure 8.2. Grace's Provider Reflection Worksheet for Margaret and Amanda.

Figure 8.2. *(continued)*

PROVIDER REFLECTION WORKSHEET *(continued)*

4. How did I provide information that may help the caregiver better understand the child's behavior?	*I have been able to introduce some information about trauma and loss and temperament style that may help the family better respond to Amanda's needs.*
5. How did I engage the caregiver to develop a response that may include a strategy to try, a resource to use, or more information to increase understanding?	*The family has been open to various ideas and is willing to set up a more defined routine and schedule. The grandmother and child care provider seem willing to partner so that the schedules complement each between home and child care.*
6. How did I provide support and emotional containment if needed?	*I have been able to support Margaret in better understanding her own strong emotions regarding having Amanda come to her home, her daughter's incarceration, and Amanda's clinginess.*
7. How do I plan to follow up on promised actions to maintain trust?	*By going to the child care setting several times, I feel I demonstrated a commitment to supporting this family in fully understanding their concerns and issues.*
8. What do I want to discuss in reflective supervision to improve my practice and outcomes with this child and caregiver?	*I want to learn more about trauma-informed work and how I can be supportive to families when young children struggle with loss. I am also curious about children's temperament and how this influences parent–child interactions. I wonder how things will go if and when Amanda has a visit with her mother Jody and if there is anything else that I could do to help the family prepare.*

KEY POINTS TO REMEMBER

- Some level of anxiety is typical for infants and young children, especially in certain developmental stages.
- Many factors may increase the chances that a child develops anxious behaviors, including temperament factors and trauma exposure.
- Home visitors can help caregivers learn strategies that allow young children to feel safe and to gain skills needed to manage anxious feelings.

SUGGESTED FURTHER READING

Daniels, N. (2015). *How to parent your anxious toddler.* Jessica Kingsley Publishers.

Pincus, D. (2012). *Growing up brave: Expert strategies for helping your child overcome fear, stress, and anxiety.* Little, Brown.

Rice, K. F., & Groves, B. M. (2005). *Hope and healing: A caregiver's guide to helping young children affected by trauma.* ZERO TO THREE Press.

Wilson, R., & Lyons, L. (2013). *Anxious kids, anxious parents: 7 ways to stop the worry cycle and raise courageous and independent children.* Health Communications.

9

What Else Might This Be?

Family Challenges

Jackie, a physical therapist in an early intervention system, arrives for her scheduled visit with Chloe, a 10-month-old girl with motor delays and torticollis. The door is opened by Chloe's 10-year-old sister, Olivia, who is holding her and helping her with a bottle. Jackie is surprised to see Olivia, as it is a school day. Looking in, Jackie notices that the floor is covered with piles of clothing, stacks of toys, and many partially filled boxes and trash bags. Olivia tells her, "We are moving to grandma's apartment. They have a pool!"

Chloe's mother, Desiree, appears, carrying a box of dishes. She seems surprised to see Jackie, and says, "Is it Wednesday already?" Jackie feels irritated and wonders why Desiree did not tell her about this move last week! She also wonders where Chloe's father is, as he is typically present for sessions. He does not often participate, but Jackie has noticed that he does usually listen in. "So, Olivia says you are moving. It seems pretty busy here with all this activity. Would another time be better?" Desiree takes the baby and tells Olivia to take the box into a different room. In a low voice, she explains to Jackie that they were evicted and will be going to her mother's apartment for a few days. After that, she is unsure where they will be. Olivia thinks they are packing up, but actually Desiree is sorting their things because she has no place to keep most of it. "If you want to work with Chloe today, that would be okay. I'm just not sure when we'll be able to see you again," Desiree says.

Jackie feels overwhelmed by the young family's situation and unsure if she could or should try to help. Thoughts and ideas come quickly. She wonders where Chloe's father is in all this, if she should offer to contact the service coordinator or maybe a social worker, or whether someone at her church could help. Feeling even more uncomfortable, Jackie tells Desiree that she is sorry for her troubles and agrees to go ahead with the session. As she sits down with Chloe, Jackie is relieved to be focused on something familiar.

In the last few chapters, we focused on how to explore difficult child behavior with families using the PAUSE problem-solving approach, incorporating reflection and relationship-based methods. Throughout, we recognized the possibility that caregiving behaviors may contribute to difficulties in children's behaviors. In this chapter, we delve into some of the more common stressors that families face, discuss how these stressors affect caregiving behavior and child outcomes, and present some suggestions for home visitors working with families in these situations.

Home visitors must bear in mind that families that experience risk factors may be reluctant to disclose their struggles due to concerns about being labeled or judged. Those with identified issues related to mental illness (MI) or substance use concerns may fear asking for help with their children due to recognition of potential for reporting to authorities and fear of having children removed (Boursnell, 2014). When home visitors are able to work with families over the long term, the potential for building a positive relationship is increased. Over time, the professional can get to know the family in a deeper way that includes recognition of their strengths and their successful ways of coping. When home visitors take the time to get to know families and to begin to understand them within a cultural and community context, families are more likely to experience the relationship with the home visitor as supportive, which may increase their willingness to take advantage of offered help. These steps are important for all families including when supporting the mental health needs of diverse families. Recent research on evidence-based home visiting programs shows that some keys to success with diverse families include recruiting home visitors who can form close connections with families, tailoring screening strategies to fit families' culture, and helping families access both concrete supports and mental health interventions when needed (Ferguson et al., 2023).

Before we cover specific stressors, it is important to acknowledge that many families that use early childhood services may experience more than one stressor across time or concurrently. For example, trauma experience is associated with substance abuse as well as mental health conditions that could include anxiety, depression, or borderline personality disorder (BPD). In addition, some groups, such as military and returning veteran populations, have much higher rates of depression, anxiety, and suicide than the general public (Creech et al., 2014; Lieberman & Van Horn, 2013). Individuals from minoritized communities are also at higher risk for trauma, including those related to experiences of discrimination. Combinations of risk factors may reduce the effectiveness of home visiting programs. In one study, children of mothers who had either depression or who lacked trust in the home visiting providers showed improvement in cognition and behavior. However, children whose mothers had both concerns did not improve, even though both groups received the same number of visits (Cluxton-Keller et al., 2014).

In some home visiting programs, screening for certain types of risk factors is part of standard activities. This can include screening for caregiver mental health concerns and the presence of stressors (Ferguson et al., 2023). Knowing which stressors and risk factors are related may help the home visitor to be more alert to other potential issues after screening identifies a concern. For example, prenatal and postnatal maternal screening for depression is helpful, but we may miss other important information if the screening ends there. In this instance, mothers with depression may also benefit from screening to check for coexisting stressors, trauma, or anxiety as well as the availability of resilience factors, including social supports (Price & Masho, 2014).

Although it is important to find safe ways for families to share the issues that concern them, it is also fair to say that the presence of multiple risk factors that complicate families' lives will also complicate the home visitor's work with them. It may be difficult to determine where to start when the problems are so interconnected (Monahan et al., 2012). Providers may have long-term goals related to program requirements, often tied to grant funding, that differ from priorities that families might identify as preferred. Families are often distracted from long-term goals by acute issues (Boursnell, 2014). Historically, some approaches may have used deficit models; more recent models focus on family strengths and understanding a family's cultural context (Walsh & Mortensen, 2020).

In the following sections, we apply strategies from a range of approaches that align well with the relationship-based and reflective practice principles that underlie much of the work of home visitors. We next discuss application of several such strategies to home visiting, including providing emotion support, sharing knowledge of resources, helping family members develop resilience, providing content flexibly, and recognizing cultural contexts (Ferguson et al., 2023; Substance Abuse and Mental Health Services Administration [SAMHSA], 2014, 2021). First let's see how Jackie is progressing with Chloe's family as we begin to discuss what it is like for home visitors to interact with families whose needs are many.

On the way to her next visit, Jackie calls Chloe's service coordinator to alert her to the family's impending homelessness. "I feel so terrible that I missed this. I knew money was tight when Desiree lost her child care job during COVID, but thought things were getting better." The service coordinator has several ideas about how to help and agrees to call the family. Jackie feels relieved but wonders if she should have been able to take more direct action while with the family. She is also concerned that Chloe's family might be hard to contact in the future. As she prepares for her next visit, Jackie wonders if she will ever see the family again.

SORTING THROUGH MYRIAD POSSIBLE FAMILY RISK FACTORS

Jackie, the home visitor in the chapter vignette, is faced with helping this family gain some much-needed supports for issues outside her direct work with Chloe but that very much influence Chloe's development. Home visitors see many different caregivers and families and are likely to encounter a variety of challenging situations like Jackie's experience with Chloe's family. The following subsections identify some of the potential issues that families face and describe some ways the home visitor can support the child and family. Table 9.1 summarizes some potential strategies a home visitor might consider when parents or other caregivers experience MIs or disability or are at risk for environmental challenges. As always, the home visitor should strive to provide information, make appropriate referrals to other resources when needed, and modify their plan to best suit the needs and abilities of the child and family.

Parents with Mental Illness and Disability

MIs of any kind are common. According to surveys (SAMHSA, 2021), nearly a quarter of adults had a MI in the last year, 16.5% of those over 12 years met criteria for a substance use disorder (SUD), and having both was not uncommon (SAMHSA, 2021). Census data indicates that about a third of adults and half of those under 25 years reported symptoms of anxiety and/or depression, with younger people most affected (KFF, 2023). People less than 25 years of age and people of color may be less likely to receive treatment for these conditions (KFF, 2023). Because many of these individuals

Table 9.1. Home visitor responses to assumptions about children

Caregiver expectation of child's development	Home visitor response
A caregiver tells the home visitor that they believe their 2-month-old baby is ready to eat solid foods such as cereal, saying, "She should be sleeping through the night by now and I'm exhausted!"	"A lot of caregivers I talk with are tired and wonder about how to help their baby sleep better. Usually, I hear doctors talk about adding cereal when babies are a little older, but you could check with your doctor to see what is recommended. I wonder if you would like to talk about some ideas to help you get some more rest."
A caregiver shouts angrily at a 30-month-old child who is running off in a park, "You are doing this on purpose to embarrass me!"	"It's hard when little kids have so much energy! Even though running off is pretty normal, sometimes caregivers worry that other people think you are not doing your job."
A caregiver cries when their toddler hits them during discipline. They say, "He is bad and will never be good."	"I know it is frustrating for you when he hits. I wonder if he is frustrated too. Maybe he is really trying to tell us what he wants, but he doesn't have the words yet."

are of child-bearing age, it is likely that many children grow up with a caregiver with SUD, MI, or both conditions (Boris et al., 2019).

The majority of interest and research on parental MI has focused on mothers, and specifically on maternal depression. There is also a sizable body of research on the effects of borderline personality disorder and trauma, which are related to each other and to depression. In recent years, researchers and clinicians have begun to consider the needs of caregivers with schizophrenia and substance abuse. Recent reviews of research on paternal MI show its impact on child development and both internalizing and externalizing behaviors (Scarlett et al., 2023). Although knowledge of the effects of caregiver MI is growing and expanding, for the purposes of this discussion we briefly consider anxiety, depression, and BPD, as these are among the most common and best studied MIs and most likely to be encountered by home visitors. As we review these potential risks, keep in mind that caregivers who have MI and other risks are able to take care of their children, but they may need additional supports to do so effectively.

Depression and Caregiving

Depression is common in the general population and more likely in people who have other life stressors. For example, 40% to 60% of low-income mothers report depression, which is twice the rate in general samples (National Center for Children in Poverty, 2008). Unfortunately, most of these women do not seek treatment (Knitzer et al., 2008). Women are especially vulnerable to depression during pregnancy and the postpartum period. (This is discussed later in the chapter.) Early childhood programs along with primary health care providers have often attended to depression and especially maternal depression, due to their high association with negative child outcomes. Depression and the often co-occurring anxious symptoms may interfere with a mother's performance of many daily activities, including appropriate caregiving behaviors. With infants, the main concern is the mother's low reciprocity and sensitivity, which can impair attachment. With toddlers, concerns center on discipline and behavior management styles that can lead to ongoing challenging behaviors. The research on these concerns is extensive and complex, with efforts to consider both direct effects and interplay among many factors, including child characteristics such as temperament and delays in development, parental histories, and stressful family context and overall environment (Alvarez et al., 2015). To address these types of concerns, the home visitor should focus on the following:

- Keep goals simple to avoid overwhelming the caregiver with depression.

- When working with families with infants, support parents to read and respond to babies' cues to maximize positive attachments.

- When working with families with toddlers, provide support related to appropriate behavior management.

Borderline Personality Disorder

All people have personality styles or traits that might include tendencies toward eccentric, dramatic, or fearful thinking and behavior (American Psychiatric Association [APA], 2022). When a person's typical ways of thinking and feeling about themself and others significantly interfere with daily life, a personality disorder (PD) may be present (APA, 2022). Many people display more than one PD, and it is common for PD to be present concurrent with other psychiatric disorders (Zimmerman et al., 2005), such as depression and anxiety. Often the PD is not diagnosed, leading to less effective treatments.

One of the best known and most researched forms of personality challenges is borderline personality disorder (BPD) (Mendez-Miller et al., 2022). Important for home visitors who use a relationship-based model, BPD includes feelings and behaviors that interfere with all close relationships. Understanding BPD is particularly critical for workers in early childhood fields, as it also is related to problems with caregiving behaviors that affect relationships with the child and discipline methods that may result in adverse child outcomes (Tomlin, 2002). Finally, BPD frequently co-occurs with anxiety, depression, trauma, and substance abuse, meaning that home visitors should consider it when working with families with these other risk factors.

The core features of BPD include intense and conflictual relationships, poor control of impulses and emotions, and problems with thinking and sense of self (APA, 2022; Mendez-Miller et al., 2022). Because BPD includes problems with affect regulation and unusual beliefs, the person may show impulsive behaviors and a low level of consistency. Due to the extreme level of inconsistency that caregivers with BPD may demonstrate, their children are at high risk for insecure attachment patterns and subsequent challenging behaviors. Caregivers with BPD, unable to manage their own emotions, lack the skills to scaffold child emotional experiences. They are likely to need help to learn how to accurately recognize, tolerate, and respond to child emotions. When faced with negative child emotions such as fear or sadness, caregivers with BPD frequently push away the feelings with criticism and mocking. At the extreme, disorganized attachment may occur (Keren et al., 2018; Petfield et al., 2015). Mothers with BPD are likely to need assistance to recognize typical child development and to have appropriate expectations. In addition, due to the potential for extreme emotional and behavioral swings, help in maintaining a stable and nurturing environment—including guidance on how to establish and sustain a routine and to be consistent in setting limits—may be needed (Keren et al., 2018; Petfield et al., 2015).

Interpersonal characteristics that interfere with the caregiver–child relationship can also significantly challenge the provider's ability to form and maintain an effective working relationship with affected caregivers (Tomlin, 2002). Inappropriate perceptions about other people can lead caregivers to react strongly to a home visitor's attempts to set limits or boundaries, typically interpreting these behaviors as abandonment. As a result of these misperceptions, caregivers may demonstrate maladaptive behaviors that can include apparent self-sabotage and behaviors that seem to push the home visitor away. These behaviors may include not answering or returning calls, failing to follow through with recommendations, or refusing to continue services. At other times, the caregiver may behave in ways that seem intended to force the home visitor to give more attention, commonly with threats of self-harm or attempted suicide. In these types of instances, the home visitor should take the following steps:

- Set limits and keep strong boundaries (e.g., let the person know when you can accept phone calls and resist adding extra appointments when caregivers are highly stressed).

- Help the caregiver to build routines and consistently set limits with their child.

- Monitor their own feelings and behaviors, as people with BPD may provoke feelings of frustration and anger.

- Work with a supervisor to enact a safety plan if a caregiver is threatening self-harm.

Anxiety

Anxiety disorders are diagnosed when a person displays fear, worry, or avoidance behavior of objects or situations to a degree that is out of proportion to actual danger, interferes with functioning, is hard to control, and is not culturally compatible (American Psychiatric Association, 2022). Anxieties can be narrow, such as phobias (fear of specific objects and situations), or broad, such as generalized anxiety (e.g., worry about a number of events or activities). These disorders often begin in childhood and can persist if not treated. As we discussed in Chapter 8, anxieties and fears in young children are often related to caregiver anxiety; therefore, screening and addressing caregiver anxiety is important for overall child and family functioning. Furthermore, anxiety disorders commonly occur with other issues, including depression and substance use.

Many people had anxiety related to the COVID-19 pandemic and experiences of lockdown. Although in most places emergency practices are suspended, some people continue to have anxious feelings related to the chances of becoming ill, going to public spaces, inviting persons into their home, or sending children to child care. Increased anxiety has been noted as one of the symptoms of long COVID in around 25% of affected persons (Pavli et al., 2021). Both of these situations may be more likely in females and are associated with other anxiety and mood disorders. Home visitors can support caregivers with anxiety by providing appropriate screening, using the strategies for depression discussed in this chapter, and making referrals to mental health providers when needed. Review the strategies presented in Chapter 8 when both caregivers and children are affected.

Caregivers with Disability

More than 4.4 million parents in the United States have one or more disability conditions (National Research Center for Parents with Disabilities, 2022). There is increasing recognition that having a disability does not mean that caring for a child is impossible, and research on the effects of disability on caregiving, though limited, is growing (Kleinmann & Songer, 2009). Disability alone does not present risk for successful caregiving; instead, those with disabilities who have problems in caregiving most likely also struggle with additional issues, including poverty, trauma histories, and other risk factors (Kirshbaum & Olkin, 2002; National Research Center for Parents with Disabilities, 2022). Home visiting services, when properly individualized and adapted, can be one of the supports that help parents with all types of disabilities retain custody of their children and parent safely and successfully (Kleinmann & Songer, 2009).

People with disabilities including motor or sensory impairment, or intellectual disability, can become parents and may need specialized supports (Keren et al., 2018). Individuals who have sensory impairment, including vision or hearing loss, may successfully care for their children with few accommodations and community supports. Home visitors can help caregivers identify supports, including the following:

- Technology, such as visual alarms for people who are deaf, to allow independent caregiving.

- Other providers such as occupational therapists and physical therapists who can provide adaptive equipment to increase mobility and accessibility.

- Community programs to access housing, transportation, and other resources.

Parents with intellectual disability may concern home visitors the most, as they are more likely to have involvement in the child welfare system. However, evidence suggests that most parents with intellectual disability, given sufficient support, can successfully care for their children (Coren et al., 2018). Home visitors can support caregivers with intellectual disability by doing the following:

- Breaking down tasks into steps and planning for frequent repetition and practice.

- Providing information in alternative formats that match literacy levels, including picture supports and video recordings.

- Supporting caregivers to develop routines to accomplish necessary caregiving tasks and activities (e.g., daily hygiene, getting ready for daily activities, administering medications, keeping appointments).

Autism is a lifelong neurodevelopmental disorder that is characterized by difficulties in social and social communication skills in combination with strong preferences for sameness or repetition (APA, 2022). Given that rates of autism are increasing and that understanding of the spectrum of autism is greatly expanded, home visitors may encounter parents with autistic characteristics or formal autism diagnoses (APA, 2022). As with other conditions discussed, autism can co-occur with other neurodevelopmental disorders as well as with disorders such as anxiety and depression. Although it is known that autism is a lifelong condition, limited research has been conducted on parents with autism to date (Adams, 2021). A recent community-based study compared experiences of mothering for women with and without autism (Pohl et al., 2020). Autistic mothers in the study reported that being a parent was rewarding while also reporting more concerns for depression, anxiety, and coping at home than mothers without autism. Relevant to home visiting, these mothers were also more likely to feel isolated, judged, and unable to get support from others for parenting. Home visitors should be aware that sensory processing challenges are common in autism and can impact pregnancy and early parenting experiences such as breast feeding or tolerating infant cries. Recommended supports for caregivers with autism include using clear communication and help with planning and task management. Caregivers with autism may also benefit from using the CDC's *Learn the Signs. Act Early.* materials including the free, downloadable phone app as a source of easily accessible information about child development. As with other conditions, consulting with providers such as a mental health, speech, or occupational therapist may be needed when supporting parents who have autism.

Substance Use Disorder

Home visitors are increasingly supporting families affected by substance misuse, many of whom are also involved in child welfare systems (Bosk et al., 2019). The misused substances include alcohol, opioids, methamphetamines, heroin, and marijuana. Excessive use of substances, whether legal or not, is likely to impair a person's daily functioning across all areas of life, including caregiving. When substances are used during pregnancy, there are also a variety of possible effects on the unborn child, many of which result in lifelong developmental, behavioral, and physical effects (Boris et al., 2019).

Home visitors should recognize the potential effects of drugs on the child directly and through impaired caregiving behavior (Lowell et al., 2021; Boris et al., 2019). Alcohol, though legal, is the most commonly used addictive substance. Use of alcohol during pregnancy is known to lead to serious birth defects that include problems in growth and the nervous system, leading to a cascade of developmental and behavioral problems. Smoking cigarettes during pregnancy has become less common, but still occurs and can lead to many problems for the fetus, including prematurity, miscarriage, and small size, which are risk factors for medical and learning issues (Hackshaw et al., 2011). Use of e-cigarettes (vaping) is less common during pregnancy but may have similar risk (Schilling et al., 2021). Similar concerns have been reported for second-hand exposure to smoke for children, fetuses, and pregnant people (Hayashi et al., 2011; Schilling et al., 2021).

Many people are familiar with the effects of prenatal exposure to opioids, including neonatal abstinence syndrome (NAS), a medical condition that includes a range of symptoms and may require expensive and lengthy medical care (Boris et al., 2019). In addition to opioids, babies exposed to substances such as alcohol and cocaine during pregnancy may be physically dependent on the drug, leading to withdrawal symptoms (Boris et al., 2019). Depending on the drug used, the baby might have physical symptoms such as breathing problems, vomiting, diarrhea, trembling, excessive sleeping, or behaviors such as crying and irritability (Baldwin et al., 2009; Boris et al., 2019). Early on, babies born with substances in their systems may have feeding and sleep problems that make them hard to care for. Continuing irritability and problems with soothing can interfere with bonding, especially when parents' confidence is undermined by a lack of success (Baldwin et al., 2009). As children grow older, both behavioral and learning issues may become apparent. These child behaviors can present especially difficult problems for caregivers who continue to misuse substances.

Substance use impacts a range of caregiving behaviors and may result in child welfare involvement (Bosk et al., 2019; Lowell et al., 2021). For example, caregivers who continue to use substances may engage in risky behaviors that lead to concerns for child safety. Examples include driving while under the influence or allowing children to be exposed to dangerous chemicals through second-hand smoke or ingestion. Some caregivers who are impaired by the effects of drugs or alcohol may fail to provide needed supervision or, in some instances, they use funds for drugs instead of providing sufficient food and other needed resources. Caregivers who misuse substances may also have difficulty providing a basic routine or a stable home environment. Substance use may impact behaviors needed for sensitive caregiving. Caregivers may miss or misread babies' cues, lack feelings of joy and pleasure when interacting with their baby, and be less resilient to caregiving stressors (Suchman, 2008).

When a caregiver has a substance disorder that results in child welfare involvement, they may be required to engage in separate interventions for caregiving and for addiction, often without consideration of possible trauma

(Bosk et al., 2019). Recently, it has been recognized that treatment methods that include attention to their role as a parent/caregiver may be more effective than approaches that rely on skill building, educational, or behavioral models and may also contribute to maintaining sobriety (Bosk et al., 2019; Lowell et al., 2021). Although many home visitors do use a relational approach, they may still find that people with SUD are harder to engage and retain in services. Recently, researchers used data from focus groups to identify barriers persons with SUD encounter when participating in home visiting (Lowell et al., 2021). The study found that many people think home visiting is only for children with delays. The Lowell study suggests that because individuals with SUD often worry that their use has affected their child, they may be reluctant to accept early intervention or other services that seem to confirm this fear and contribute to their feelings of being stigmatized or judged. The researchers proposed that to work effectively with families affected by SUD, home visitors would benefit from additional training and consultation around attachment, reflective practice, and adult mental health and SUD issues. One program that addresses these concepts is Mothering from the Inside Out (MIO), which is an intervention specifically for women affected by SUD who are mothers (Lowell et al., 2021; Suchman et al., 2008). The intervention uses relationship to encourage the caregiver to increase their interest in the child's emotional experience, resulting in improvement in caregiver reflective functioning, child behavior, and the relationship. The intervention has additional benefits including improved symptoms of depression and anxiety and less chance of relapse.

Home visitors can expect to encounter families living with SUD and can consider the following guidelines and strategies to enhance their skills with these families:

- Because SUD is so common, make questions about the use of alcohol and other drugs part of regular assessment activities.

- Be prepared to offer resources and referral for information, assessment, diagnosis, treatment, family counseling, self-help groups, and other community-based supports when family members disclose problematic use.

- Provide complete information about the focus and goals of the home visiting program to dispel common misperceptions.

- Discuss and agree with families about the limits and boundaries regarding contact and appointment.

- Prioritize relationship building between the home visitor and the caregiver and to strengthen the caregiver–child relationship.

- Seek additional consultation and training to gain knowledge and skills in SUD and associated MI, including trauma.

- If abuse and/or neglect are observed, contact authorities, as defined by federal and state statutes and your agency policies.

- Discuss reactions to families experiencing substance abuse issues in reflective supervision and consultation (RSC).

Traumatic Experiences

We discussed how young children respond to trauma exposure in Chapter 8. In this subsection, we acknowledge that caregivers can also be affected by trauma in several ways. Caregivers may be directly affected by traumatic events that occurred during their own childhood or events that are currently occurring. Common examples of such trauma include community or interpersonal violence, loss, accidents, natural disasters, immigration, and exposure to discrimination and racism. Caregivers can also be indirectly affected, showing symptoms after their children experience a traumatic event (Wilcoxon et al., 2021). For some families, trauma is pervasive and chronic, including chaotic and unsafe environments and poverty, and historical and ongoing experiences such as discrimination, racism, and stigmatization.

Because trauma has the potential to affect all aspects of functioning, skills related to caregiving, especially emotional availability and discipline methods, are likely to be affected (Roell & Neal-Barnett, 2021; Slade et al., 2023). Trauma may reduce a person's ability to engage in relationships, dampen cognitive skills, and reduce emotion regulation, all of which may be important to sensitive and effective caregiving. Parents and other caregivers may struggle with decision making and planning, for example. When both the caregiver and the child are traumatized, the caregiver may respond in several maladaptive ways: becoming withdrawn and unavailable, becoming overprotective, and repeatedly talking about or even actually reenacting the events (Scheeringa & Zeanah, 2001). Home visiting services such as the Michigan Infant Mental Health Home Visiting Model services have been shown to improve social and emotional outcomes in toddlers whose mothers experienced trauma and had current PTSD symptoms.

Providing stability and routine is frequently recommended as a strategy to help young children begin to heal when trauma occurs. Unfortunately, for some children this is not possible, when poverty and domestic violence combine to result in homelessness. Women who are homeless are highly likely to have experienced violence or trauma. About 90% reported at least one trauma event, with up to 50% of homelessness in women due to interpersonal trauma (Bassuk et al., 2014). More than 2.5 million American children experienced homelessness in 2014, with about half of these reported to be under 6 years of age (Bassuk et al., 2014; Samuels et al., 2010; Yamashiro & McLaughlin, 2021). These figures include families that do not have their own homes but "double up" with friends or extended families, with frequent moves from place to place, as well as families that live in cars, shelters, or the open. As might be expected, parents and other caregivers who are homeless may have other stressors or risk factors, including anxiety, depression, trauma disorders, and substance use. These issues are known to have the potential to affect caregiving behavior, and homelessness on its own can also have an impact on a person's ability to support their children.

When families have experienced trauma, home visitors can help the family prioritize immediate and longer-term needs, such as the following:

- Physical safety, including a safe place to live and protection from injury or threat
- Return to routines and schedule
- Access to therapies needed to heal from the trauma experience

Stress and Mental Health Conditions During Pregnancy

The stressors that we have discussed so far are likely to be present prior to the child's birth, meaning that many pregnant people experience stress during their pregnancies. In addition, mental health conditions can present during pregnancy. According to the World Health Organization, about 1 in 5 women has a mental health condition during pregnancy or in the year following birth. The training and advocacy group Postpartum Support International, reports that 1 in 5 mothers and 1 in 10 fathers have postpartum depression. More severe disorders, including other mood disorders, anxiety, and psychosis, can also occur in this period. Findings on racial and ethnic differences in perinatal mood disorders are mixed. Compared to white women, Black women are more than twice as likely to have a perinatal mental health condition and half as likely to receive treatment (Feldman & Pattani, 2019; Sethi, 2020).

Because perinatal mental health conditions are common, researchers have been interested in understanding if and how maternal stress and mental health conditions during pregnancy affect the fetus and if these effects are long lasting. Fetal exposure to maternal stress has been related to higher infant reactivity or vulnerability to stress (Davis & Thompson, 2014; Martinez-Torteya et al., 2018). This increased reactivity is proposed to occur through fetal programming, a process in which the prenatal environment permanently affects the baby's development, putting them at risk for physical and health issues that can be long lasting (Barker, 1998). Although more research is needed, some studies suggest that babies exposed to maternal stress in utero appear more fearful, react more strongly to novelty, and are at higher risk for depression and anxiety later as preteens or teens. For pregnant people whose anxiety or depression is in the top 15% in terms of severity, the risk for the fetus to have behavior problems in childhood or adolescence is doubled from 5% to 10% (O'Donnell et al., 2014). Some gender differences have been reported. For example, boy babies exposed to prenatal stress are less likely to survive and are more likely to have developmental problems; girl babies were more prone to anxiety and affective disorders (Davis & Thompson, 2014).

Pregnant people may have many types of worries and concerns; some are related specifically to the pregnancy and others are more general. When discussing worries during pregnancy, home visitors may notice that some caregivers worry about the pregnancy itself, such as whether it was planned or desired, about the health of the baby, and about the experience of delivery. Pregnant people tend to worry about miscarriage early in pregnancy, switching to concern about the fetus in the middle and then, near the end, about the delivery.

Anxiety that is related to the pregnancy has been linked with premature birth and child outcomes such as problems in cognition, emotion, temperament, anxiety, and executive functions (Guardino & Schetter, 2014). Pregnant people who are younger, have less education, and have lower incomes are more likely to have pregnancy-related anxiety, as are pregnant people who are in relationships that end more quickly. African American and Latina pregnant people may be more vulnerable to this kind of anxiety. Of note, Black women experience maternal mortality rates as high as 4 times the rate for white women, creating additional stress and worry in this population (Parker, 2021). In addition, pregnant people's personal characteristics, including lower self-esteem, lower mastery and optimism, and less social support (especially from a partner), are also risk factors for pregnancy-related anxiety (Guardino & Schetter, 2014).

Supports to families during pregnancy can help in the present moment and may reduce the environmental and physiological risks related to stressors for the caregiver and the child down the road. These supports should include the following:

- Providing education and resources to help pregnant people stay healthy, such as nutrition and prenatal care
- Contributing to a supportive social environment through building a positive relationship
- Screening for caregiver depression, anxiety, and pregnancy-specific anxiety

Supports that help prevent anxiety and depressive symptoms related to pregnancy include the following:

- Providing childbirth education resources to alleviate worries
- Giving support related to diagnostic tests

- Encouraging healthy practices balanced with assurances that most babies are born healthy
- Being aware of and acknowledging racism and cultural oppression as well as the potential for bias in health care when supporting families of color

Environmental Risk Factors: Social Determinants of Health

Many families face economic uncertainties that can dramatically affect their ability to be in the present moment to meet the needs of their children. When a family is struggling to make ends meet (e.g., pay rent, utilities, car notes, and insurance; purchase food and diapers), it can be challenging for caregivers to notice the developmental nuances that occur in very young children. Families can be affected by stressors in their personal lives and more systematic ones. For example, following the 2007 economic recession and slow recovery, many families continued to struggle with economic conditions that led to unemployment, underemployment, and a shift from the middle class to poverty. As a result of the fiscal crisis, a staggering number of children lived in poverty and were food insecure. According to the National Center for Children in Poverty, in 2010 more than 20% of American children lived in families with incomes below the poverty level, and another 25% lived in families with significantly low incomes (Wight et al., 2010). Recent research is beginning to identify similar family financial impacts related to the COVID-19 pandemic, with families in lower to middle income levels disproportionately affected (Pew Research Center, 2022; Rodriguez et al., 2023). When considering family financial instability, home visitors should recognize that it may be related to several other common stressors discussed earlier, including caregiver mental health and substance use concerns; family situations, including incarceration and divorce; and experiences that can include living with domestic violence and bias or discrimination.

More recently, the COVID-19 emergency led to a cascade of challenges that affected everyday life and overall well-being. In addition to general worries about safety, families with young children often lost access to child care, leading to many caregivers trying to balance working from home while caring for their children. Many home visiting as well as health care services shifted to virtual means during this time. As a result, both caregivers and providers had to learn new ways of being together during an unprecedented emergency (Traube et al., 2022). Although the emergency is officially over, many families may continue to experience ramifications, including significant loss of available child care slots nationally (Swigonski et al., 2021). Regardless of the source of the stresses, home visitors are likely to be very aware of the struggles of such families, feeling the tension of how to balance attention to program goals with fulfilling basic needs for accessing safe child care, housing, food, and medical care.

EXTENDING YOUR SKILL SET
TO SUPPORT PARENTS AND CAREGIVERS

In addition to knowledge of specific risk factors and how they interact, home visitors can provide supports for families who struggle with chronic stressors. In the following subsections, we detail a set of strategies that are targeted for helping individuals in recovery and that complement home visitors' efforts to provide relationship-based and reflective approaches (Ferguson et al., 2023; SAMHSA, 2014, 2021).

Provide Emotion Support

Home visitors must be aware that, for many families, additional time and effort will be needed to even make initial contacts, in addition to the time required for the family to develop enough trust in the relationship to accept emotional and other supports. Programs may use partnerships with other trusted entities such as places of worship to connect with harder to reach families, including those who are undocumented and speak languages other than English (Ferguson et al., 2023). Expectations about what relationships with home visitors might be like are formed through prior experiences with all kinds of relationships, whether personal (e.g., parents, friends, partners) or professional (e.g., teachers, doctors, case managers). Individuals with MI and disability often reported believing that others do not understand their problems and that they lack trust in their ability to be helped. Reports of being criticized about parenting or other skills in ways that damage confidence were also noted (Kleinmann & Songer, 2009; Perera et al., 2014; Pohl et al., 2020). As discussed in earlier chapters, experiences related to racial and other forms of discrimination may lead some caregivers to be wary in professional relationships. As a result, such individuals may need more time and support in order to feel comfortable with the home visitors. Home visitors can use the relationship-building strategies outlined in Chapter 1, understanding that forming the relationship may take longer.

Everyone has biases of some kind or the other. Biases about common risk factors may interfere with the home visitor's ability to demonstrate emotional supports needed to build relationships. Some home visitors may have negative attitudes or beliefs about MI (e.g., believing that people with MI are unable to care for children) that are likely to interfere with building positive partnerships (Perera et al., 2014). Attitudes about substance use problems, such as viewing it as a weakness rather than an illness, might also lead to misunderstandings about caregivers' intentions, or abilities to meet their children's needs. Stigma related to MI and disabilities may lead home visitors to have lowered expectations for affected individuals. Negative views about families with child welfare involvement might interfere with supporting positive reunification efforts with the child's primary caregivers. Also, hearing about caregivers who are in prison may bring up biased ideas about these individuals' abilities to care for their children and to watch out for their best interests. Home visitors who are aware of their own bias can monitor their reactions to family characteristics and behaviors and explore these reactions in supervision/consultation. Research about specific populations can be used as a starting place in learning about individual families, but in the end, to avoid stereotyping, every family must be understood as unique.

Within a positive relationship, home visitors can provide emotional support to families who experience risk and stressors. In Chapter 1, we discussed the importance of developing relationships and how home visitors can act in ways that build relationships through consistent and reliable responses. For families that have multiple risk factors and have had few positive relationships with professionals, behaviors that signal respect and recognition of family strength are needed. Home visitors can demonstrate respect by behaviors such as the following:

- Arriving on time
- Respecting family boundaries
- Asking permission to be in the family's home
- Asking what name to use when referring to the child and family members
- Talking openly and honestly with the family
- Asking permission to share and gather information

Jackie texts and calls Desiree several times over the next couple of weeks but does not hear back. She checks in with the service coordinator, who fortunately has the grandmother's contact information. When Jackie reaches Desiree, Desiree expresses surprise to hear from her. Desiree lets Jackie know that she is not in a position to meet, but she tells Jackie how much she appreciates hearing from her. "I thought you would just forget about us," she says. Jackie assures her that she has not forgotten Chloe or her and that she would like to restart in person or virtual visits when possible.

Gain Skills With Difficult Topics

As we discussed in earlier chapters, much of home visiting work relies on the provider's capacity to engage in relationship with the caregiver (Walsh & Mortensen, 2020). In order to be able to help families who live with many stressors or risk factors, home visitors must be able to recognize and talk about the issues. For example, many programs attend to maternal depression through screening and referral. When staff have additional training about these topics, they and caregivers are more satisfied and communicate more about concerns such as MI and its effect on caregiving (Knitzer et al., 2008).

Attaining this skill level necessitates gaining a level of comfort with difficult topics through training, experience, and practice. Training needs to include content knowledge and, more important, ideas for assessing family readiness to discuss an issue, practice so that information can be shared smoothly, and supports for professional development including supervision and self-reflection so that home visitors can assess their own level of comfort (Monahan et al., 2012; Walsh & Mortensen, 2020). When talking about these topics, try to find a balance of words that are professional yet understandable to families. Using the same words that the family uses can be productive. Introducing new words, just like introducing new ideas, can be successful when done with care and support. Appendix 9A provides examples of how to discuss challenging topics and an opportunity to capture your own ideas.

Have Reasonable Expectations

Families with severe or multiple challenges may make progress at slower rates than others, may experience repeat problems, and may require more of the home visitor's time overall. For example, caregivers with depression or autism may have a hard time following through to implement strategies shared by the home visitor (Alvarez et al., 2015). In parallel, the home visitor may need additional training and support to be effective (Ferguson et al., 2023; Lowell et al., 2021; Monahan et al., 2012; Slade et al., 2023). Home visitors would be wise to strive to tolerate patterns that involve ups and down, or one step forward, one back, as this is the nature of work with families with complex lives and multiple stressors. Being able to recognize and celebrate small changes can help home visitors tolerate the slower pace that these families have. These small changes are often quite meaningful for a specific family. For example, the home visitor can help the family celebrate trying out a bedtime routine, even if they do not yet implement it every night. A caregiver might demonstrate a great use of time-out during one visit and then go back to yelling at the child during the next. In this situation, the home visitor can remind the caregiver of the previous success and encourage them to try again next time. These acts of acknowledging and highlighting small changes can contribute to a positive relationship with the family. In turn, the caregiver is better able to hear and act on recommendations that are made after the home visitor has joined them in seeing and appreciating this small improvement (Landy & Menna, 2006).

Often, the home visitor may think that their own effectiveness is lacking when families make slow progress. Being clear about one's scope of practice and learning to see one's role as part of the bigger web of support that is needed can be beneficial (Walsh & Mortensen, 2020; Yoches et al., 2012). For example, your role may be to get the family to the point that they could choose to use another service. A component of a person's MI, disability, substance use disorder, or trauma response can include lashing out at providers, blaming them for problems, or accusing them of not helping enough. It is important to learn not to take these emotional responses personally and to avoid letting them get in the way of the work to be done (Landy & Menna, 2006). Talking over these experiences with a supervisor can help. We review more about these and other benefits of supervision in Chapter 10. For more details on reflective supervision and consultation, including how to make the most of your supervision experience, please see the supplement "Reflective Supervision and Consultation: What Is It, Why Do I Need It, and How Can I Use It Most Effectively?" included in this book.

Share Information

Families with multiple challenges have many needs, and these can be experienced by the family as well as the home visitor as emergencies. Having referral information and resources for a variety of potential issues can help build your relationship with the family, as it allows the family to see you as a responsive and reliable source of support. It can also help you, as the provider, to feel calmer and better prepared.

Although the need to provide concrete supports and help in a crisis is very real, it is not the only form of information that can be shared. Information about child development and behavior is also an important component of most home visiting programs. Many home visitors and early intervention providers have very detailed knowledge about child development and may not be aware of how little some parents and other caregivers know about expected skills for babies and toddlers. Lack of knowledge about typical development can lead caregivers to have inappropriate expectations. One important role of the home visitor is to gently challenge perceptions or assumptions about children in general or about the specific child (Landy & Menna, 2006). There are times when a home visitor and a caregiver have different ideas about when specific skills can be expected. For example, a home visitor may be surprised to hear a caregiver say, "She is 18 months old already and should be ready to potty train." The home visitor might respond in one of the following ways:

"What does her doctor recommend?"

"In your experience, when do children usually learn toileting?"

"Tell me more about how you plan to teach her."

"How has she shown you she is ready to learn this new skill?"

Questions or statements like these lead to a conversation in which the home visitor and the caregiver can think together about the issue

> Access caregiver-friendly, free and accessible resources to promote tracking early childhood development in both English and Spanish by using the CDC's *Learn the Signs. Act Early.* materials in your work with children and their families. Visit cdc.gov/actearly for easy access.

from different perspectives. In this example, perhaps the home visitor may learn that children in the caregiver's community typically learn some parts of toilet training at this age. The home visitor may find that they agree with the caregiver, once they better understand. Or perhaps the home visitor will learn that the caregiver's motivation to potty train at this age is to save money on diapers. By knowing this information, the home visitor can identify a resource that addresses this concern while working on an appropriate potty-training plan. Table 9.1 provides some additional examples of how a home visitor might respond when sharing information about child development in ways that are congruent with different community values and expectations.

Build Problem-Solving Skills

At times, rushing to solve problems and providing resources is not the answer. When a home visitor provides a resource or solution too quickly, there is a risk that they are not on the same page as the family. The solution the home visitor identifies may not be one the family would have chosen. Even less helpful, the home visitor might not even know what the family thinks is the main problem, meaning that their suggestions are not aligned with family goals and are likely to be ignored. Furthermore, when the home visitor is always the problem solver, families lose a chance to build problem-solving skills and to have a sense of efficacy that comes from taking charge of issues themselves.

Caregivers with the risk factors we have discussed may have difficulty with planning and problem solving; as a result, their normal life may involve moving from crisis to crisis. Slowing down and providing opportunities to help a family work through a problem step by step can help families gain skills in these areas. This is likely to require more flexibility in how and at what pace program content is delivered (Ferguson et al., 2023). Depending on the family, a home visitor may need to be patient and provide support as the family moves at their own pace. So, the family may miss appointments, lose important forms, or forget to apply a strategy that the home visitor suggested. It may feel counterintuitive, but at these times slowing down even more may be needed to allow space to think about what might be getting in the way, such as being too stressed, sad, or angry (Landy & Menna, 2006).

As she drives to a visit with Maureen and her family, Kathryn thinks about the plan they made the previous week to talk to the family doctor about the baby's hearing. Kathryn reviews in her mind the steps they agreed that Maureen would follow and feels relieved that this will finally be resolved. Kathryn has been worried about the baby's ability to hear for months.

When Maureen answers the door, Kathryn immediately asks about the doctor's appointment. Maureen looks a little embarrassed. She tells Maureen, "I never called the doctor. We had some other things come up. Our heat got shut off, and then my mom's car broke down. It's been wild." Kathryn feels disappointed and concerned. She doesn't understand how Maureen can be so disorganized. At the same time, she recognizes that Maureen's family has encountered some unavoidable stressors. She wonders if Maureen is aware of the importance of getting the baby's hearing checked.

Kathryn says, "Well, it sounds like you have had a wild week. I can understand how things got away from you." "Yes, they did," Maureen answers. She seems to relax. "I thought you would be mad since I didn't get the call made to the doctor. I know you think it's important. This is like the second or third time we made a plan about it."

Kathryn realizes that Maureen may have reasons other than the ones that she stated for not making the call. She decides to work toward getting a conversation started about things that get in the way instead of just making another plan, starting with better understanding the family's priorities. She says, "Yes, I do think it is important. But now I am wondering if we should try to think about this in another way. I'd interested to hear what you think is most important now." Maureen smiles and says, "I'd really like that."

At this point, Kathryn may learn a number of different reasons for Maureen's failure to make the call. Maureen really might have been distracted by the stressful events that happened. She may be uncomfortable talking on the phone, or she may be afraid to find out whether the baby has a hearing problem. Maureen also may not be worried about the baby's hearing at all, leaving her little motivation to go for a checkup. By starting a conversation instead of continuing to repeat the plan, Kathryn may learn more about how Maureen sees things.

Accept the Unexpected: What Is Needed Now?

Once home visitors step across the threshold into a family's home, anything can happen. As much as a home visitor would like to have a good plan for a session, circumstances may interfere so that the plan may no longer be appropriate. Many home visitors report that flexibility is an important key to working with families who have many stressors. Being willing to give up the planned session in favor of what the family needs right now or is capable of doing may be the right and most effective strategy. This requires a willingness to step outside of one's role, at times. Although some home visiting models incorporate flexibility and individualization, others may require fidelity to a program model. Home visitors may feel caught between an action that supports relationship and adherence to the program model (Barak, Spielberger, & Gitlow, 2014). When this happens, home visitors should discuss the situation with a supervisor, as their agency may have general policies or guidance for this issue. If there is no policy, the home visitor and supervisor can discuss acceptable options.

Providers and agencies should consider whether it is a good use of resources to continue providing training or curriculum as planned when a caregiver is overwhelmed in a way that interferes with meaningful participation (Alvarez et al., 2015). Instead, stopping to ask questions and creating a space for exploring the current concern or family priority is needed. If family priorities are left unaddressed, the family is unlikely to be willing or able to attend to issues they believe are less important. The case presented in the previous subsection reviewed a few examples of the caregiver and the home visitor having different agendas. Examples of helpful responses a home visitor might try include shifting the plan to better attend to the caregiver's concern or helping to identify resources that would be effective to address an immediate need (e.g., helping the family to get the heat turned back on or to locate a source for help with transportation). In other situations, the home visitor could discover that the family is working with another agency. Coordinating plans between agencies would be useful in this situation; we talk more about coordination in Chapter 10.

Know Your Limits

The potential for home visiting services to address the mental health needs of caregivers and young children is of high interest (Zeanah & Korfmacher, 2019) and may increase the program's capacity to meet other goals (Ferguson et al., 2023). Although home visitors may not think they have the specialized skills needed to help caregivers with significant stressors, one of the main wishes of mothers who struggle with MI is long-term in-home supports by someone who could provide practical help and be available to talk about problems (Krumm et al., 2013). This combination of a long-term relationship, good listening skills, and practical knowledge is certainly in the repertoire of a home visitor or early intervention professional and will be enough to meet the needs of many families. Additional training and support are needed for home visitors to contribute to family needs in this way (Ferguson et al., 2023). However, even with training and supervision, there will be times when referrals and coordination with other professionals are essential (Yoches et al., 2012).

One difficulty is that participants in home visiting and early intervention programs often do not view the caregiver–professional relationship in the same way. This may lead to differences in expectations about what will and can occur. About three quarters of participants in home visiting programs report viewing the visitors as a friend. This differs from the perspective of the home visitor, who is more likely to describe their role as a resource for information, a person who cares or helps, or a friend with boundaries (Mills et al., 2012; Riley et al., 2008). Agency policies are likely to address boundary issues; if they do not, this should be part of supervision. Overall, it can be helpful to know that even though caregivers and professionals see the roles differently, there tends to be a high level of family satisfaction with home visits. We return to this issue in more detail in Chapter 10.

HOW WE ENGAGE WITH FAMILIES

Despite the home visitor's best efforts and skill, some families will continue to resist offers of relationship, support, and concrete help. When families seem hard to engage, disengaged, distant, or overwhelmed, home visitors may become frustrated and discouraged by their perceived lack of effectiveness. To cope, the provider may push too hard or let go too soon. Unfortunately, these responses may be all too familiar to the family, which has many times experienced personal and professional relationships that do not meet its needs. It is not surprising, then, if the family implements a coping strategy from its own past, such as choosing to terminate the relationship. This result may reinforce the home visitor's view that the family did not want help after all. For these families, the emphasis should be on building relationship, in a very basic way, by being reliable, consistent, and containing. Frequently, this will start with attention to the caregiver's emotional experience.

Many of the caregivers that home visitors work with may have trouble with emotion regulation. They may lack an ability to tolerate negative emotions along with difficulties recognizing positive ones. These caregivers will benefit from provider actions aimed at their own emotional experience. This suggestion may send up a red flag, with home visitors running off shouting, "I'm no therapist!" It is true that early intervention workers are unlikely to have backgrounds or licenses that prepare them to deliver psychotherapy, and that careful attention to professional boundaries and appropriate scope of practice are important. However, with training and supervision, a home visitor can function in a way that provides some emotional containment, not as a friend or as a therapist, but in a way that lets the caregiver share their emotions that are directly related to their child and about what it is like for them to be a parent (Ferguson et al., 2023; Tomlin et al., 2016; Weatherston, 2000).

A home visitor sits listening to a mother and father discuss their concerns about the behavior of their 14-month-old son, who had been biting peers at child care. The mother states, "He is so mean; kind of like a bully." The home visitor, who has been listening to the parents' complaints about this boy for 45 minutes, notices that her own response to this statement was a flash of annoyance or even anger. She realizes that she believes the parents' expectations are unreasonable and that she is irritated because this topic has been discussed many times before. Although her initial impulse is to remind the parents of her previous teaching about typical development, instead she decides to respond to their emotional states. The worker asks, "What is it like for you to see your son act like a bully?" This question leads to a discussion of the mother's fears that her son would hurt someone and what would happen if he was kicked out of child care.

Caregivers who have multiple challenges may not respond as well to structured teaching activities as others. Some caregivers, especially young mothers, for example, are more open to information when it is presented "in the moment" (Dozier & Bernard, 2019). Caregivers who have cognitive challenges due to trauma or intellectual disability may need tasks broken down and repeated. Home visitors who can be flexible, who use active strategies such as demonstration or modeling directly with the child, who adapt material to be culturally congruent, and who choose topics based on what is currently happening with the family may be more effective in engaging harder to reach parents (Ferguson et al., 2023; Mills et al., 2012). Allowing the family to be "the driver" may increase attention and future application of learning, as the family more clearly recognizes the relevance of the information shared to its daily life.

We have often discussed the importance for young children to implement a caregiving strategy that blends routine and limit-setting with warmth. Similarly, home visitor behaviors such as expressive, animated, and warm interactions with caregivers are favored. In addition, these warm interactions between caregiver and home visitor are likely to increase their responsiveness to babies, which is related to enhanced child developmental outcomes (Trivette, Dunst, & Hamby, 2010).

In a related vein, we advise caregivers to provide labeled praise for their children, meaning to talk specifically about behaviors that they are happy to see. An example of labeled praise to encourage sharing in a young child might be, "I like it when you let Karen have a turn with the ball." In parallel, home visitors can specifically point out or emphasize caregiver strengths, with statements such as "It's so great how you are using that bedtime routine we talked about" or "That was a really terrific redirection you just gave to Tina." Home visitors who express confidence in a caregiver's competence help them recognize what they are doing well; this in turn builds confidence in parenting skills (Landy & Menna, 2006; Mills et al., 2012).

In Chapter 6 we discussed how for many good reasons some diverse families may use different caregiving methods with positive results. For example, praising one's children may not be comfortable for Black families due to historical experiences related to surviving enslavement (Ghosh Ippen, 2018). Similarly, other methods of connecting with caregivers may be desirable. Some programs prioritize hiring home visitors who share racial, ethnic, and cultural backgrounds or who are from similar communities from the families they serve (Ferguson et al., 2023). When home visitors and families do not share these traits, the providers should seek opportunities to openly discuss how it feels to work with a person from a different race or culture even when these conversations may feel uncomfortable (Ghosh Ippen, 2018). These types of discussions are useful when first meeting families and can be revisited over time as the relationship grows.

USING THE PAUSE FRAMEWORK

The vignette presented in this chapter depicts a home visitor encountering a family facing homelessness. Consider how Jackie had to shift her perception of her role and stretch to find resources to support Chloe and her family. Think about how you might have to adjust the strategies you chose and your evaluation of success in such a circumstance. For more on how Jackie might process her experiences with Chloe and her family, see Figures 9.1 and 9.2.

WHAT'S NEXT?

In Chapter 10, we reflect on taking care of ourselves, establishing good boundaries in our work, and participating in reflective supervision or consultation.

TIPS FOR PRACTICE

- Be aware that a family with one risk factor is likely to also be experiencing others that may require different kinds of attention.

- Home visitors who can step back, evaluate situations, and consider multiple perspectives, using methods such as PAUSE, will be most effective with families that have multiple risk factors and stressors.

- When the home visitor experiences strong feelings, they should notice them and also take time to wonder how the situation is being experienced by the caregiver and the child.

KEY POINTS TO REMEMBER

- A large number of American families are living with significant stressors that may make it difficult to meet basic needs. These families may need to obtain concrete supports before they are able to fully attend to the emotional needs of their young children.

- Caregiver stressors including those related to national and global crisis and personal issues such as mental health concerns, disabilities, and substance use may interfere with caregiving behaviors. Nevertheless, individuals with these challenges most likely can successfully care for their children with supports, including home visiting.

- Relationship-based practices and reflective skills can help home visitors find ways to engage families who struggle with stressors that challenge caregiving.

PAUSE WORKSHEET

Child: **Chloe**   Date: **August 21, 2024**

Caregiver: **Desiree**   Provider: **Jackie**

PERCEIVE—Explore what is happening.

Caregiver perspective:	Provider perspective:
The family is overwhelmed with being evicted and having to move quickly.	I am unclear what my role should be in this situation. Do I focus on my role as a physical therapist or should I offer to help in a concrete way to address the emergency situation?

ASK—Clarify what is happening.

Starting with the caregiver's priorities and concerns, ask more detailed/specific questions to clarify what is happening.

The family has been evicted. What are their immediate needs? How can I help?

They are moving in with Desiree's mother. Will visits continue there? How long will they live in that location?

Where is Chloe's father? What is the plan for all of their belongings?

Who else could help the family at this time?

How can the team minimize the impact of the move on the children and their development?

UNDERSTAND—Explore why it is happening.

With the caregiver, explore explanations for what is happening. Consider possible explanations that include the environment, the child, and the caregiver. Listen and observe closely as you explore the situation in conversation with the family.

Caregiver perspective:	Provider perspective:	Child's perspective:
The family is in crisis now and does not have time to address Chloe's specific needs. Desiree has to look out for the entire family.	There is a short window to help Chloe reach her developmental milestones. Is there a way to continue to	It might be confusing for Chloe to be moving so quickly. Is there any way I can help her with the transition while still

(continued)

Figure 9.1. Jackie's PAUSE Worksheet for Desiree and Chloe.

Figure 9.1. *(continued)*

PAUSE WORKSHEET *(continued)*

UNDERSTAND *(continued)*

Caregiver perspective:	Provider perspective: offer physical therapy services? Do I have any other roles to play?	Child's perspective: including therapeutic goals?

STRATEGIZE and EVALUATE—Identify possible responses/solutions.

1. Solution/action to try: Refer this family to a local resource for supports and services.	How will we know if it works? The family will have their needs met. When will we evaluate if it works? By phone when scheduling the next visit.
2. Solution/action to try: Ask the family how the home visitor could have been more helpful.	How will we know if it works? Team members will learn ways to help in similar situations. When will we evaluate if it works? When a similar situation occurs.

PROVIDER REFLECTION WORKSHEET

Provider Reflection Worksheet

Child: **Chloe**   Date: **August 22, 2024**

Caregiver: **Desiree**   Provider: **Jackie**

1. How did I follow the caregiver's lead to learn what is most pressing or important to them?	It was very difficult for me to know how to respond to this family's crisis. I felt uncomfortable and uncertain. I did ask if I should leave or continue with the session.
2. How did I ask clarifying questions that help me to understand the problem better? How did I inquire about the caregiver's values and beliefs related to the issue?	When I arrived they seemed very busy, so I asked if there might be a better time to meet. This question allowed me to find out more about what happened. I think the family felt heard.
3. How did I reflect on and offer to discuss similarities and differences between me and the caregiver? These might include race, ethnicity, language, gender, sexual orientation, religious and other beliefs, values, experiences, etc.	I have been through a similar situation, and I feel pulled to tell Desiree it will all be okay and what to do next. But I know I need to maintain my role as the PT and get other help from the team. How can I connect with her and support her in this tough situation? Is it ok to share some of my own story with her? I know this is hard but don't know how to help!

(continued)

Figure 9.2. Jackie's Provider Reflection Worksheet for Desiree and Chloe.

Figure 9.2. (continued)

PROVIDER REFLECTION WORKSHEET (continued)

4. How did I provide information that may help the caregiver better understand the child's behavior?	I was surprised and unsure how to respond. I did not think to ask about Chloe's experience in this situation.
5. How did I engage the caregiver to develop a response that may include a strategy to try, a resource to use, or more information to increase understanding?	I don't feel I did a good job managing my own feelings, so I did not problem-solve with the family. I actually felt relieved when Desiree suggested I just have my session with Chloe, as that was familiar, and I felt competent. How can I learn from this experience in case something like this happens again?
6. How did I provide support and emotional containment if needed?	I had trouble with my own feelings, so I did not support the family. I was surprised at my strong reaction of irritation. I am worried that the family sensed my discomfort with not knowing how to help.
7. How do I plan to follow up on promised actions to maintain trust?	I did offer to explore some resources and called the family when I got back to the office, after speaking with some other staff members.
8. What do I want to discuss in reflective supervision to improve my practice and outcomes with this child and caregiver?	I want to explore my reaction to this situation, learn about possible resources for families, and discuss how to better react in these kinds of situations.

SUGGESTED FURTHER READING

Hanson, M. J., & Lynch, E. W (2013). *Understanding families: Supportive approaches to diversity, disability, and risk* (2nd ed.). Paul H. Brookes Publishing Co.

Slade, A., Sadler, L. S., Eaves, T., & Webb, D. L. (2023). *Enhancing attachment and reflective parenting in clinical practice: A Minding the Baby Approach.* Guilford.

APPENDIX 9A

PRACTICE DISCUSSING DIFFICULT TOPICS

Use this form to think about words and questions to discuss and learn more about difficult topics parents and caregivers face. Review the sample wording and add your own ideas in the space provided. It might be helpful to discuss your ideas with a colleague or in reflective supervision or consultation sessions.

Topic	Sample wording	Your turn
Depression	How have you been feeling lately? Are there times when you feel down or not able to enjoy your baby?	
Incarcerated family member	I understand that Sally's father is incarcerated at this time. How has that been for you and your child? How might you talk with Sally about this?	
Family struggling economically	How are you getting your everyday needs met? What kinds of help could your family use (e.g., food, shelter, transportation, health care)?	
Domestic violence	Do you feel safe? Is your child safe? Is anyone hurting you? Are there weapons in your home? Do you have a place to go if you feel unsafe? Do you have someone to call to help you?	

(continued)

APPENDIX 9A **PRACTICE DISCUSSING DIFFICULT TOPICS** *(continued)*

Topic	Sample wording	Your turn
Substance use/abuse	Does anyone in the home use alcohol or other substances? Does anyone have a problem with using?	
Parent deployment	Is anyone serving in the military? If yes: What has been shared with the rest of the family about the deployment? How might you talk with the children about this?	
Parent relationship problem	How do you both get along? How do you solve problems? How much do you agree about parenting and other important family decisions?	
Other topics		

10

You Can't Do This Alone

Boundaries, Self-Care, and Supervision

Anna drives away from a home visit with a mix of feelings. She notices how tight her shoulders are feeling and tries to relax her jaw, as she is gritting her teeth. "This family is so difficult!," she thinks. Every time Anna thinks she has a handle on things with this family, something else comes up. Anna started working with Anthony's mother, Tessa, during her pregnancy. Reflecting back, Anna realizes that she has worked with the family for 8 months so far in her role as a home visitor for a prevention program. Over this time period, Anna has found herself frustrated and even angry many times. Honestly, some days Anna wishes that Tessa would just fire her.

Anna cannot understand how Tessa can be so engaged and cooperative one day and then appear completely unmotivated and disinterested the next time she sees her. Sometimes Tessa tells Anna she does not remember things that have been discussed many times. At other times, she calls Anna multiple times in a day with questions and demands. Often, this is followed by missed appointments and calls for several weeks. Luckily, Anthony is an adorable and responsive baby that Anna very much enjoys seeing and playing with. Whenever Anna thinks about asking to have the family reassigned, she remembers Anthony and his needs. "Someone needs to put this baby first," she often says to herself.

This week, Tessa was completely disconnected during the appointment. The apartment was cluttered and dirty. Anthony was in a car seat and needed a change. Anna feels a little surge of anger when she recalls seeing Anthony sleeping in the car seat. She feels sure they have reviewed safe sleep practices a few times. Anna did not even try to address the issue with Tessa this time; she took the baby from the car seat, gave him a bath, and put him in clean clothes. As she bustled around doing these tasks, Anna did not notice that Tessa sat quietly and just watched her.

As she pulls into her own garage, Anna remembers noticing that Anthony had grown and that many of his clothes were too small. "I'll have to remember to bring those outfits I got for Anthony next week," Anna thinks. She suddenly realizes she cannot recall whether she confirmed the next appointment with Tessa. Anna thinks back to when she left. She remembers that Tessa had followed her to the door and recalls saying to Tessa, "Did you want something?" in a voice that she now thinks might have been a little rough. Anna has a picture of Tessa pulling back slightly and shaking her head no. "I wonder what her problem was today, anyway," Anna thinks briefly as she begins her own evening routine.

In this chapter, we return to the topics of relationship and reflective practice, including challenges to maintaining these practices, such as secondary trauma, setting limits and boundaries, finding personal and professional balance, and avoiding burnout. These are important issues for all kinds of providers; you can't do your best work if you don't take care of yourself. As part of this discussion, this chapter details how reflective supervision and consultation (RSC) can provide support to home visitors as well as serve as a form of professional development (Jones Harden, 2010; Susman-Stillman et al., 2020; Watson et al., 2014; Watson et al., 2016). Increasingly, researchers and practitioners are seeking to use RSC as a tool to promote competence with diverse families (Noroña et al., 2023). Finally, we explore ideas to manage miscommunication and conflicts between team members as well as between provider and family, with suggested steps for repair when things go wrong.

Increased emphasis on serving children in early childhood has resulted in an expansion of home visiting in general. Across the county, more programs are available, serving a variety of families. Increasingly, these programs are considering how home visiting can support both caregiver and child mental health (Ferguson et al., 2023). For most participating families, a risk factor led to their eligibility for services. Risk factors vary widely and can include having a child with a disability or delay (Part C of the Individuals with Disabilities Education Improvement Act of 2004, PL 108-446), being a young or vulnerable parent, or having experience with or risk for child welfare involvement (Maternal, Infant, and Early Childhood Home Visiting Program Act of 2022, PL 117-328). In addition to the challenges that this work with families brings, the characteristics of the work itself may be difficult for home visitors for several reasons (Tomlin et al., 2016).

Some home visitors trained in models that involve working with individual clients may have trouble shifting to working with a dyad (Tomlin et al., 2016). In fact, many home visitors and early education providers may have had training that was primarily child-focused; these providers may subsequently struggle when required to deliver services to caregivers (Lowell et al., 2021; Tomlin, 2002). Additional training in working with adults is needed to learn to effectively partner with caregivers (Walsh & Mortensen, 2020). Caregivers may also expect the provider to "do work" with their child. As a result, although research supports the value of providers coaching caregivers, in practice, service delivery may most often involve the home visitor interacting with the child while the caregiver watches but does not have a chance to practice the methods being demonstrated (Jones Harden et al., 2010; Romano & Schnurr, 2022).

Often, home visitors speak about the frustration of figuring out facilitating the caregiver–child relationship when other things seem more important, such as getting basic needs met (Jones Harden et al., 2010). Early intervention workers have much information and many resources to share with families and may get impatient for caregivers to start taking advantage of those resources. The previous chapters highlight the importance of developing a relationship with families that will serve as a vehicle for sharing knowledge, skills, and resources. This link between the caregiver–provider relationship and the delivery of the services is at the core of successful intervention (Ferguson et al., 2023; Lee et al., 2013; Lowell et al., 2021). It's helpful to consider three interrelated sets of strategies or actions borrowed from infant mental health practice that build relationship and skills in caregivers across time (Ferguson et al., 2023; Tomlin & Viehweg, 2003; Weatherston, 2000, 2005). These sets of strategies include those that 1) provide support, 2) build skills, and 3) promote positive interactions.

First, the home visitor should plan and intentionally act in ways that provide support. Needed supports include those that are concrete and practical, such as helping a family to obtain resources (e.g., diapers) or an advocate (e.g., access a waiver program, find a child care program). Home visitors can also provide psychological or emotional supports simply by being consistent and reliable, actions that are foundational to forming a positive relationship. When caregivers experience the home visitor as a supportive presence, they are better able to participate in activities needed for the next type of interaction, teaching, and skill building to improve outcomes in child behavior and development. Activities to improve outcomes may include noticing a baby's cues, gently introducing new ideas, speaking for the baby, highlighting strengths of the relationship, noticing and encouraging positive caregiving skills, and explaining and modeling those skills when needed. Ultimately, once the caregiver feels safe in concrete and psychological ways and has a basic skill base, then they are more ready to apply the skills and build their own relationship and positive interactions with the child (Tomlin & Viehweg, 2003; Weatherston, 2000; Woods et al., 2011). This sequence should not be thought of as a linear one. Providers should not anticipate getting to an "end," but instead should view working through these three strategies as a process. It is important to remember that with very complex family situations or with young children who have significant needs, it is very unlikely that any one family–provider relationship will be all that is needed to achieve every family goal. Home visitors would do well to understand their role in helping a family as only a piece of the work to be done (Walsh & Mortensen, 2020).

BOUNDARIES AND ETHICS IN EARLY CHILDHOOD WORK

Home visitors are sometimes unprepared for the level of difficulty that some families live with (Tandon et al., 2008; Zeanah et al., 2006). As reviewed in earlier chapters, families may struggle with a range of problems on a daily basis (e.g., parental incarceration, domestic violence, unsafe housing, extreme poverty, debilitating substance use, or mental illness). Home visitors who grew up in more secure circumstances may have little or no frame of reference for understanding these types of experiences.

Similarities between home visitor and family characteristics, including race, ethnicity, or lived experiences, can be advantageous. However, sharing characteristics with family does not guarantee that a home visitor will avoid the kind of personal biases that may interfere with the work (Zeanah et al., 2006). For example, a home visitor who overcame difficult life circumstances may have the attitude that anyone could do the same, leading to frustration with clients who are not making progress that the provider believes is appropriate (Jones Harden, 2010). Other times, home visitors may unexpectedly become reactive to challenging family circumstances that remind them of their own difficult times. It can be hard for the provider to separate out what is happening to the family from their own experiences (Hubel et al., 2020; Seligman, 2014; Zeanah, Korfmacher, et al., 2023).

There is a level of intimacy that is part of working with families with very young children (Tomlin & Viehweg, 2003; Watson & Gatti, 2012). For many providers and families, the fact that the work occurs in the family's home adds another layer of closeness to the work and the relationship (Zeanah, Korfmacher, et al., 2023). Family members may view the home visitor, who has worked diligently from a relationship-based perspective as a friend, rather than as a professional (Mills et al., 2012; Riley et al., 2008). Home visitors need to clearly define the relationship, providing boundaries that protect the family and themselves. This could include having written explanations of the home visitor's role and expectations about family participation in sessions. It can be helpful to specify how and when communication will occur, such as when the caregiver can expect that the home visitor will answer calls. The home visitor may also need to discuss program policies regarding the use of texting and social media to clarify up front what communication methods will be used. Home visitors may be invited to family gatherings such as a child's birthday party or may be offered a meal or snack. Families may ask for favors such as a ride to the store or an offer to watch the children while the caregiver takes a shower or runs an errand.

Home visitors may struggle to balance the apparently competing needs of the caregiver and the infant, or to understand unfamiliar contexts related to a family's culture (Zeanah, Korfmacher, et al., 2023). Understanding professional ethical standards and agency policies and guidelines can help the home visitor know how to respond to situations and requests like these (Walsh & Mortensen, 2020). Home visitors must make the best decisions possible for each situation based on their understanding of their role, their program's policies, and the specific family. It may be helpful to talk through these kinds of situations with a supervisor to gain clarity and direction.

Early childhood providers' consideration of boundaries and ethics varies. Recently, there have been calls for the development of an ethical code specific to infant mental health, raising the question of this need in other early childhood serving programs (Zeanah, Steier, et al., 2023). In one study with Early Head Start home visiting staff, some providers reported that they think about boundaries and are aware of the need to avoid crossing them. These providers also reported attending to their own emotional involvement with families. However, others in the sample reported directly helping families in concrete ways, such as providing a ride to the store or even giving cash in an emergency. Others reported making an effort to solve a family problem that was clearly outside of their scope of practice. For example, one provider barred an abusive partner from participating in the home visit (Jones Harden et al., 2010). Behaviors such as these may be considered ethical violations in many professional disciplines. In these examples, the home visitor has moved from a professional to a more personal relationship, which can set up inappropriate expectations, interfere with achieving the planned outcomes, and miss opportunities for caregivers to build skills to solve problems on their own. Maintaining awareness about one's scope of practice and skill set and clarity about the role and responsibilities of a home visitor can help avoid ethical errors and dilemmas.

Home visitors also need to be clear about roles and responsibilities when families are working with multiple providers and agencies, especially when differences in practices among professionals or between professional practices and community expectations are present (Zeanah, Steier, et al., 2023). For example, families with caregivers who have substance use issues or those with mental illness or developmental disorders may be involved with multiple professionals from early intervention, mental health, and child welfare, among other programs. Tensions can arise when providers working together or in supervisory relationships have different professional backgrounds (Zeanah, Steier, et al., 2023). Beeber and Canuso (2012) state that home visitors should request clarification of the "margins of authority" (p. 164) from supervisors or program managers in order to fully understand where their own authority starts and ends. In some cases, agencies have articulated agreements that explain how their staff communicate and work together. It is helpful to have clear communication about when and by whom various decisions are made. Understanding the roles and activities of other providers can also help the home visitor or other early childhood provider maintain awareness of when and how they may appropriately make changes to their specific work to accommodate the needs of a family in crisis or with chronic issues before the problems undermine their effectiveness. Clear communication and coordination within and across agencies and professionals are crucial. However, it's important to emphasize that information sharing for coordination efforts needs to be done sensitively and with permission. Home visitors who struggle to understand or hold information that caregivers may share should avoid the temptation to process this information with other workers, respecting the family's privacy across all aspects of this work and especially when discussing trauma and other difficult subjects (Yoches et al., 2012). However, it is certainly appropriate to discuss challenging situations in reflective supervision or consultation sessions, where confidentiality can be assured.

Another aspect of the intensity and closeness of this work occurs when the home visitor and parent have similar characteristics or backgrounds. Some home visiting programs have emphasized similarities between workers and the populations they serve, such as ethnicity and, especially, languages spoken (Ferguson et al., 2023). The shared experience of being a caregiver or parent can establish helpful common ground between the home visitor and family and may help facilitate trust (Mills et al., 2012). Regardless of the type of similarity a home visitor and family share, there are times when the use of a personal story is thought to have some benefit, such as increasing provider credibility and showing an understanding of caregiver feelings in a way that may help them accept a suggestion. Sharing a personal story may not always be useful, however. Some caregivers may feel less competent if the home visitor seems to know everything. When self-disclosing, it is probably best to keep the focus on the child and family, sharing only your experiences that are directly related to the work. It might be appropriate to share the activities you experienced at the zoo with your own child to promote learning about animals, but not the shopping trip you had with your best friend. When using this method, monitor how comfortable the parent seems to feel and make sure that the sharing is not a distraction (Woods et al., 2011). Refer to Box 10.1 for some suggestions about how to develop and maintain appropriate boundaries.

Lack of clear boundaries may increase the stress and likelihood of experiencing burnout in those who work with young families (Tandon et al., 2008; Zeanah et al., 2006). However, it is also true that the higher the level of risk and the more problems that the family has, the greater the likelihood that the home visitor will have strong feelings about the family (Seligman, 2014; Watson & Gatti, 2012). As a result, the home visitor may feel pressed to do more and maybe to stretch a boundary. For example, nurses in a Nurse Family Partnership program reported that families in which parents

> **Box 10.1. Suggestions for Developing and Maintaining Appropriate Boundaries**
>
> - Know and follow ethical guidelines of the profession.
> - Know personal preferences regarding boundaries in relationships with families.
> - Understand how a family's sense of boundaries might affect the home visitor.
> - Consider the preferences of families and what will help them feel safe and engaged.
> - Discuss issues of boundaries with families as necessary in certain situations.
>
> From Weldum, J. R., Songer, N. S., & Ensher, G. S. (2009). The family as foreground. In G. L. Ensher, D. A. Clark, & N. S. Songer (Eds.), *Families, infants, and young children at risk* (pp. 39–58). Paul H. Brookes Publishing Co.; reprinted by permission.

have mental health issues need more time and that it was harder to stay on the planned schedule (Zeanah et al., 2006). When difficult topics must be addressed, home visitors may struggle with concern that they do not have the background or training to address these areas adequately (Tandon et al., 2008; Tomlin et al., 2016; Yoches et al., 2012). It can be helpful to focus on what the home visitor provides that is helpful, such as child guidance and general supports, while maintaining the perspective that one is not responsible for every challenge a family faces. Reflective supervision or consultation can help the home visitor manage these feelings and worries.

MANAGING MISSTEPS

No matter how carefully home visitors approach their work, mistakes will happen. These mistakes can include something as simple as a misunderstanding or communication problem about a scheduled appointment or something more serious that threatens the relationship. Caregivers can become frustrated with a home visitor who has to set a limit due to an agency rule, disappointed and disengaged when the service does not meet their expectations, or angry when a home visitor brings up a concern about an issue. For their part, home visitors may have similar feelings of disappointment when a family does not attain set goals, frustration when a family misses appointments, and anger when a family does something the home visitor perceives as potentially dangerous for the child. When working in collaboration with other professionals, similar breaches are possible. For example, workers can experience frustration when a task is incomplete due to lack of clarity about role responsibility. At other times, workers from different backgrounds may view a family differently, causing disagreement about what approach is likely to be most effective (Capacity Building Center for States, 2017).

When partners have strong feelings or do not take care in communicating, relationships can suffer. It is important to note that occasional "ruptures," such as disagreements, miscommunications, or one partner having hurt feelings, are a completely normal part of any close relationship. Acknowledging and addressing a rupture is needed to move toward repair of the breakdown in the relationship (Friedlander, 2014). For many families partnering with home visitors, the notion that such a repair is possible is foreign. Naming and taking steps to mend a misstep or misunderstanding can provide an example of being responsive and correcting an error that the caregiver can use with their child or within other relationships. To round out the parallel process, this type of rupture and repair can occur in other relationships, including those with colleagues and supervisors (Heffron & Murch, 2010). Participating in RSC can help home visitors recognize and prepare to make repairs when these kinds of mistakes inevitably happen (Lingas, 2022).

Addressing breaks in a relationship requires more than technical skills. It also necessitates an openness and willingness to discuss what happened and one's own role in it (Friedlander, 2014; Lingas, 2022). It's possible to notice a change in another person without recognizing what started it. Being willing to address that change and to consider your own possible role are good steps toward repair. Friedlander (2014), a psychologist who often writes about therapeutic and supervision processes, offers an approach to managing relationship ruptures that can be helpful for home visitors: Once you have noticed and pointed out that something seems to be happening, make a statement about what you think could be occurring. Next, ask if the other person is willing to discuss the situation. Last, take responsibility for your part in the situation. The next part of the vignette gives an example of how this might look in an early childhood context.

In virtual group supervision later that week, Anna vents her frustration about Tessa's lack of engagement during the visit. She shares that she had only focused on the baby and his needs. Instead of just reminding Anna that her role was to help both caregiver and child, Anna's supervisor listens carefully and sympathizes with how frustrated she must have felt. "It is difficult to feel that you are working so hard and no one is listening," the supervisor says. After a bit, the supervisor asks Anna to provide more details about what was happening during the visit. The supervisor adds that she does not have a good feel for what Tessa was doing or how she was reacting while Anna helped Anthony. Anna again recalls that Tessa was quiet and describes Tessa following her to the door at the end of the visit. "This seems a little different from what you usually describe about Tessa. What was that like for you when you noticed her difference?" the supervisor asks.

"Well, actually, I did not notice that at the time. I thought about it later when I got home," Anna admits. "Right now, I guess I kind of think she wanted to say something." After talking with her supervisor, Anna recognizes that she missed some cues that Tessa was giving during the last visit. When she arrives for the next visit, Tessa is still cool and distant. Anna tries out the plan she developed with her supervisor.

Observe/notice:

A: "I feel like you seem a little upset today."

T: "I am okay."

State what you think or feel might have happened (if you think you know):

A: "I am concerned that I was not very responsive to you the last time we met."

T: "You were kind of rude."

Ask if the person is willing to discuss what happened or is happening:

A: "Would it be okay if we talked about what is happening between us?"

T: "I guess."

Self-correct when needed:

A: "In thinking back to last week, I feel like I missed that you wanted to tell me something. I am sorry about that. Is there something that you would like to say?"

T: "I was feeling down and then you just went straight to Anthony. I know I should not have him in the seat. I could tell you were mad and that made me more down."

A: "You are right that I was frustrated about the car seat. But I should have asked about it so I could understand what was going on with you. Are you still feeling down today? If it's okay, I'd like to hear what is going on with you."

SECONDARY TRAUMA AND BURNOUT

Many types of professionals who function in challenging environments can develop a prolonged response to chronic stressors inherent in their work. This response is called *burnout*. Burnout is typically defined as having three components: emotional exhaustion, cynicism or depersonalization, and inefficacy (Maslach et al., 2001). Worker burnout is very common in high-stress human service fields such as nursing and child welfare. Burnout characteristics such as feelings of being emotionally overwhelmed and ineffective may contribute to worker turnover. When experiencing burnout, workers report a number of physical and psychological symptoms, including headaches, stomach pain, panic symptoms (e.g., heart racing, dry mouth), problems sleeping, and changes in appetite (Denmark & Jones Harden, 2012). Trauma responses are also possible for professionals. This can happen when the professional directly experiences a traumatic event, such as a personal or on-the-job experience of being threatened, or when the provider sees someone else being hurt or threatened. In addition, workers who spend time with traumatized individuals and hear the stories and see the results of traumatic events may eventually develop trauma symptoms (Denmark & Jones Harden, 2012).

Although a good deal of work has been done on secondary trauma and burnout in other fields, these phenomena are only now beginning to be explored among home visitors or other early intervention professionals (Carolan & Fishel, 2023; Lee et al., 2013). This is unfortunate, as the intensity and quality of this work, especially with populations that experience more risk factors, means that home visitors who serve young families may be vulnerable to these experiences. Several aspects of home visiting work contribute to potential burnout, including those connected to the setting, family and caregiver characteristics, worker preparation, and worker response to the work (Tomlin et al., 2016). In one study, home visiting nurses acknowledged feelings of satisfaction that come with seeing things work out for families and knowing that they helped, along with many negative emotions, such as disappointment or sadness when a family cannot reach its own potential, struggling with one's own feelings when a family's goals and worker's goals are not aligned, and the overall problem of laying down the work at the end of the day (Zeanah et al., 2006). In another study, Early Head Start providers reported system-related concerns, including the burden of large caseloads and limited ability to make decisions and take actions (Jones Harden et al., 2010). Finally, in recent years, early care and education workers reported a range of stress-related symptoms in response to pandemic conditions (Swigonski et al., 2021).

There are several ways to address the stress of this work in order to reduce the potential for and address symptoms of burnout and secondary trauma when needed. Basic self-care should be a priority for all who work with families with very young children and especially those whose caseloads are high or include multi-risk families. Most people are able to name the main areas of self-care, including taking care of oneself physically and emotionally. These main areas typically include getting enough sleep, eating a reasonably healthy diet, and making room for some relaxation, exercise, and fun. Others frame this as creating a healthy work–life balance so that both work and personal activities are pleasurable and enjoyable. Home visitors can be supported by policy- and program-derived methods that help as well (Carolan & Fishel, 2023; Simpson et al., 2018). These include providing equitable compensation, flexible work environments, and opportunities for professional development, ensuring safety protocols are in place, offering stress management classes, providing emotional supports such as retreats and mental health days, acknowledging accomplishments, and providing formal mental health supports as needed (Carolan & Fishel, 2023; Denmark & Jones Harden, 2012; Simpson et al., 2019). It is helpful to spend some time reflecting on your own work–personal-life balance. Appendix 10A is one way you can examine your current work and life activities and consider whether you are in balance.

In one study, home visitors specified a desire for more supervision that included emotional support provided by someone able to understand the work (Jones Harden et al., 2010). Workers who serve families with multiple issues may benefit from reflective supervision or consultation over time to manage their own feelings. When emotions are high and distressing, single or inconsistent sessions are often not enough to manage the worker's response. To be most effective, supervision needs to be ongoing and include both social and organizational supports. Without these types of supports, home visitors can feel "isolated and overwhelmed" (Yoches et al., 2012, p. 95) and, as a result, the work does not move forward. In the next section, we discuss reflective supervision and consultation as a way to gain support for these kinds of situations as well as a useful method of professional development.

REFLECTIVE SUPERVISION AND CONSULTATION (RSC)

The literature on RSC emphasizes three characteristics: collaboration, regularity, and reflection (Fenichel, 1992; Tomlin et al., 2014). A supervisory relationship that is collaborative is intended to be egalitarian. The supervisor, though typically more experienced, does not provide a prescriptive or directive approach. Instead, the supervision is characterized by the pair working together with an emphasis on the supervisee's exploration and discovery with support. Recently, it has been noted that the supervisor or consultant position may carry privilege that can make achieving a truly collaborative or nonhierarchical relationship difficult. Research from the perspective of supervisees suggests that a supervisor or consultant's actions that promote feelings of safety, including holding a nonjudgmental stance, are important (Barron et al., 2022a).

Regularity or consistency in supervision has been cited by supervisors and supervisees as a key attribute of the RSC process (Barron et al., 2022a; Tomlin et al., 2016). Consistency may be a higher priority for supervisees who are white compared to those who identify as Black, Asian, Latinx, or Native American (Shivers et al., 2022). Regularity in supervision has several meanings. From a practical standpoint, the supervision should be regularly scheduled. The time should be set aside and interruptions or cancellations avoided. The supervisee should come to experience the supervisor as consistent and reliable. Finally, the supervision must include a reflective component that allows the supervisee to have time and support to consider their own responses to the work, to link those responses back to previous experiences, to consider how those responses may guide future action, to wonder about what is happening to the caregivers and the baby, and to consider a variety of possible links between all of these factors (Heffron & Murch, 2010; Shahmoon-Shanok, 2010; Watson, 2022; Weatherston & Barron, 2010).

This consideration of links and influences between various facets of the work, especially among relationships, is related to the concept of parallel process. *Parallel process* describes how relationships are interconnected (Heffron & Murch, 2010). It has been described for more than 100 years in the psychotherapy literature, and an understanding of it is now a conventional component of reflective practice and supervision or consultation. Recent empirical work with psychotherapists has demonstrated the theory that interaction patterns that occur in supervision are taken back to work with clients (Tracey et al., 2012).

Most home visitors would agree that we are changed by our experiences, both personal and professional. When we are able to use reflection, we make connections between experiences and learn what works and what doesn't, changing what we do based on experience (Heatherington et al., 2014). A good reflective coach, supervisor, consultant, or facilitator is typically a more experienced practitioner who will help the supervisee improve their ability to step back and reflect. This involves gaining skills in the ability to think broadly and deeply in order to combine internal knowledge (including one's own experience of thoughts, feelings, and reactions) with external knowledge (e.g., scientific knowledge, best practice guidelines) in a way that improves or advances practice (Brandt, 2014). Being able to integrate information at this level takes time and experience and is often achieved through a supervisory relationship that takes a reflective approach. In reflective supervision, the supervisor will assist the supervisee to move between considering different relationships using many methods. A coach or supervisor may accomplish this feat through a variety of means, ranging from more direct activities (e.g., providing direct instruction, modeling, asking questions, providing feedback, facilitating problem solving) and less obvious ones (e.g., remaining silent in order to provide space for the supervisee's own thoughts to emerge) (Brandt, 2014; Heffron & Murch, 2010; Knoche et al., 2013; Shahmoon-Shanok, 2010; Watson, 2022; Weatherston & Barron, 2010).

BENEFITS OF REFLECTIVE SUPERVISION AND CONSULTATION

As mentioned, the empirical research basis for reflective coaching, supervision, and facilitation, although an active area of growth, remains relatively small (Watson et al., 2014; Tomlin & Heller, 2016). In infant and toddler fields, including home visiting, there is a growing effort to explore how RSC supports the workers and improves the work (Simpson et al., 2018; Susman-Stillman et al., 2020; Watson & Gatti, 2012; Watson et al., 2014; Weatherston et al., 2010). To date, there is some evidence not only of how it works, but also of how it may improve recipient skills and benefit organizations. Reflective supervision and coaching have been associated with more effective implementation of programming (McAllister & Thomas, 2007), transformed practice for providers, and more positive outcomes for young children (Knoche et al., 2013). In home visiting and early education and care, the importance of reflective supervision generally, and especially with more vulnerable families, has been highlighted (Ferguson et al., 2023; Jones Harden, 2010; Watson & Gatti, 2012). RSC supervisors reported benefits, including enhanced relationships and emotional, reflective, and coping skills, as a result of participation in the practice (Susman-Stillman et al., 2020). Similarly, participants in RSC reported benefits related to their personal wellness (e.g., less burnout and better engagement), personal growth in self-regulation and reflective capacity, and effects on their practice, such as those related to building relationship, observing, and bringing up difficult topics (Barron et al., 2022a).

Everyone has an individual point of view that comes from a blend of many things: personal characteristics and experiences, training, personality, values, and beliefs (Weldum et al., 2009). Although it is not possible or even desirable for home visitors to keep their own responses and views out of the work, sometimes those views or responses can get in the way. Reflective supervision or consultation provides a way to address thoughts and feelings of the home visitor in order to better address family and young child needs (Watson & Gatti, 2012). Content to examine may include material related to personal biases. Examples of some of the benefits of reflective supervision have been summarized as "clarifying the family situation, increasing self-awareness regarding one's work with families, debriefing and regrouping after a crisis, and gaining new perspectives for use in refining interventions" (McAllister & Thomas, 2007, p. 205).

Reflective supervision is likely to be particularly important for areas in which home visitors or other early childhood professionals may not be formally prepared, such as caregiver mental illness (Jones Harden et al., 2010). Even when a home visitor suspects the problem, without opportunities for reflective consultation they may not know what to do or may fail to appreciate the need to take actions such as making community referrals (Jones Harden et al., 2010; Tandon et al., 2008). Similarly, younger and less experienced home visitors, who are more likely to report burnout symptoms (Lee et al., 2013), are seen as likely to significantly benefit from supervision. The quality of the supervision is also important. When workers are satisfied with supervision and feel more empowered in work, less burnout is reported (Lee et al., 2013).

Beyond benefits to individual workers, supervision is also useful for employers and agencies. Supervision has been associated with enhanced worker-reported job satisfaction and lower burnout (Mena & Bailey, 2007), and with better worker retention (McGuigan et al., 2003). Less frequent turnover of workers benefits families, enhancing the consistency of the service provided. Agencies also benefit through the cost savings realized by avoiding the expenses associated with recruitment and retraining.

Reflective supervision, consultation, and coaching methods, although valuable and increasingly recognized as effective, are not universally implemented for a variety of reasons. Barriers include practical concerns, such as making time for the sessions, and worries or fears about self-examination and the potential for being judged (Heffron & Murch, 2010; Norman-Murch & Ward, 1999). There are several emerging areas of study in RSC, particularly related to the needs and preferences of supervisees within the increasingly diverse workforce (Lingas, 2022; Noroña et al., 2023; Simpson et al., 2018). In a recent large national study, most providers of RSC were white women (97%), suggesting that most individuals of color could not access a supervisor of their own race or ethnicity (Shivers et al., 2022). In the same study a top priority was creating pathways to open opportunities for more diverse practitioners to become supervisors (Shivers et al., 2022).

Home visitors should take time to make sure they understand what RSC involves and clearly understand how it is different from other workforce development methods including coaching, as well as individual supports, such as personal therapy. Providers of RSC should build the skills needed to support a diverse workforce, particularly as emerging data suggest some preferences in supervision methods connected to race (Shivers et al., 2022). For example, in one sample, half of Native American providers endorsed a preference for group supervision that incorporates specific cultural practices, while about a third of Black participants reported a desire for creativity in supervision session format and practices (Shivers et al., 2022). Implemented skillfully and with attention to diversity, inclusion, and antiracist principles, reflective supervisory relationships will increase the ability to slow down, back up, take a careful look at the whole picture, examine implicit bias, explore emotions as part of the work, and learn new skills (Barron et al., 2022b; Lingas, 2022; Neilsen Gatti et al., 2011; Shahmoon-Shanok, 2010; Shivers et al., 2022; Susman-Stillman et al., 2020; Weatherston & Barron, 2010). For more information on reflective supervision and consultation, please see the supplement "Reflective Supervision and Consultation: What Is It, Why Do I Need It, and How Can I Use It Most Effectively?" included in this book.

USING THE PAUSE FRAMEWORK

Using the vignettes in this chapter, let us see how Anna processes her experiences with Anthony and his mother, Tessa. See Figures 10.1 and 10.2 for examples of how this might look.

PAUSE WORKSHEET

Child: **Anthony**   Date: **October 30, 2024**

Caregiver: **Tessa**   Provider: **Anna**

PERCEIVE—Explore what is happening.

Caregiver perspective:	Provider perspective:
Tessa has a lot on her plate. She seems to love Anthony and want the best for him. She has periods where she seems very engaged and other times when she is preoccupied.	I am worried about Anthony getting everything he needs. Tessa seems to miss some of the important cues he gives her about his needs. I feel frustrated when she misses appointments or doesn't call to cancel, and also when she calls multiple times in a row asking for something.

ASK—Clarify what is happening.

Starting with the caregiver's priorities and concerns, ask more detailed/specific questions to clarify what is happening.

I could ask more about how things are going for Tessa now, such as "How are you handling all of the things you have to do with Anthony?"

I might start a conversation about how much he is growing and changing. I could reflect that I remember when my own children outgrew their clothes so quickly.

UNDERSTAND—Explore why it is happening.

With the caregiver, explore explanations for what is happening. Consider possible explanations that include the environment, the child, and the caregiver. Listen and observe closely as you explore the situation in conversation with the family.

Caregiver perspective:	Provider perspective:	Child's perspective:
Tessa may have worries about finances or other family issues. She may not have enough information about Anthony's development.	Tessa may be struggling with family or other issues I am not aware of.	Anthony may be confused by his mother's varied and inconsistent responses to his needs.
		(continued)

(continued)

Figure 10.1. Anna's PAUSE Worksheet for Tessa and Anthony.

Figure 10.1. (continued)

PAUSE WORKSHEET (continued)

UNDERSTAND (continued)		
Caregiver perspective: *She may not know how to support him to reach his next developmental milestones.*	Provider perspective:	Child's perspective:

STRATEGIZE and **EVALUATE**—Identify possible responses/solutions.

1. Solution/action to try: *Explore how Tessa sees Anthony and his current development to find out more about what she would like to see happen so we can update his plan.*	How will we know if it works? *Tessa's perspective about Anthony is shared.* *New needs are identified.* When will we evaluate if it works? *By the next regular plan review date.*
2. Solution/action to try: *Discuss adding a social worker to our team to gather more information and identify resources.*	How will we know if it works? *Social work is added.* When will we evaluate if it works? *When we review the assessment report from the social worker together.*

PROVIDER REFLECTION WORKSHEET

Provider Reflection Worksheet

Child: _Anthony_   Date: _October 30, 2024_

Caregiver: _Tessa_   Provider: _Anna_

1. How did I follow the caregiver's lead to learn what is most pressing or important to them?	I missed her lead this time. I realize I am struggling to understand what is most important for Tessa. She seems inconsistent and sometimes not attentive enough to Anthony's needs.
2. How did I ask clarifying questions that help me to understand the problem better? How did I inquire about the caregiver's values and beliefs related to the issue?	I did not ask questions. Instead, I jumped to solve the immediate issues and didn't even realize Tessa was watching me. I wonder what she was thinking. I don't think I even confirmed our next appointment.
3. How did I reflect on and offer to discuss similarities and differences between me and the caregiver? These might include race, ethnicity, language, gender, sexual orientation, religious and other beliefs, values, experiences, etc.	I guess I assumed Tessa thinks like me and would always keep her baby first in mind. But maybe something is keeping her from doing that or maybe she does think about Anthony but I am missing it.

(continued)

Figure 10.2. Anna's Provider Reflection Worksheet for Tessa and Anthony.

(continued)

Figure 10.2. *(continued)*

PROVIDER REFLECTION WORKSHEET *(continued)*

4.	How did I provide information that may help the caregiver better understand the child's behavior?	*I did not share any information other than simply doing what needed to be done. I have no idea whether Tessa will learn from my simply bathing and changing Anthony when he needed that.*
5.	How did I engage the caregiver to develop a response that may include a strategy to try, a resource to use, or more information to increase understanding?	*I did not engage with Tessa. I think we might need to invite another service to the team. Maybe a social worker could help us better understand what is happening with this family and whether other resources are necessary.*
6.	How did I provide support and emotional containment if needed?	*I did not do very well with containing emotions, as I realize I was too upset myself when Tessa did not take proper care of Anthony. How can I be more present in the moment and then more helpful to Tessa?*
7.	How do I plan to follow up on promised actions to maintain trust?	*I made a plan to provide clothing, but I did not discuss it with Tessa. I will discuss the clothing plan with my supervisor to make sure that is allowed. I need to contact the family to confirm the next appointment. I wonder how I can check in with Tessa on how she is feeling about our working relationship.*
8.	What do I want to discuss in reflective supervision to improve my practice and outcomes with this child and caregiver?	*It feels very discouraging to read what I wrote and see so many mistakes, assumptions, and judgments! I want to better understand Tessa's ups and downs, my own reactions to her, and why this is so challenging for me. I know I am motivated to stay involved because I like Anthony, although I secretly wish the family would "fire" me or just exit the program. Why am I so frustrated?*

What's Next?

After working through these chapters, the "what's next" question is now directed to you. What will you do with this information, and how will you incorporate the PAUSE framework into your work with families and children?

TIPS FOR PRACTICE

- Mistakes happen in any relationship. Home visitors can learn to repair breaks in relationships that occur with families they serve.
- In order to effectively serve caregivers and prevent burnout, home visitors must attend to their own emotional responses and practice self-care.
- Reflective supervision is a way for home visitors to receive support to grow professionally and better serve caregivers with challenging situations.

KEY POINTS TO REMEMBER

- Due to the intense nature of home visiting with vulnerable caregivers, home visitors are at risk for experiencing strong emotional responses such as burnout or secondary trauma.
- Self-care is necessary to be most effective in this work.
- Attention to boundaries is difficult due to the intensity and intimacy of the work of home visitors. Boundary issues may be present with families, co-workers, and supervisors as well as across agencies. Clear communication of roles and responsibilities can avoid boundary violations.
- Mistakes and missteps are normal in all relationships, and the relationships between home visitors and families are no exceptions. These types of missteps can be addressed and repaired.
- Home visitors are working in a complex environment and may experience strong emotions and other responses related to the work. Reflective supervision and consultation can help home visitors manage their feelings, allow for integration of emotion and thinking, and build skills that improve practice.
- Despite some consensus about the core features of RSC that are shared across samples of providers and recipients, emerging evidence suggests preferences for RSC formats and methods are not universal across ethnic and racial groups.

SUGGESTED FURTHER READING

Childress, D. C. (2021). *Pause and reflect: Your guide to a deeper understanding of early intervention practice.* Paul H. Brookes Publishing Co.

Heffron, M. C., & Murch, T. (2010). *Reflective supervision and leadership in infant and early childhood programs.* ZERO TO THREE Press.

Heller, S. S., & Gilkerson, L. (Eds.). (2010). *A practical guide to reflective supervision.* ZERO TO THREE Press.

Summers, S. J., & Chazan-Cohen, R. (2012). *Understanding early childhood mental health: A practical guide for professionals.* Paul H. Brookes Publishing Co.

APPENDIX 10A

REFLECTION ON WORK-LIFE BALANCE

Exercise: Review your calendar for at least 2–4 weeks, placing each event into one of the three columns. Total the number in each column and compare; consider the balance between what you do for others and what you do that supports your own well-being. Discuss your results with a trusted colleague or in reflective supervision.

Things I do for work	Things I do for others outside work	Things I do for me
Ex: Meetings with colleagues	Ex: Drive children to sports event	Ex: Doctor appointment
Ex: Sessions with clients	Ex: Volunteer at church	Ex: Go to a movie with spouse or friend
Ex: Paperwork	Ex: Serve on local board for not-for-profit organization	Ex: Plan a family vacation
Ex: Research resources and useful information for families	Ex: Lawn care for aging parents	Ex: Massage, exercise, pedicure/manicure

(continued)

APPENDIX 10A **REFLECTION ON WORK-LIFE BALANCE** (continued)

Things I do for work	Things I do for others outside work	Things I do for me
TOTAL:	TOTAL:	TOTAL:

Last Reflection

As a home visitor, you know that your work is extremely important in helping caregivers provide the best they can for their children by promoting their strengths, capacities, and resilience while living with sometimes quite difficult and complex circumstances. We hope that you have found the PAUSE framework—as well as the other ideas, resources, and concepts provided here—helpful as you seek to improve your practice and partnerships with caregivers.

Throughout this book, we encouraged you to slow down, think more deeply, consider multiple perspectives, and use reflective supervision or consultation. We hope that reading this book has provided space for you to think and wonder about your own practice as a home visitor. Maybe you have found validation for some of your current practices, new ideas for improving practice, and even permission to ask for help when something is outside of your scope of responsibilities. Please accept one final invitation to pause and think about what you will take from your reading and reflection and consider what steps you might take next in your journey as a practitioner. Here are some questions to help you organize your thoughts:

What else do you want to know about?

Which suggested books and resources will you read and refer to?

What strategies will you incorporate into your home visiting practice?

What might you do differently now?

Which ideas will you share with your colleagues and supervisor?

How did you see yourself in the examples provided? What does this tell you?

Which practices were affirmed for you or help you know you are on the right track?

Finally, we encourage you to find ways to continue to expand your skills and knowledge by participating in reflective supervision/consultation. Through the support of such a learning relationship, you will achieve better understanding of your own and other people's perceptions of situations and events, and you will increase your ability to support caregivers to address the needs of their children. Thank you for your work as a home visitor!

Reflective Supervision and Consultation

What Is It, Why Do I Need It, and How Can I Use It Most Effectively?

PART 1: WHAT IS RSC?

Reflective supervision and consultation (RSC) is a professional development practice that has become standard in early childhood fields, including most major home visiting models (Ferguson et al., 2023; West et al., 2022). RSC is understood as a professional relationship that, when engaged in regularly over time, builds reflective and relationship skills and supports emotional well-being. In fact, one of the most enduring descriptions of RSC comes from Rebecca Shahmoon-Shanok (2006) who succinctly called it "a relationship for learning."

An early effort to define RSC identified three key features: supervision that is *consistent, collaborative, and reflective* (Fenichel, 1992). This triad of features was borne out in a study that sought expert opinions of the essential characteristics of RSC (Tomlin et al., 2016). More recent research has also suggested that those receiving RSC value similar features of the relationship (Barron et al., 2022a, 2022b).

Consistency can mean structural aspects of supervision, such as that which occurs on a regular schedule and has a standard agenda. A reliable "frame" to the RSC session provides a sense of predictability that allows the participant freedom to consider their often complex thoughts, feelings, and responses to this work (Heffron et al., 2016). Consistency can also refer to how the supervisor/consultant is with the supervisee, typically meaning a person who is reliable or can be counted on. Interpersonal consistency builds trust and a sense of safety in a relationship. We understand that consistent behavior of caregivers underpins a child's developing attachment relationship and that this consistent relationship contributes to the child's growing self-regulation. Similarly, consistency on the part of home visitors and other providers is key to establishing trusting relationships with caregivers. In parallel, consistency in the RSC relationship builds and facilitates a sense of safety for the worker. This sense of safety allows the recipient to explore their own reactions to the work in a way that deepens understanding. In current best practice guidelines, RSC is described as differing from other forms of professional support, such as coaching or mentoring, due to its explicit attention and exploration of the parallel process (e.g., how relationships affect relationships) (Alliance for the Advancement of Infant Mental Health, 2018; Watson et al., 2022). This emphasis underscores the importance of relationships in early childhood work and keys in on the ability to recognize the connections among relationships in ways that deepen understanding.

In RSC, the supervisor/consultant strives to offer a relationship that is more collaborative and less hierarchical. Signifiers of this partnering approach occur at the onset of the relationship through agreement on the basics like scheduling the session and continue within sessions through the co-creation of the agenda or plan for each session. A collaborative model may be most clearly demonstrated as the supervisor makes space for the supervisee to explore and discover rather than impose their own views about a situation. For this reason and others, it can be desirable to separate administrative types of supervision (e.g., tasks such as guidance on report writing or monitoring of productivity) from RSC. This is because it is more difficult to achieve collaboration when relationships are unequal. In recent years, it has become clear that aspects of power and privilege can be present in supervisory relationships despite our best intentions (Bobes, 2017; Hause & Lemoine, 2022; Shivers et al., 2022). Providers of RSC should take the initiative to discuss these issues openly and regularly over time, increasing the chances that the relationship will feel and function as an equal partnership (Bobes, 2017; Clark et al., 2019; Shivers et al., 2022; Stroud, 2010).

Another main classic characteristic of RSC is that it seeks to make space for and build the participants' reflective skills. The ability of the supervisor or consultant to listen, wait, and hold a safe space is emphasized as a best practice in RSC in a recent guideline (Alliance for the Advancement of Infant Mental Health, 2018; Watson et al., 2022). Of note, RSC is unique in that attention to the emotional content of the work is prioritized. Specifically, the emotional responses of the supervisee (and the supervisor) are identified, addressed, and used to further practice (Williams et al., 2019; Alliance for the Advancement of Infant Mental Health, 2018). Specifically, RSC should offer an opportunity to step back and slow down in order to fully consider experiences in the work with infants and young children and families. This includes identifying and exploring one's own thoughts, feelings, and responses, being open to possible thoughts, feelings, and responses of the caregiver and child, and wondering about how these may connect. Over time, regularly practicing reflection with the support of another builds this "muscle" and increases a person's ability to be reflective in the moment with clients. And in turn through the parallel process, it is expected that a more reflective provider can help their client grow their own reflective skills that are needed as a primary caregiver for young children (Shahmoon-Shanok, 2009).

Our understanding of RSC has been evolving in parallel with efforts to re-imagine infant and toddler work from more diverse perspectives (Noroña et al., 2023; Paradis et al., 2021; Thomas et al., 2019). Much of the initial explorations around definition and description of RSC was from the point of view of experts or supervisors, primarily from mental health backgrounds (Tomlin et al., 2016). Given that literature suggests that most RSC supervisors in early childhood fields are white and female, this perspective may not fully represent much of the current workforce (Shivers et al., 2022). More recently, there has been an increased emphasis on the perspective of supervisees (Barron et al., 2022a). In this work, supervisees reported that participation in RSC impacted their work with families, how they view themselves as professionals, and their overall personal growth. In a companion article (Barron, 2022b), the authors described a developmental process of growth in participating in RSC that may parallel supervisees' professional development growth.

A recent multimodal design study that sought to investigate reflective supervision competencies and practices from an equity lens yielded some insight into recipients' experiences and preferences for RSC (Shivers et al., 2022). When asked to identify their top priorities for transforming reflective supervision, nearly half of all responders identified a desire for more pathways for diverse practitioners to become supervisors. Similarly, 57% of all respondents prioritized training for supervisors on understanding and addressing topics such as talking about their own culture and identities and recognizing and naming privilege. This is important to do well, since other work indicates that the responsibility for bringing up these topics rests with the supervisor (Bobes, 2017; Clark et al., 2019; Stroud et al., 2010). Differences in preferences for topics and supervision modalities were also noted among different ethnic and racial groups surveyed in the study. For example, about a third of Black and Latinx participants expressed a preference for supervisors who used creativity (e.g., movement, art, breathing) in supervision formats and practices. Half of Native American supervisees reported preferring supervision in groups, with incorporation of cultural traditions and practices.

Shivers and colleagues also considered the experiences of supervisors (2022). They found no differences in racial and ethnic groups in acknowledging that it is the supervisor's responsibility to facilitate learning about culture and race. Other data suggest that there might be differences in fulfilling this responsibility. For example, Black supervisors reported feeling more open to discussing culture and race, whereas white supervisors were less confident than either Black or Latinx supervisors in discussing culture and race. These findings are interesting, given that supervisees in the Barron research (2022b) reported that being able to bring up diversity as needed was important to their feelings of safety in the relationship.

Much work remains to be done as we seek to understand which components are most key to making supervision or consultation reflective and effective across early childhood sectors and what variations are needed to best meet the needs of an increasingly diverse workforce. Gaining a richer understanding of the range of processes that promote reflection in diverse participants will require intentional inclusion of a broader range of voices as we seek to improve our research and training methods.

Why is RSC needed in infant-early childhood home visiting work?

Home visiting is an intense, intimate, and at times highly emotional field. The effects of working in this field can be moderated by participating in RSC. Sources of stress in the work include the setting, the clients, the structure and culture of the agency, and the worker's own history (Tomlin et al., 2016). Working in homes puts the home visitor in the tricky position of being an "expert" and a "guest" at one time (Simpson et al., 2018). The worker finds themselves on the family's "turf," creating tensions around issues that could include the potential for cultural missteps or concerns about the provider's safety.

Work with young children and families is inherently relationship-based. Furthermore, young children have higher needs for sensitive and stable care, meaning that the emotional status of the provider of that care—whether the primary or other caregiver for the child—is of great importance (Kwon et al., 2020). In many cases, the work of home visiting centers on supporting caregivers who have significant challenges bringing the prospect of experiencing secondary stress or trauma to the forefront (Tomlin et al., 2016). Working closely with clients who have had challenging experiences may trigger a workforce that has been historically female, underpaid, and at times burdened with their own challenging histories (Ruprecht et al., 2020; Simpson et al., 2018). Studies have shown that various sectors of the infant-toddler and family workforce have themselves experienced higher numbers of adverse childhood experiences (ACES), experiences of discrimination and violence, and increased mental health challenges such as depression (Simons, 2022; Simpson et al., 2018). Individuals who work in early childhood education and other early childhood fields may often come from populations that have experienced more stress and trauma than others, including women and those identifying as persons of color (Hubel et al., 2020; Simons et al., 2022). These studies clearly show that the infant-toddler workforce needs support to address their own psychological well-being in order to be available to clients (Simons et al., 2022).

In addition to aspects of work with the family, early care professionals can struggle with stress that comes from the culture of the agency or experiences with colleagues. Considerations include structural aspects of employment such as work hours, benefits and pay, and even physical labor related to caring for small children. Burdens related to documentation and feelings of lacking control over one's schedule can contribute to stress and even burnout in this worker population (Eaves et al., 2022; Simpson et al., 2018). Furthermore, given the fact that early care and education work may be team-based, relationships with colleagues could be sources of either support or of friction. RSC can help workers with these concerns to a degree; however, it is acknowledged that changes at an agency level may be a more appropriate way to alleviate stresses of this nature and that even larger cultural or system issues may underlie many of these stressors (Simpson et al., 2018).

What are the benefits of RSC?

Broadly, RSC is thought to have two main functions: skill-building and wellness. Recent reviews identified concerns about research RSC methods and critiqued it as limited by being primarily theoretical, descriptive, and correlational (Huffhines et al., 2023; West et al., 2022). Acknowledging these limitations, the research does show some promise in demonstrating that RSC benefits the workforce in key ways. Research with early care and education providers, home visitors, early intervention providers, and infant mental health specialists suggests that participation in RSC yields concrete improvements in skills such as insightfulness, productivity, reflection, understanding and ability to support others, and relationship skills (Bernstein & Edwards, 2012; Huffhines et al., 2023; Simpson et al., 2018; Subramaniam & Oliveira, 2023; Susman-Stillman et al., 2020; Virmani & Ontai, 2010). Participation in RSC has also been shown to support well-being, emotional regulation, increase ability to cope with stress, reduce burnout, and decrease emotional exhaustion (Huffhines et al., 2023; Pavkov & Wells, 2023; Susman-Stillman et al., 2020; Watson et al., 2014).

These benefits of RSC are clearly of value to the individual worker. Provider well-being has become of interest to employers, given that it predicts intent to stay in the workforce as well as the quality of the work (Kwon et al., 2020). Furthermore, families with young children also obviously benefit from access to well-trained and emotionally regulated providers. Watson and colleagues suggest that clients benefit when workers access RSC because the practice results in different thinking and therefore different and often more effective actions (Watson et al., 2014). Reduced staff burnout and secondary trauma are also connected to lower staff turnover, resulting in cost savings for employers and the ability to enjoy a more stable relationship with a provider for families and children (Denmark & Harden, 2012; Shea et al., 2020).

What is RSC like?

An RSC session is typically scheduled on a regular and consistent basis, such as once a week or once a month. Sessions typically last 60–90 minutes. Some supervisors/consultants may begin a session with a centering activity, such as offering a brief meditation, reading a poem, or leading a movement activity, like stretching or some chair yoga. Consultants or supervisors may use a standard agenda or the beginning of a session to co-construct the agenda with the supervisee. Supervisees can expect to be given space to speak, wonder, and reflect on the work they are doing with clients. The supervisor/consultant may ask questions, make comments, or at times share their own responses to the material shared. A frustration to some when they are new to RSC is that the supervisor/consultant most likely will not give solutions, or as one participant memorably put it, "She don't fix nothing" (B. Eisenhut, personal communication, October 27, 2023).

RSC can be delivered in groups or individually, with a few structural and format differences. For example, individual RSC is usually an hour, whereas group sessions are typically 90 minutes. Group sessions may be structured so that members take turns sharing their experiences in the work; this can be planned ahead or might be determined at the beginning of the session. This format means that a participant might be sharing a story one time and listening and responding to another person's story another time. Some group norms or guidelines may be offered by the consultant or developed by group members. Any guidelines offered can help structure the process and ensure that participants have a meaningful and safe experience. Groups offer advantages including opportunities to hear other stories, ideas, and perspectives. Facilitating a group RSC session means that the supervisor or the consultant is tasked with attending to the individual group members, their own response to the content shared, and the overall emotional tone of the group (Heffron et al., 2016). This can make group supervision richer and more challenging at the same time!

RSC, like many home visiting services, was often by necessity offered virtually during COVID. Although the pandemic has subsided, many groups continue to meet virtually, due to advantages such as eliminating travel time, increased access for those in lower resourced areas, opportunity to meet with participants from a broader geographical area, and ability to attend when weather is bad, to name a few. Some best practices when participating virtually have been generated (Alliance for the Advancement of Infant Mental Health, 2018; McCormick et al., 2019). For example, virtual participants should keep their cameras on to increase engagement and reduce the temptation to multitask. Some groups like the use of chat features in the virtual platform; others find these types of sidebars to be distracting. These conventions should be discussed when beginning a virtual group and should be reviewed often.

PART 2: ACCESSING AND MAXIMIZING THE BENEFITS OF RSC IN MY PRACTICE

How can I tell if the supervision or consultation that I receive is "reflective"?

A good first step to finding high-quality RSC is to choose a qualified consultant or supervisor. Qualifications can include training and credentials as well as lived or earned expertise. Some important qualifications might include knowledge about families with infants and young children, knowledge of adult learning styles, training in supervision, consultation, and mentorship, and work experience in the field. Some may prefer a supervisor who is like themselves in training background, gender, race, ethnicity, or languages spoken. You may wish to choose a supervisor who has an earned credential, such as the various Endorsements offered by the Alliance for the Advancement of Infant Mental Health, offered in many states and other countries (2018). Depending on the setting in which you work or your own personal goals for supervision, there may be other preferred or required supervisor/consultant characteristics.

How is RSC evaluated?

Another way of ensuring high-quality RSC is to conduct regular evaluations. Evaluations should help clarify if the RSC meets expectations for components such as structure and content. The methods should provide for examination of factors such as what the supervisor does, what the supervisee does, and what interactions happen between them. An evaluation can also consider if the intended outcomes of professional development and wellness are achieved. Questions to consider include whether the supervisee gains knowledge and skills. Does the supervisee report better ability to manage feelings and emotions related to the work? Ultimately, it would be desirable to connect the changes in the supervisee with better family outcomes; however, this research is not yet available. As we have discussed, our definitions of RSC have been expanding and changing; therefore, assessments will also need to change over time. With this caveat, we can consider some of the more readily available assessment tools.

Available methods for evaluating RSC include observational measures, supervisor ratings, and self-reports of the experience by participants (Tomlin & Heller, 2016; Heller & Ash, 2016; Watson, 2022). Some of these tools are designed for research, requiring training to use, but can provide a broad outline to organize our thinking about what we can expect to think about and do when participating in high-quality RSC. For example, the Provider Reflective Process Assessment Scales (PRPAS) measure change in reflective capacity over time via rating a 5-minute speech sample about work with a challenging family. The speech sample is then rated for evidence of reflective processes, such as self-knowledge and self-regulation. Christopher

Watson and colleagues have developed a research tool to assess RSC, the Reflective Interactive Observation Scale (RIOS; Watson, 2022). The RIOS is structured around the topics of conversation (Elements) and the activities (Collaborative Tasks) that occur between supervisor/consultant and supervisee. A trained rater uses the RIOS when viewing a recorded section of an RSC session (see the textbox). When viewing these components, bear in mind that you may not use all of them in every session.

Essential Tasks (Watson et al., 2022)	Collaborative Tasks
Understanding the Family Story	Describing
Holding the Baby or Child in Mind	Responding
Professional Use of Self	Exploring
Parallel Process	Linking
Reflective Alliance	Integrating

Several more accessible tools have been developed that supervisors and supervisees can use to rate RSC experiences and reflective skills. For example, the Reflective Supervision Rating Scale (RSRS) (Ash, 2010; Gallen et al., 2016) has been used in several studies, adapted for different providers and is readily available. The RSRS includes 17 items completed by the supervisee to rate the frequency with which the supervision includes activities related to reflective processing and skills, mentoring, supervision structure, and mentalization. Shea, Goldberg, and Weatherston (2016) created the Reflective Supervision Self-Efficacy Scale for Supervisors, a 17-item measure that asks supervisors to rate their confidence in their own reflective supervision skills. A companion scale, the Reflective Supervision Self-Efficacy Scale for Supervisees, is a 17-item assessment of the degree to which the supervisees are confident that they can engage in reflective practice activities. Both of these tools include items that reflect common reflective practice skills and activities expected in RSC, and they have been used in a recent evaluation of a home visitation model (see Shea et al., 2020). Finally, Hardy (2017) provided a set of tools based on their Multicultural Relational Perspective (MRP) approach, a comprehensive supervision approach from family therapy that prioritizes relationships and cultural competence. These tools are for both supervisor and supervisee and focus on supervisor competence, supervisor and supervisee experience and satisfaction, and supervision outcomes.

How long can I expect to take part in RSC? Will I "graduate" from it at some point?

Professional training in any field typically includes two types of experiences: didactic or direct teaching and applied practice with mentoring from someone who is more experienced. This supported practice is understood as the way that a learner successfully transfers knowledge to practice, and it is sometimes thought of as the difference between "knowing" and "doing" the work. Often, we may think of this type of coaching, mentoring, or clinical supervision as time limited or perhaps no longer needed once one has attained an independent practice level. Because infant–early childhood professionals know there is always more to learn, and due to the expectation that RSC has some self-care benefits, professionals in the early childhood workforce are encouraged to engage in RSC throughout their careers. For those who pursue Endorsement, a credential in infant and early childhood mental health through the Alliance for Infant Mental Health (2018), RSC may be an initial requirement and an ongoing expectation, reflecting the value placed on RSC throughout one's career.

How can I prepare to benefit from RSC, or what is my role in RSC as a supervisee?

Participation in RSC requires some of the same actions that we ask of supervisors—consistent attendance, open stance, and active engagement. In fact, there may be a signed agreement outlining these and other expectations. Participants should come prepared to perform many of the same functions that we have described as key for practice with families and abbreviated as PAUSE, meaning Perceive, Ask, Understand, Strategize, and Evaluate. In addition to these basic strategies that we can "do," there are some other ways that supervisees can seek to "be" to get the most from RSC participation. Below, we rewrite the PAUSE acronym to review some best practices for recipients of RSC:

Be Prepared—think about what you may want to share in supervision/consultation about your experiences in the work and consider what questions you will bring to the session. The burden of planning and engaging in the session is to be shared between or co-constructed by the supervisees and the consultant. Expect and be ready to be an active contributor.

Be Assertive—Discuss your preferences for the structure and content of RSC sessions with the supervisor or consultant. Supervisors and consultants are encouraged to initiate conversations about diversity. If this conversation is not offered, it is recommended that the supervisee bring it up. If something is offered that isn't comfortable or culturally congruent for you, let the supervisor know. For example, some people are uncomfortable with centering activities that involve closing the eyes. Others may want to incorporate some movement, such as chair yoga or a walking practice. Use of creative activities and materials from the arts, such as poetry, writing, or visual art, may appeal to others. It is acceptable and encouraged for supervisees to let the consultant know what works for them.

Be Unbiased—Everyone has biases, so being totally unbiased is not really possible. We can, however, work toward awareness of our biases. Similarly, we can best engage in a reflective process that leads to growth when we are willing to "color outside the lines," to consider alternate perspectives and be able to tolerate uncertainty or "not knowing." Do your best to be honest and open regarding these sometimes uncomfortable moments.

Be Self-compassionate—RSC is a learning relationship, and that means that we don't know it all—and likely never will! Making mistakes is part of the process of our work and sometimes may lead to some of our most valuable learning. Similarly, in RSC sessions, as you share stories and experiences, it's helpful to consider what went well and to explore what you might choose to do differently next time. These "oops" moments are not shared to be judged, but are learned from with vulnerability, humility, and compassion for ourselves.

Be Engaged—Take an active role before, during, and after the session. This may include activating your reflective skills ahead of supervision/consultation as well as when you enter the space. During the session, stay present in order to consider your own responses to this work, taking care to attend to both thoughts and feelings. When your consultant or other group members offers a response or reflection, stay open to their contributions. As you exit a session, reflect on what you will take with you including how you may apply ideas that were shared and discussed.

You may find that participation in RSC is a developmental process, meaning that you participate in different ways over time. Carla Barron and colleagues (2022b) note that it takes time to become used to some RSC practices, such as adopting a stance of wondering and exploring thoughts and feelings versus seeking answers. The same researchers noted that for some workers, it may be that you are just as new to the work of home visiting as you are to RSC! Therefore, you may feel that it is hard to take a deep look at your work when you are just building your skill sets. Don't worry if it feels you are just scratching the surface; with practice, you will improve.

A Caveat: RSC will not fix all the things.

It is thought that RSC contains a self-care component. However, RSC, although a wonderful practice with many benefits, can only go so far in building skills and in contributing to the wellness of the early childhood workforce. In terms of growing your skills, there is still a place for other forms of professional development such as direct work experience, continuing education, or earning a degree. And although RSC has been shown to serve some wellness functions, it will not entirely replace other forms of self-care, including those that help with physical well-being (e.g., accessing concrete resources; nutrition, exercising, or getting enough sleep), mental well-being (e.g., personal therapy; stress reduction methods), or spiritual well-being (e.g., meditating or participating in a place of worship). In addition, we must acknowledge that there are very real, complex, and challenging structural factors in our agencies, communities, and our larger society that may affect the wellness of all of us. When informed by awareness of the reality of systemic racism and other forms of discrimination and improved by practices connected to cultural humility, participation in RSC can contribute to our efforts to manage our responses to these larger concerns.

PART 3: TAKING THE NEXT STEPS IN YOUR RSC AND WELLNESS JOURNEY

We hope that reading this supplement has helped you understand what RSC is and why and how it can help your practice. We also hope you understand that although there are some core components of RSC, there is no one-size-fits-all approach. Now, we invite you to consider your personal preferences and needs related to RSC and to use the RSC Preparation Worksheet (Form 1) to document your personal action plan.

FORM 1 (page 1 of 2)

RSC PREPARATION WORKSHEET

Name: _____ Date: _____

Reasons I want to access RSC:
- ❑ Gain/build skills partnering with families
- ❑ Explore my experiences working with young children and caregivers
- ❑ Improve my own emotional regulation
- ❑ Required to earn or maintain a credential
- ❑ Other: _____

RSC Structural Preferences:
- ❑ Format:
  - ○ Individual
  - ○ Group
  - ○ Combination
- ❑ Platform:
  - ○ In person
  - ○ Virtual
  - ○ Combination
- ❑ Periodicity
  - ○ Weekly
  - ○ Bi-weekly
  - ○ Monthly
- ❑ Timing
  - ○ 60 minutes
  - ○ 90 minutes
  - ○ Morning
  - ○ Midday
  - ○ Afternoon
  - ○ Evening
  - ○ Day(s) of the week preferred: _____
- ❑ Includes creative activities such as movement, art, or incorporates cultural practices
  - ○ What this looks like for me: _____
- ❑ Cost
  - ○ Provided by employer
  - ○ Personal professional development
- ❑ Rate I am able to pay: _____
- ❑ Other preferences: _____

(continued)

FORM 1 **RSC PREPARATION WORKSHEET** *(continued)*

Supervisor/Consultant qualities most important to me:
- ❏ Personal characteristics or identities (e.g., race, gender, age, language spoken)
- ❏ Other interpersonal characteristics (e.g., warmth, sense of humor, passion about the work)
- ❏ Credentials/qualifications (e.g., degrees, endorsements)
- ❏ Employment or field experiences (e.g., geographic location, agency based, private practice)

Strategies I will try:
- ❏ I will learn more about RSC by (e.g., reading, talking to colleagues, contacting my state infant mental health association).
- ❏ I will initiate a conversation with my supervisor consultant to discuss:
    1. Making some adjustments to my current supervision/consultation to be more reflective or better aligned with my personal needs.
    2. Getting support and buy-in for me to engage in RSC (e.g., protected time, funding)
- ❏ I will improve my own engagement in RSC sessions by:
    1. Protecting the time for meetings and attending regularly
    2. Taking steps to be fully present such as putting my phone on silent and avoiding multi-tasking during sessions
    3. Practicing active listening skills
    4. Other _____
- ❏ Other strategies: _____

Timeline for accessing RSC: _____

REFERENCES

Alliance for the Advancement of Infant Mental Health. (2018). *Best practice guidelines for reflective supervision/consultation.* www.allianceaimh.org/reflective-supervisionconsultation

Ash, J. (2010). *Reflective Supervision Rating Scale.* Unpublished measure.

Barron, C. C., Dayton, C. J., & Goletz, J. L. (2022a). From the voices of the supervisees: What is reflective supervision and how does it support their work (Part I). *Infant Mental Health Journal, 43,* 207–225.

Barron, C. C., Dayton, C. J., & Goletz, J. L. (2022b). From the voices of the supervisees: A theoretical model of reflective supervision (Part II). *Infant Mental Health Journal, 43,* 226–241.

Bernstein, V., & Edwards, R. C. (2012). Supporting early childhood practitioners through relationship-based, reflective supervision. *NHSA: Dialog A Research-to-Practice Journal for the Early Intervention Field, 15*(3), 286–301.

Bobes, T. (2017). A developmental model of personal and professional growth. In K. V. Hardy & T. Bobes (Eds.), *Promoting cultural sensitivity in supervision: A manual for practitioners* (pp. 15–20). Routledge.

Clark, R., Gehl, M., Heffron, M. C., Soliman, S., Shahmoon-Shanok, R., & Thomas, K. (2019). Mindful practices to enhance diversity-informed reflective supervision and leadership. *Zero to Three, 40*(2), 18–27.

Denmark, N., & Harden, B. J. (2012). Meeting the mental health needs of staff. In S. J. Summers & E. Chazan-Cohen (Eds.), *Understanding early childhood mental health: A practical guide for professionals* (pp. 217–226). Paul H. Brookes Publishing Co.

Eaves, T., Robinson, J. L., Brown, E., & Britner, P. (2022). Professional quality of life in home visitors: Core components of the reflective supervisory relationship and IMH-E® Endorsement engagement. *Infant Mental Health Journal, 43,* 242–255.

Fenichel, E. (1992). *Learning through supervision and mentorship to support the development of infants, toddlers and their families: A source book.* ZERO TO THREE Press/National Center for Clinical Infant Programs.

Ferguson, D., Smith, S., Granja, S., Nguyen, U. S., Berstein, J., Atkins, N., & Lasala, O. (2023). *Infant-early childhood mental health in home visiting programs serving diverse families: Promising strategies to support child and family well-being.* National Center for Children in Poverty, Bank Street Graduate School of Education. https://www.nccp.org/wp-content/uploads/2023/09/NCCP-HV-Report_FINAL.pdf.

Gallen, R. T., Ash, J., Smith, C., Franco, A., & Willford, J. A. (2016). How do I know that my supervision is reflective? Identifying factors and validity of the Reflective Supervision Rating Scale. *Zero to Three, 37*(2), 30–37.

Hardy, K. V. (2017). The Multicultural Relational Perspective Supervision Outcome Tools for Mental Health Professionals. In K. V. Hardy & T. Bobes (Eds.), *Promoting cultural sensitivity in supervision: A manual for practitioners* (pp. 117–132). Routledge.

Hause, N., & Lemoine, S. (2022). *Beyond reflection: Advancing reflective supervision/consultation (RS/C) to the next level: A professional innovations discussion paper.* ZERO TO THREE Press.

Heffron, M. C., Reynolds, D., & Talbot, B. (2016). Reflecting together: Reflective functioning as a focus for deepening group supervision. *Infant Mental Health Journal, 37*(6), 628–639.

Heller, S. S., & Ash, J. (2016). The Provider Reflective Process Assessment Scales (PRPAS): Taking a deep look into growing reflective capacity in early childhood providers. *Zero to Three, 37*(2), 22–29.

Hubel, G. S., Davies, F., Goodrum, N. M., Schmarder, K. M., Schnake, K., & Moreland, A. D. (2020). Adverse childhood experiences among early care and education teachers: Prevalence and association with observed quality of classroom social and emotional climate. *Children and Youth Services Review, 111.* https://doi.org/10.1016/j.childyouth.2020.104877

Huffhines, L., Herman, R., Silver, R. B., Low, C. M., Newland, R., & Parade, S. H. (2023). Reflective supervision and consultation and its impact within early childhood-serving programs: A systematic review. *Infant Mental Health Journal, 44*(6), 803–836. https://doi.org/10.1002/imhj.22079

Kwon, K., Ford, T. G., Salvatore, A., Randall, K., Jeon, L., Malek-Lasater, A., . . . Han, M. (2020). Neglected elements of a high-quality early childhood workforce: Whole teacher well-being and working conditions. *Early Childhood Education Journal,* 1–12.

McCormick, A., Eidson, F., & Harrison, M. (2019). Reflective consultation with groups via virtual technology: What is best practice? *Zero to Three, 40* (3), 64–71.

Noroña, C. Raskin, E., Flores, E, Fernandez-Pastrana, I., Anderson-Phou, S., & Saulnier, M. (2023). Diversity-informed reflective consultation and radical healing: A new paradigm for infant and early childhood mental health providers serving immigrant families. *Zero to Three, 43*(3), 33–54.

Pavkov, T. W., & Wells, L. (2023). The Relationship between reflective supervision/consultation and reduced burnout among early education professionals. *Zero to Three, 43*(4), 50–57. https://doi-org.proxy.ulib.uits.iu.edu/https://www.zerotothree.org/resources/zero-to-three-journal/zero-to-three-journal-archive/

Paradis, N., Johnson, K., & Richardson, Z. (2021). The value of reflective supervision/consultation in early childhood education. *Zero to Three, 41*(3), 68–75.

Ruprecht, K., Tomlin, A., Perkins, K. J., & Viehweg, S. (2020). Understanding secondary trauma and stress in the early childhood workforce. *Zero to Three, 40*(4), 41–50.

Shea, S. E., Goldberg, S., & Weatherston, D. J. (2016). A community mental health professional development model for the expansion of reflective practice and supervision: Evaluation of a pilot training series for infant mental health professionals. *Infant Mental Health Journal, 37*(6), 653–662.

Shea, S. E., Jester, J. M., Huth-Bocks, A. C., Weatherston, D. J., Muzik, M., & Rosenblum, K. L. (2020). Infant mental health home visiting therapists' reflective supervision self-efficacy in community practice settings. *Infant Mental Health Journal, 41*(2), 191–205.

Shahmoon-Shanok, R. (2006). Reflective supervision for an integrated model: What, why and how? In G. M. Foley & J. D. Hochman (Eds.), *Mental health in early intervention: Achieving unity in principles and practice* (pp. 343–382). Paul H. Brookes Publishing Co.

Shahmoon-Shanok R. (2009). What is reflective supervision? In S. S. Heller & L. Gilkerson (Eds.), *A practical guide to reflective supervision* (pp. 7–23). ZERO TO THREE Press.

Simons, C., Jones Harden, B., Leed, K. A., & Tirrell-Corbin, C. (2022). Infant-toddler teachers' early adversity, current wellbeing, and engaged support of early learning. *Early Childhood Research Quarterly, 61,* 158–169.

Simpson, T. E., Robinson, J. L., & Brown, E. (2018). Is RS enough? An exploration of workforce perspectives. *Infant Mental Health Journal, 39*(4), 478–488.

Stroud, B. (2010). Honoring diversity through a deeper reflection: Increasing cultural understanding within the reflective supervision process. *Zero to Three, 31*(2), 46–50.

Subramaniam, A., & Oliveira, A. G. (2023). Breaking new ground Massachusetts' efforts to build diversity-informed, reflective, and relationship infant and early childhood systems. *Zero to Three, 43*(4), 21–26.

Susman-Stillman, A., Lim, S., Meuwissen, A., & Watson, C. (2020). Reflective supervision/consultation and early childhood professionals' well-being: A qualitative analysis of supervisors' perspectives. *Early Education and Development, 31*(7), 1151–1168.

Thomas, K., Noroña, C. R, & Seymour-St. John, M. (2019). Cross-sector allies together in the struggle for social justice: Diversity-informed tenets for work with infants, children, and families. *Zero to Three, 39*(3), 44–54.

Tomlin, A., & Heller, S. S. (2016). Measurement development in reflective supervision: History, methods, and next steps. *Zero to Three, 37*(2), 4–13.

Tomlin, A. M., Sturm, L., & Hines, E. (2016). Reflection in home visiting: The what, why and a beginning step toward how. *Infant Mental Health Journal, 37*(6), 617–627.

Tomlin, A. M., Weatherston, D. J., & Pavkov. T. (2016). Critical components of reflective supervision: Responses from expert supervisors in the field. *Infant Mental Health Journal, 35*(1), 70–80.

Virmani, A., & Ontai, L. L., (2010). Supervision and training in child care: Does reflective supervision foster caregiver insightfulness? *Infant Mental Health Journal, 31*(1), 16–32.

Watson, C., with Harris, M., Hennes, J., Harrison, M., & Meuwissen, A. (2022). *RIOS guide for reflective supervision and consultation in the infant and early childhood field.* ZERO TO THREE Press.

Watson, C., Neilsen, G. S., Cox, M., Harrison, M., & Hennes, J. (2014). Reflective supervision and its impact on early childhood intervention. *Early Childhood and Special Education: Vol 18. Advances in Early Education and Day Care.* Emerald Group.

West, A., Madariaga, P., & Sparr, M. (2022). *Reflective supervision: What we know and what we need to know to support and strengthen the home visiting workforce* (OPRE Report No. 2022-101). Office of Planning, Research, and Evaluation; Administration for Children and Families; U.S. Department of Health and Human Services.

Williams, M. E., Joyner, K., Matic, T., & Lakatos, P. P. (2019). RS: A quantitative program evaluation of a training program for infant and early childhood mental health supervisors. *The Clinical Supervisor, 38*(1), 158–181.

References

AAP Council on Early Childhood, AAP Committee on Psychosocial Aspects of Child and Family Health, AAP Section on Developmental and Behavioral Pediatrics. (2016). Addressing early childhood emotional and behavioral problems. *Pediatrics, 138*(6), e20163023.

Adams, D., Stainsby, M., & Paynter, J. (2021). Autistic Mothers of Autistic Children: A Preliminary Study in an Under-Researched Area. *Autism in adulthood: Challenges and management, 3*(4), 339–346. https://doi.org/10.1089/aut.2020.0078

Ainsworth, M. D. S. (1979). Infant–mother attachment. *American Psychologist, 34*(10), 932–937.

Aktar, E., Majdandzic, M., de Vente, W., & Bogels, S. M. (2014). Parental social anxiety disorder prospectively predicts toddlers' fear/avoidance in a social referencing paradigm. *Journal of Child Psychology and Psychiatry, 55*(1), 77–87.

Alink, L. R., Mesman, J., van Zeijl, J., Stolk, M. N., Juffer, F., Koot, H. M., Bakermans-Kranenburg, M. J., & van Ijzendoorn, M. H. (2006). The early childhood aggression curve: Development of physical aggression in 20- to 50-month-old children. *Child Development, 77*(4), 954–966.

Alliance for the Advancement of Infant Mental Health. (2018). *Best practice guidelines for reflective supervision/consultation.* www.allianceaimh.org/reflective-supervisionconsultation.

Alvarez, S. L., Meltzer-Brody, S., Mandel, M., & Beeber, L. (2015). Maternal depression and early intervention: A call for an integration of services. *Infants and Young Children, 28*(1), 72–87.

American Academy of Pediatrics Task Force on Sudden Infant Death Syndrome. (2011). SIDS and other sleep-related infant deaths. Expansion of recommendations for a safe infant sleep environment. *Pediatrics, 128*(5), 1030–1039.

American Academy of Sleep Medicine. (2014). *International classification of sleep disorders* (3rd ed.). American Academy of Sleep Medicine.

American Psychiatric Association. (2013). *Diagnostic and statistical manual of mental disorders* (5th ed.). Author.

American Psychiatric Association. (2022). *Diagnostic and statistical manual* (5th ed., text rev.). *(DSM-5-TR).* Author.

Bahtiyar-Saygan, B., & Berument, S. K. (2022). The role of temperament and parenting on anxiety problems among toddlers: Moderating role of parenting and mediating role of attachment. *Infant Mental Health Journal, 43*(4), 533–545.

Baldwin, H. A., Songer, N. S., & Ensher, G. L. (2009). The cycle of substance abuse. In G. L. Ensher, D. A. Clark, & N. S. Songer (Eds.), *Families, infants, and young children at risk: Pathways to best practice* (pp. 249–272). Paul H. Brookes Publishing Co.

Bandura, A. (1977). *Social learning theory.* General Learning Press.

Barak, A., Spielberger, J., & Gitlow, E. (2014). The challenge of relationships and fidelity: Home visitors' perspectives. *Children and Youth Services Review, 42*, 50–58.

Barker, D. (1998). In utero programming of chronic disease. *Clinical Science, 95*, 115–128.

Barker, L. H., & Berry, K. (2009). Developmental issues impacting military families with young children during single and multiple deployments. *Military Medicine, 174*, 1033–1040.

Barron, C. C., Dayton, C. J., & Goletz, J. L. (2022a). From the voices of the supervisees: What is reflective supervision and how does it support their work (Part I). *Infant Mental Health Journal, 43*, 207–225.

Barron, C. C., Dayton, C. J., & Goletz, J. L. (2022b). From the voices of the supervisees: A theoretical model of reflective supervision (Part II). *Infant Mental Health Journal, 43*, 226–241.

Bassani, D. G., Padoin, C. V., Philipp, D., & Veldhuizen, S. (2009). Estimating the number of children exposed to parental psychiatric disorders through a national health survey. *Child and Adolescent Psychiatry and Mental Health, 3*(6). doi:10.1186/1753-2000-3-6

Bassuk, E., DeCandia, C., Beach, C., & Berman, F. (2014). *America's youngest outcasts: A report card on child homelessness.* The National Center on Family Homelessness at American Institutes for Research. http://www.homelesschildrenamerica.org/mediadocs/280.pdf

Beauchamp, G. K., & Mennella, J. (2011). Flavor perception in human infants: Development and functional significance. *Digestion, 83* (Supplement 1), 1–6.

Beeber, L. S., & Canuso, R. (2012). Intervening with parents. In S. J. Summers & R. Chazan-Cohen (Eds.), *Understanding early childhood mental health: A practical guide for professionals* (pp. 159–177). Paul H. Brookes Publishing Co.

Belden, A., Thompson, N. R., & Luby, J. L. (2008). Temper tantrums in healthy versus depressed and disruptive preschoolers: Defining tantrum behaviors associated with clinical problems. *Journal of Pediatrics, 152*(1), 117–122.

Belli, A., Breda, M., di Maggio, C., Esposito, D., Marcucci, L., & Bruni, O. (2022). Children with neurodevelopmental disorders: How do they sleep? *Current Opinion in Psychiatry, 35*(5), 345–351.

Bernier, A., Carlson, S., & Whipple, N. (2010). From external regulation to self-regulation: Early parenting precursors of young children's executive functioning. *Child Development, 81*, 326–339.

Bernstein, V. J., & Edwards, R. C. (2012). Supporting early childhood practitioners through relationship-based, reflective supervision. *National Head Start Association Dialog, 15*(3), 286–301.

Biedzio, D., & Wakschlag, L. (2019). Developmental emergence of disruptive behaviors beginning in infancy: Delineating normal-abnormal boundaries to enhance early identification. In C. Zeanah (Ed.), *Handbook of Infant Mental Health* (2nd ed., pp. 407–425). Guilford Press.

Bishop, D. V. M., Snowling, M. J., Thompson, P. A., Greenhalgh, T., & CATALISE Consortium. (2016). CATALISE: A multinational and multidisciplinary Delphi consensus study. Identifying language impairments in children. *PLoS One, 11*(7). e0158753. 10.1371/journal.pone.0158753 [PubMed: 27392128]

Blanchard, S. B., Coard, S. I., Hardin, B. J., & Mereoiu, M. (2019). Use of parental racial socializations with African American toddler boys. *Journal of Child and Family Studies, 28*, 387–400.

Bocknek, E. L., Richardson, P. A., McGoron, L., Raveau, H., & Iruka, I. U. (2020). Adaptive parenting among low-income black mothers and toddlers' regulation of distress. *Child Development, 91*(6), 2178–2191. https://doi.org/10.1111/cdev.13461

Bonuck, K. A., Hyden, C., Ury, G., Barnett, J., Ashkinaze, H., & Briggs, R. D. (2011). Screening for sleep problems in early intervention and early childhood special education: A systematic review of screening and assessment instruments. *Infants and Young Children 24*(4), 295–308.

Bos, K. J., Fox, N., Zeanah, C. H., & Nelson, C. A. (2009). Effects of early psychosocial deprivation on the development of memory and executive function. *Frontiers in Behavioral Neuroscience, 3*, 16. https://doi.org/10.3389/neuro.08.016.2009

Bordin, E. S. (1979). The generalizability of the psychoanalytic concept of the Working Alliance. *Psychotherapy: Research, Theory, and Practice, 16*(3), 252–260.

Boris, N., Renk, K., Lowell, A., & Kolomeyer, E. (2019). Parental substance abuse. In C. H. Zeanah (Ed.), *Handbook of infant mental health* (4th ed., pp. 171–179). Guilford Press.

Borowitz, K. C., & Borowitz, S. M. (2018). Feeding problems in infants and children: Assessment and etiology, *Pediatric Clinics of North America, 65*, 59–72.

Bos, K. J., Fox, N. Zeanah, C. H., & Nelson, C. A. (2009). Effects of early psychosocial deprivation on the development of memory and executive function. *Frontiers in Behavioral Neuroscience, 3*(16), 1–7.

Bosk, E. A., Paris, R., Hanson, K. E., Ruisard, D., & Suchman, N. E. (2019). Innovations in child welfare for caregivers with substance use disorders and their children. *Child and Youth Services Review, 101,* 99–112.

Bourne, S. V., Korom, M., & Dozier, M. (2022). Consequences of inadequate caregiving for children's attachment, neurobiological development, and adaptive functioning. *Clinical Child and Family Psychology Review, 25,* 166–181.

Boursnell, M. (2014). Assessing the capacity of parents with mental illness: Parents with mental illness and risk. *International Social Work, 57*(2), 92–108.

Brandt, K. (2014). Transforming clinical practice through reflection work. In K. Brandt, B. D. Perry, S. Seligman, & E. Tronick (Eds.), *Infant and early childhood mental health: Core concepts and clinical practice* (pp. 293–307). American Psychiatric Publishing.

Brazelton, T. B., & Sparrow, J. (2006). *Touchpoints Birth to Three* (2nd ed.). De Capo Lifelong Books.

Bridgett, D. J., Oddi, K. B., Laake, L. M., Murdock, K. W., & Bachman, M. N. (2013). Integrating and differentiating aspects of self-regulation: Effortful control, executive functioning, and links to negative affectivity. *Emotion, 13*(1), 47–63.

Briggs-Gowan, M. J., Carter, A. S., & Ford, J. D. (2012). Parsing the effects violence exposure in early childhood: Modeling developmental pathways. *Journal of Pediatric Psychology, 37,* 11–22.

Bronfenbrenner, U. (2005). The bioecological theory of human development. In U. Bronfenbrenner (Ed.), *Making human beings human: Bioecological perspectives on human development* (pp. 3–15). Sage Publications Ltd.

Brooker, R. J., Buss, K. A., Lemery-Chalfant, K., Aksan, N., Davidson, R. J., & Goldsmith, H. H. (2013). The development of stranger fear in infancy and toddlerhood: Normative development, individual differences, antecedents, and outcomes. *Developmental Science, 16*(6), 864–878.

Brown, L. F., Pridham, K. A., & Brown, R. (2014). Sequential observation of infant regulated and dysregulated behavior following soothing and stimulating maternal behavior during feeding. *Pediatric Nursing, 19,* 139–148.

Brownell, C. A., Svetlova, M., Anderson, R., Nichols, S. R., & Drummond, J. (2013). Socialization of early prosocial behavior: Parents' talk about emotions is associated with sharing and helping in toddlers. *Infancy, 18*(1), 91–119.

Bruer, J. T., & Greenough, W. T. (2001). The subtle science of how experience affects the brain. In D. B. Bailey, J. T. Bruer, F. J. Symons, & J. W. Lichtman (Eds.), *Critical thinking about critical periods* (pp. 209–232). Paul H. Brookes Publishing Co.

Bruns, D. A., & Thompson, S. D. (2010). Feeding challenges in young children. *Infants and Young Children, 23*(2), 93–102.

Bryant-Waugh, R. (2019). Feeding and eating disorders in children. *Psychiatric Clinics of North America, 42,* 157–167.

Bull, M. J. (2014). Car safety seats and the First Steps provider. *UTS Training Times, 10*(2), 8–9. http://www.in.gov/fssa/files/TT_2014_2_May.pdf

Buss, K. (2011). Which fearful toddlers should we worry about? Context, fear, regulation, and anxiety risk. *Developmental Psychopathology, 47*(3), 804–819.

Callejas, E., Byrne, S., & Rodrigo, M. J. (2021). Parental self-regulation and the promotion of healthy routines in early childhood. *Journal of Child and Family Studies, 30,* 1791–1802.

Capacity Building Center for States. (2017). *Creating and sustaining cross-system collaboration to support families in child welfare with co-occurring issues: An administrator's handbook.* Children's Bureau, Administration for Children and Families, U.S. Department of Health and Human Services. https://capacity.childwelfare.gov/states/resources/creating-sustaining-administrator-handbook

Carbonneau, R., Vitaro, F., Brendgen, M., Boivin, M., & Tremblay, R. E. (2022). Early risk factors associated with preschool developmental patterns of single and co-occurrent disruptive behaviors in a population sample. *Developmental psychology, 58*(3), 438–452. https://doi.org/10.1037/dev0001295

Carolan, M. E., & Fishel, A. P. (2023). The early childhood workforce across disciplines: Incorporating experiences from health, child welfare, and education to build a sustainable workforce. *Zero to Three, 43*(3), 5–,13.

Charlot-Swilley, D., Condon, M. C., Rahman, T. (2022). At the feet of storytellers: Implications for practicing early relational health conversations. *Infant Ment Health Journal, 43*(3):373–389. doi: 10.1002/imhj.21981

Chess, S., & Thomas, A. (1996). *Temperament: Theory and practice.* Brunner/Mazel.

Child Trends Data Bank. (2019). *In 2017, the rate of children in foster care rose in 39 states.* https://www.childtrends.org/blog/2017-the-number-of-children-in-foster-care-rose-in-39-states

Clark, L. (2020). *SOS for parents: A practical guide for handling common everyday behavior problems* (5th ed.). SOS Programs and Parent Press.

Clarkson Freeman, P. A. (2014). Prevalence and relationship between adverse childhood experiences and child behavior among young children. *Infant Mental Health Journal, 35*(6), 544–554.

Cluxton-Keller, F., Burrell, L., Crowne, S. S., McFarlane, E., Tandon, S. D., Leaf, P. J., & Duggan, A. K. (2014). Maternal relationship insecurity and depressive symptoms as moderators of home visiting impacts on child outcomes. *Journal of Child and Family Studies, 23,* 1430–1443.

Coard, S. I. (2022). Race, discrimination, and racism as "growing points" for consideration: attachment theory and research with African American families. *Attachment & Human Development,* 24:3, 373–383, doi: 10.1080/14616734.2021.1976931

Cohen, J., & Scheeringa, M. (2009). Post-traumatic stress disorder diagnosis in children: Challenges and promises. *Dialogues in Clinical Neuroscience, 11*(1), 91–99.

Colonnesi, C., Napoleone, E., & Bogels, S. M. (2014). Positive and negative expressions of shyness in toddlers: Are they related to anxiety in the same way? *Journal of Personality and Social Psychology, 106*(4), 624–637.

Comer, J. S., Hong, N. Poznanski, B., Silva, K., & Wilson, M. (2019). Evidence base update on the treatment of early childhood anxiety and related problems. *Journal of Clinical Child & Adolescent Psychology, 48*(1), 1–15.

Condon, M. C., Charlot-Swilley, D., & Rahman, T. (2022). At the feet of storytellers: Equity in early relational health conversations. *Infant Mental Health Journal, 43*(3), 390–409. https://doi.org/10.1002/imhj.21979

Cook, F., Mensah, F., Bayer, J. K., & Hiscock, H. (2019). Prevalence, comorbidity and factors associated with sleeping, crying and feeding problems at 1 month of age: A community-based survey. *Journal of Paediatrics and Child Health, 55*(6), 644–651. https://doi.org/10.1111/jpc.14262

Coren, E., Ramsbotham, K., & Gschwandtner, M. (2018). Parent training interventions for parents with intellectual disability. *Cochrane Database Systematic Reviews, 7*(7), CDC007987.

Cozza, S. J., Guimond, J. M., McKibben, J. B. A., Chun, R. S., Arata-Maiers, T. L., Schneider, B., Maiers, A., Fullerton, C. S., & Ursano, R. J. (2010). Combat-injured service members and their families: The relationship of child distress and spouse-perceived family distress and disruption. *Journal of Traumatic Stress, 23,* 112–115.

Cprek, S. E., Williamson, L. H., McDaniel, H., Brase, R., & Williams, C. (2019). Adverse Childhood Experiences (ACEs) and risk of childhood delays in children ages 1–5. *Child and Adolescent Social Work* (37), 15–24. https://doi.org/10.1007/s10560-019-00622-x

Creech, S. K., Hadley, W., & Borsari, B. (2014). The impact of military deployment and reintegration on children and parenting: A systematic review. *Professional Psychology, Research and Practice, 45*(6), 452–464. https://doi.org/10.1037/a0035055

Curtis P. R., Kaiser, A. P., Estabrook, R., & Roberts, M. (2019). The longitudinal effects of early language intervention on children's problem behaviors. *Child Development, 90*(2), 576–592. 10.1111/ cdev.12942 [PubMed: 28872672]

Dahl, A., Satlof-Bedrick, E. S., Hammond, S. I., Drummond, J. K., Waugh, W. E., & Brownell, C. A. (2017). Explicit scaffolding increases simple helping in younger infants. *Developmental Psychology, 53*(3), 407–416.

Danis, B., Hill, C., & Wakschlag, L. (2009). In the eye of the beholder: Critical components of observation when assessing disruptive behaviors in young children. *Zero to Three, 29,* 24–30.

Daro, D.A., & Harding, K.A. (1999). Healthy Families America: Using research to enhance practice. *The Future of Children, 9,* 152–176.

Davis, E.P., & Thompson, R. (2014). Prenatal foundations: Fetal programming of health and development. *Zero to Three, 34*(4), 2–22.

De Beritto, T. V. (2020). Newborn sleep: Patterns, interventions, and outcomes. *Pediatric Annals, 49*(2), e82–e87. https://doi.org/10.3928/19382359-20200122-01

de Brito, J. N., Matsumoto, M., Bonilla, Z., Loth, K. A., Geppert, J., McCoy, M. B., & Stang, J. S. (2022). Identification of positive parenting practices among parents of young children living in low-income and racially, ethnically, and culturally diverse households. *Appetite* (178), Article 196281. https://doi.org/10.1016/j.appet.2022.106281

Denham, S. A., & Couchoud, E. A. (1990). Young preschoolers' understanding of emotions. *Child Study Journal, 20,* 171–192.

Denmark, N., & Jones Harden, B. (2012). Meeting the mental health needs of staff. In S. J. Summers & R. Chazan-Cohen (Eds.), *Understanding early childhood mental health: A practical guide for professionals* (pp. 217–226). Paul H. Brookes Publishing Co.

Denno, D.M., Carr, V., & Bell, S. H. (2010). *Addressing challenging behavior in early childhood settings: A teacher's guide.* Paul H. Brookes Publishing Co.

DiStefano, G., Gino, F., Pisano, G. P., & Staats, B. R. (2014). *Learning by thinking: Overcoming the bias for action through reflection.* Harvard Business School NOM Unit Working Paper No. 14-093; Harvard Business School Technology and Operations Management Unit Working Paper No. 14-093. http://dx.doi.org/10.2139/ssrn.2414478

Doiron, K. M., Stack, D. M., Dickson, D. J., Bouchard, S., & Serbin, L. A. (2022). Co-regulation and parenting stress over time in full-term, very low birthweight preterm, and psychosocially at-risk infant-mother dyads: Implications for fostering the development of healthy relationships. *Infant Behavior and Development, 68.* doi: 10.1016/j.infbeh.2022.101731

Dosman, C., & Gallagher, S. (2022). Parenting principles primer. *Paediatric Child Health, 27*(6), 327–332.

Dougherty, L. R., Smith, V. C., Bufferd, S. J., Stringaris, A., Leibenluft, E., Carlson, G. A., & Klein, D. N. (2013). Preschool irritability: Longitudinal associations with psychiatric disorders at age 6 and parental psychopathology. *Journal of the American Academy of Child and Adolescent Psychiatry, 52*(12), 1304–1313.

Dozier, M., & Bernard, K. (2019). *Coaching parents of vulnerable infants: The Attachment Biobehavioral Catch-up approach.* Guilford Press.

Duncan, A. F. (2023). Interventions for executive function in high-risk infants and toddlers. *Clinical Perinatology, 50,* 103–119.

Dunlap, G., Ostryn, C., & Fox, L. (2011). *Preventing the use of restraint and seclusion with young children: The role of effective, positive practices.* http://challengingbehavior.fmhi.usf.edu/do/resources/documents/brief_preventing.pdf

Durrant, J., & Ensom, R. (2012). Physical punishment of children: Lessons from 20 years of research. *Canadian Medical Association Journal, 1849*(12), 1373–1377.

Eaves, T., Robinson, J. L., Brown, E., & Britner, P. (2022). Professional quality of life in home visitors: Core components of the reflective supervisory relationship and IMH-E® Endorsement engagement. *Infant Mental Health Journal, 43,* 242–255.

Edelman, L. (2004). *A relationship-based approach to early intervention.* http://cacenter-ecmh.org/wp/wp-content/uploads/2012/03/relationship_based_approach.pdf

Edwards, N. (2018). *Early social-emotional development: Your guide to promoting children's positive behavior.* Paul H. Brookes Publishing Co.

Egan, S. Z., Pope, J., Moloney, M., Hoyne, C., & Beatty, C. (2021). Missing early care and education during the pandemic: The social and emotional impact of the COVID-19 crisis on young children. *Early Childhood Education Journal, 49,* 925–934.

Egger, H., & Angold, A. (2006). Common emotional and behavioral disorders in preschool children: Presentation, nosology, and epidemiology. *Journal of Child Psychology and Psychiatry, 47,* 313–337.

Ellwood, J., Draper-Rodi, J., & Carnes, D. (2020). Comparison of common interventions for the treatment of colic: A systematic review of reviews and guidelines. *British Medical Journal Open, 10*(2), e035405.

Ensher, G. L., & Clark, D. A. (2016). *Foundations for best practice with special children and their families*. ZERO TO THREE Press.

Ensher, G. L., & Clark, D. A. (2020). Relationships and interactions: Mental health strategies and solutions for infants, young children, and their families. In G. L. Ensher, D. A. Clark, & M. M. Luke (Eds.), *Mental health in the early years: Challenges and pathways to resilience* (pp. 109–118). Washington, DC: ZERO TO THREE.

Evanoo, G. (2007). Infant crying: A clinical conundrum. *Journal of Pediatric Health Care, 21*, 333–338.

Feldman, N., & Pattani, A. (2019). *Black mothers get less treatment for postpartum depression than other moms*. https://kffhealthnews.org/news/black-mothers-get-less-treatment-for-postpartum-depression-than-other-moms/

Felitti, V. J., Anda, R. F., Nordenberg, D., Williamson, D. F., Spitz, A. M., Edwards, V., Koss, M. P., & Marks, J. S. (1998). Relationship of childhood abuse and household dysfunction to many of the leading causes of death in adults. The Adverse Childhood Experiences (ACE) Study. *American Journal of Preventive Medicine, 14*(4), 245–258.

Fenichel, E. (Ed.). (1992). *Learning through supervision and mentorship to support the development of infants, toddlers, and their families: A source book*. ZERO TO THREE Press.

Ferguson, D., Smith, S., Granja, S., Nguyen, U. S., Berstein, J., Atkins, N., & Lasala, O. (2023). *Infant-early childhood mental health in home visiting programs serving diverse families: Promising strategies to support child and family well-being*. National Center for Children in Poverty, Bank Street Graduate School of Education. https://www.nccp.org/wp-content/uploads/2023/09/NCCP-HV-Report_FINAL.pdf.

Fleming, P. J., & Blair, P. S. (2015). Making informed choices on co-sleeping with your baby. *BMJ, 350*:h563. doi: http://dx.doi.org/10.1136/bmj.h563

Fonagy, P., Gergely, G., Jurist, E., & Target, M. (2002). *Affect regulation, mentalization, and the development of the self*. Other Books.

Fonagy, P., Steele, H., Steele, M., Leigh, T., Kennedy, R., Mattoon, G., & Target, M. (1995). Attachment, the reflective self, and borderline states: The predictive specificity of the Adult Attachment Interview and pathological emotional development. In S. Goldberg, R. Muir, & J. Kerr (Eds.), *Attachment theory: Social, developmental, and clinical perspectives* (pp. 233–278). Analytic Press.

Fonagy, P., & Target, M. (1998). Mentalization and the changing aims of child psychoanalysis. *Psychoanalytic Dialogues, 8*, 8–114.

Forman, D. (2007). Autonomy, compliance, and internalization. In C. A. Brownell & C. B. Kopp (Eds.), *Socioemotional development in the toddler years: Transitions and transformations* (pp. 285–319). Guilford Press.

Friedlander, M. L. (2014). Use of relational strategies to repair alliance ruptures: How responsive supervisors train responsive psychotherapists. *Psychotherapy, 52*(2), 174–179. http://dx.doi.org/10.1037/a0037044

Frosch, C., Mitchell, Y., Hardgraves, L., & Funk, S. (2019). Stress and coping among early childhood intervention professionals receiving reflective supervision: A qualitative analysis. *Infant Mental Health Journal, 40*(4), 443–458.

Garcia Coll, C., Crnic, K., Lamberty, G., Wasik, B. H., Jenkins, R., Garcia, H. V., & McAdoo, H. P. (1996). An integrative model for the study of developmental competencies in minority children. *Child Development, 67*, 1891–1914. https://doi.org/10.1111/j.1467-8624.1996.tb01834.x

García Marqués, S., Chillón Martínez, R., González Zapata, S., Rebollo Salas, M., & Jiménez Rejano, J. J. (2017). Tools assessment and diagnosis to infant colic: A systematic review. *Child: Care, Health and Development, 43*(4), 481–488. https://doi.org/10.1111/cch.12454

Garo, A., Giordano, K., Gubi, A., & Shortway, K. (2021). A consultation approach to target exclusionary discipline of students of color in early childhood education. *Contemporary School Psychology, 25*, 124–135.

Garon, N., Bryson, S. E., & Smith, I. M. (2008). Executive function in preschoolers: A review using an integrative framework. *Psychological Bulletin 134*(1), 31–60.

Geppert, U. (1986). *A coding system for analyzing behavioral expression of self evaluative emotions*. Max Planck Institute for Psychological Research.

Ghosh Ippen, C. M. (2018). Wounds from the past: Integrating historical trauma into a multicultural infant mental health framework. In C. Zeanah (Ed.), *Handbook of infant mental health* (4th ed., pp. 134–153). Guilford Press.

Gilkerson, L., Burkhardt, T., Katch, L. E., & Hans, S. L. (2020). Increasing parenting self-efficacy: The Fussy Baby Network intervention. *Infant Mental Health Journal*, 41(2), 232–245. https://doi.org/10.1002/imhj.21836

Gilkerson, L., & Gray, L. (2014). Fussy babies: Early challenges in regulation, impact on the dyad and family, and longer-term implications. In K. Brandt, B. D. Perry, S. Seligman, & E. Tronick (Eds.), *Infant and early childhood mental health: Core concepts and clinical practice* (pp. 195–208). American Psychiatric Publishing.

Gilliam, W. S., Maupin, A. N., Reyes, C. R., Accavitti, M., & Shic, F. (2016). *Do early educators' implicit biases regarding sex and race relate to behavior expectations and recommendations of preschool expulsions and suspensions.* Yale Child Study Center. https://www.jsums.edu/scholars/files/2017/03/Preschool-Implicit-Bias-Policy-Brief_final_9_26_276766_5379.pdf

Glaze, L. E., & Maruschak, L. M. (2008). *Parents in prison and their minor children.* Bureau of Justice Statistics Special Report. http://www.bjs.gov/content/pub/pdf/pptmc.pdf

Gomby, D. S., Larson, C. S., Lewit, E. M., & Behrman, R. E. (1993). Home visiting: Analysis and recommendations. *The Future of Children*, 3(3), 6–22.

Goodlin-Jones, B. L., Sitnick, S. L., Tang, K., Liu, J., & Anders, T. F. (2008). The Children's Sleep Habits Questionnaire in toddlers and preschool children. *Journal of Developmental and Behavioral Pediatrics*, 29(2), 82–88.

Gopalkrishnan, N., & Babacon, H. (2015). Cultural diversity and mental health. *Australian Psychiatry*, 23(6), 6–8.

Gopnik, A. (2010). How babies think. *Scientific American*, 303, 76–81.

Gopnik, A., Slaughter, V., & Meltzoff, A. (1994). Changing your views: How understanding visual perception can lead to a new theory of the mind. In C. Lewis & P. Mitchell (Eds.), *Children's early understanding of the mind: Early developments* (pp. 157–181). Lawrence Erlbaum.

Gottman, J. M. (1991). Chaos and regulated change in families: A metaphor for the study of transitions. In P. A. Cowan & M. Hetherington (Eds.), *Family transitions* (pp. 247–272). Lawrence Erlbaum.

Grady, J. S., & Karraker, K. (2014). Do maternal warm and encouraging statements reduce shy toddler's social reticence? *Infant and Child Development*, 23, 295–303.

Grady, J. S., Stoltzfus, J., Karraker, K., & Metzger, A. (2012). Shyness trajectories in slow-to-warm infants: Relationship with child sex and maternal parenting. *Journal of Applied Developmental Psychology*, 33(2), 91–101.

Green, M., & Palfrey, J. (2000). *Bright futures: Guidelines for health supervision of infants, children, and adolescents.* Georgetown University Press.

Guardino, C. M., & Schetter, C. D. (2014). Coping during pregnancy: A systematic review and recommendations. *Health Psychology Review*, 8(1), 70–94.

Guralnick, M. J. (2001). Connections between developmental science and intervention science. *Zero to Three*, 21(5), 24–29.

Guyon-Harris, K. L., Humphreys, K. L., & Zeanah, C. H. (2021). Adverse caregiving in early life: The trauma and deprivation distinction in young children. *Infant Mental Health Journal*, 42(1), 87–95. https://doi.org/10.1002/imhj.21892

Hackshaw, A., Rodeck, C., & Boniface, S. (2011). Maternal smoking in pregnancy and birth defects: A systematic review based on 173,687 malformed cases and 11.7 million controls. *Human Reproduction Update*, 17, 589–604.

Hardy, K. V. (2016). Mastering content talk: Practical skills for effective engagement. In K. V. Hardy & T. Bobes (Eds.), *Culturally sensitive supervision and training: Diverse Perspectives and Practical Applications.* Routledge.

Harris, Y. R., Harris, V., Graham, J. A., & Carpenter, G. J. O. (2010). The challenges of family reunification. In Y. R. Harris, J. A. Graham, & G. J. Oliver Carpenter (Eds.), *Children of incarcerated parents: Theoretical, developmental and clinical issues* (pp. 255–275). Springer.

Harrison, M. (2016). Release, reframe, refocus, and respond: A practitioner transformation process in a reflective consultation program. *Infant Mental Health Journal*, 37(6), 670–683.

Hause, N. & LeMoine, S. (2022). *Beyond reflection: Advancing reflective supervision/consultation (RS/C) to the next level.* (Professional innovations discussion paper). ZERO TO THREE Press.

Hay, D. F., & Cook, K. V. (2007). The transformation of prosocial behavior from infancy to childhood. In C. A. Brownell & C. B. Kopp (Eds.), *Socioemotional development in the toddler years: Transitions and transformations* (pp. 100–132). Guilford Press.

Hayashi, K., Matsuda, Y., Kawamichi, Y., Shiozaki, A., & Saito, S. (2011). Smoking during pregnancy increases risks of various obstetric complications: A case cohort study of the Japan Perinatal Registry Network database. *Journal of Epidemiology, 21*, 61–66.

Heatherington, L., Friedlander, M. L., & Diamond, G. (2014). Lessons offered, lessons learned: Reflections on how doing family therapy can affect therapists. *Journal of Clinical Psychology, 70*(8), 760–767.

Heffron, M. C., & Murch, T. (2010). *Reflective supervision and leadership in infant and early childhood programs*. ZERO TO THREE Press.

Heffron, M. C., Ivins, B., & Weston, D. R. (2005). Finding an authentic voice—Use of self: Essential learning processes for relationship-based work. *Infants and Young Children, 18*(4), 323–336.

Helbig, K. A., Wright, S. Derieux, J. R., Schreiber, S. R., & Radley, K. C. (2019). Behavioral interventions. In K. C. Radley & E. H. Dart (Eds.), *Handbook of behavioral interventions in schools: Multi-tiered systems of support*, pp. 14–28. Oxford University Press.

Helseth, S., Misvaer, N., Smastuen, M., Andenaes, R., & Valla, L. (2022). Infant colic, young children's temperament and sleep in a population based longitudinal cohort study. *BMC Pediatrics, 22*(163). https://doi.org/10.1186/s12887-022-03231-3

Henderson, J. M., France, K. G., Owens, J. L., & Blampied, N. M. (2010). Sleeping through the night: Consolidation of self-regulated sleep across the first year of life. *Pediatrics, 126*(5), e1081–1087. doi:10.1542/peds.2010-6875d

Hill, L., Ndugga, N., & Artiga, S. (2023). *Key data on health and health care by race and ethnicity*. KFF. https://www.kff.org/racial-equity-and-health-policy/report/key-data-on-health-and-health-care-by-race-and-ethnicity

Hirshkowitz, M., Whiton, K., Albert, S. M., Alessi, C., Bruni, O., DonCarlos, L., Hazen, N., Herman, J., Katz, E. S., Kheirandish-Gozal, L., Neubauer, D. N., O'Donnell, A. E., Ohayon, M., Peever, J., Rawding, R., Sachdeva, R. C., Setters, B., Vitiello, M. V., Ware, J. C., & Adams Hillard, P. J. (2015). National Sleep Foundation's sleep time duration recommendations: Methodology and results summary. *Sleep Health, 1*(1), 40–43.

Hu, K., & Staiano. A. E. (2022). Trends in obesity prevalence among children and adolescents aged 2 to 19 years in the US from 2011 to 2020. *JAMA Pediatrics, 176*(10), 1037–1039.

Hubel, G. S., Davies, F., Goodrum, N. M., Schmarder, K. M., Schnake, K., & Moreland, A. D. (2020). Adverse childhood experiences among early care and education teachers: Prevalence and association with observed quality of classroom social and emotional climate. *Children and Youth Services Review, 111*. https://doi.org/10.1016/j.childyouth.2020.104877

Huffhines, L., Herman, R., Silver, R. B., Low, C. M., Newland, R., & Parade, S. H. (2023). Reflective supervision and consultation and its impact within early childhood-serving programs: A systematic review. *Infant Mental Health Journal, 44*(6), 803–836. https://doi.org/10.1002/imhj.22079

Hughes, C., Foley, S., Browne, W., McHarg, G., & Devine, R. (2023). Developmental links between executive function and emotion regulation in early toddlerhood. *Infant Behavior and Development, 71*. https://doi.org/10.1016/j.infbeh.2022.101782

Individuals with Disabilities Education Improvement Act (IDEA) of 2004, PL 108-446, 20 U.S.C. §§ 1400 *et seq.*

Jeong, J., Franchett, E. E., Ramos de Oliveira, C. C., Rehmank, K., & Yousafzai, A. K. (2021). Parenting interventions to promote early child development in the first three years of life: A global systematic review and meta-analysis. *PLoS Medicine, 18*(5), e1003602. doi: 10.1371/journal.pmed.1003602

Jessen-Howard, S., & Workman, S. (2020). *Coronavirus pandemic could lead to permanent loss of nearly 4.5 million childcare slots*. Center for American Progress. https://www.americanprogress.org/issues/earlychildhood/news/2020/04/24/483817/coronavirus-pandemic-lead-permanent-loss-nearly4-5-million-child-care-slots

Jones Harden, B. (2010). Home visitation with psychologically vulnerable families: Developments in the profession and in the professional. *Zero to Three, 30*(6), 44–51.

Jones Harden, B., Denmark, N., Holmes, A., & Duchene, M. (2014). Detached parenting and toddler problem behavior in Early Head Start families. *Infant Mental Health Journal, 35*(6), 529–543.

Jones Harden, B., Denmark, N., & Saul, D. (2010). Understanding the needs of staff in Head Start programs: The characteristics, perceptions, and experiences of home visitors. *Children and Youth Services Review, 32*, 371–379.

Jones Harden, B., & Lythcott, M. (2005). Kitchen therapy and beyond: Mental health services for young children in alternative settings. In K. M. Finello (Ed.), *The handbook of training and practice in infant and preschool mental health* (pp. 256–286). Jossey-Bass

Joseph, H. M., Lorenzo, N. E., Fisher, N., Novick, D. R., Gibson, C. Rothenberger, S. D., Foust, J. E., & Chronis-Tuscano, A. (2023). Research review: A systematic review and meta-analysis of infant and toddler temperament as predictors of childhood attention-deficit/hyperactivity disorder. *Journal of Child Psychology and Psychiatry, 64*(5), 715–735.

Kagan, J., Reznick, J. S., & Gibbons, J. (1989). Inhibited and uninhibited types of children. *Child Development, 60,* 838–845.

Kaiser Family Foundation (KFF). (2023). *Latest federal data show that young people are more likely than older adults to be experiencing symptoms of anxiety or depression.* KFF. https://www.kff.org/mental-health/press-release/latest-federal-data-show-that-young-people-are-more-likely-than-older-adults-to-be-experiencing-symptoms-of-anxiety-or-depression

Kaley, F., Reid, V., & Flynn, E. (2011). The psychology of infant colic: A review of current research. *Infant Mental Health Journal, 32*(5), 526–541.

Karp, S. M., & Lutenbacher, M. (2011). Infant feeding practices of young mothers. *Maternal Child Nursing, 36*(2), 98–103.

Keiley, M. K., Howe, T., Dodge, K., Bates, J., & Pettit, G. (2001). Timing of abuse: Group differences and developmental trajectories. *Development and Psychopathology, 13,* 891–912.

Kelly, R. J., Marks, B. T., & El-Sheikh, M. (2014). Longitudinal relations between parent–child conflict and children's adjustment: The role of children's sleep. *Journal of Abnormal Child Psychology, 42,* 1175–1185.

Keren, M. (2023). Inhibition to novelty disorder: Ignes, 1 year 11 months old. In K. Mulrooney, M. Keren, & J. D. Osofsky (Eds.), *DC:0-5 casebook* (pp. 82–89). ZERO TO THREE Press.

Keren, M., Hopp, D., & Tyano, S. (2018). *Does time heal all? Exploring mental health in the first 3 years.* ZERO TO THREE Press.

Kerns, C. E., Pincus, D. B., McLaughlin, K. A., & Comer, J. S. (2017). Maternal emotion regulation during child distress, child anxiety accommodation, and links between maternal and child anxiety, *Journal of Anxiety Disorders, 50,* 52–59.

Kim, S. Y., Schwartz, S. J., Perreira, K. M., & Juang, L. P. (2018). Culture's influence on stressors, parental socialization, and developmental processes in the mental health of children of immigrants. *Annual Review of Clinical Psychology, 14,* 343–347.

Kirshbaum, M., & Olkin, R. (2002). Parents with physical, systemic, or visual disabilities. *Sexuality and Disabilities, 20*(1), 65–80.

Kleinmann, A.E., & Songer, N. S. (2009). Parents with developmental disabilities caring for infants and young children. In G. L. Ensher, D. A. Clark, & N. S. Songer (Eds.), *Families, infants, and young children at risk: Pathways to best practice* (pp. 287–315). Paul H. Brookes Publishing Co.

Knitzer, J., Theberge, S., & Johnson, K. (2008). *Reducing maternal depression and its impact on young children: Toward a responsive early childhood policy framework.* http://www.nccp.org/publications/pdf/text_791.pdf

Knoche, L. I., Kuhn, M., & Eum, J. (2013). "More time. More showing. More helping. That's how it sticks": The perspectives of early childhood coaches. *Infants and Young Children, 26*(4), 349–365.

Kochanska, G. (2002). Committed compliance, moral self, and internalization: A mediational model. *Developmental Psychology, 38*(3), 339–351.

Kochanska, G., Coy, K. C., & Murray, K. T. (2001). The development of self-regulation in the first 4 years. *Child Development, 72,* 1091–1111.

Kochanska, G., Koenig, J. Barry, R., Kim, S. & Yoon, J. (2010). Children's conscience during toddler and preschool years, moral self, and a competent, adaptive developmental trajectory. *Developmental Psychology, 46,* 1320–1332.

Kohlhoff, J., Morgan, S., Briggs, N., Egan, R., & Niec, L. (2021). Parent–child interaction therapy with toddlers: A community-based randomized controlled trial with children aged 14–24 months. *Journal of Clinical Child and Adolescent Psychology, 50*(3), 411–426. https://doi.org/10.1080/15374416.2020.1723599

Krishna, J., Kalra, M., & McQuillan, M. E. (2023). Sleep disorders in childhood. *Pediatrics in Review, 44*(4), 189–202.

Krumm, S., Becker, T., & Wiegand-Grefe, C. (2013). Mental health services for parents affected by mental illness. *Current Opinion in Psychiatry, 26*(4), 362–368.

Kuhns, C., & Cabrera, N. J. (2019). Low-income Latino mothers' and fathers' control strategies and toddler compliance. *Journal of Latinx Psychology, 8*(3), 221–237.

Laible, D. J., & Thompson, R. (2002). Mother–child conflict in the toddler years: Lessons in emotion, morality and relationship. *Child Development, 73*(4), 1187–1203.

Landy, S. (2009). *Pathways to competence: Encouraging healthy social and emotional development in young children* (2nd ed.). Paul H. Brookes Publishing Co.

Landy, S., & Menna, R. (2006). *Early intervention with multi-risk families: An integrative approach.* Paul H. Brookes Publishing Co.

Lansford, J. E. (2022). Annual research review: Cross-cultural similarities and differences in parenting. *Journal of Child Psychology and Psychiatry, 63*(4), 480–483.

Larzele, R. E. Ritchie, K. L., Knowles, S. J. Curtis, J., Lin, H., Oliver, M. G., Bigler, J. F., & Larzelere, W. A. (2023). Immediate and longer-term effects of modeling desired behavior and collaborating when toddlers are non-compliant. *Journal of Child and Family Studies, 32,* 2063–2082.

Lee, E., Esaki, N., Jeehoon, K., Greene, R., Kirkland, K., & Mitchell-Herzfeld, S. (2013). Organizational climate and burnout among home visitors: Testing mediating effects of empowerment. *Children and Youth Services Review, 35,* 594–602.

Leitjen, P., Gardner, F., Melendez-Torres, G. J., Knerr, W., & Overbeek, G. (2019). Parenting behaviors that shape child compliance: A multilevel meta-analysis. *PLoS ONE, 13*(10), e0204929. https://doi.org/10.1371/journal.pone.0204929

Lieberman, A., Ghosh Ippen, C., & Van Horn, P. (2015). *Don't hit my mommy* (2nd ed.). ZERO TO THREE Press.

Lieberman, A., & Van Horn, P. (2008). *Psychotherapy with infants and young children: Repairing the effects of stress and trauma on early attachment.* Guilford Press.

Lieberman, A., & Van Horn, P. (2013). Infants and young children in military families: A conceptual model for intervention. *Clinical Child and Family Psychology Review, 16,* 282–293.

Lieberman, A. F., Chu, A., Van Horn, P., & Harris, W. W. (2011). Trauma in early childhood: Empirical evidence and clinical implications. *Development and Psychopathology, 23*(2), 397–410.

Lieberman, A. F., Compton, N. C., Van Horn, P., & Ghosh Ippen, C. (2003). *Losing a parent to death in the early years: Guidelines for the treatment of traumatic bereavement in infancy and early childhood.* ZERO TO THREE Press.

Lingas, K. A. (2022). Mind the gap(s): Reflective supervision/consultation as a mechanism for addressing implicit bias and reducing our knowledge gaps. *Infant Mental Health Journal, 43,* 638–652.

Livas-Dlott, A., Fuller, B., Stein, G. L., Bridges, M., Mangual Figeuroa, A., & Mireles, L. (2010). Commands, competence, and cariño: Maternal socialization practices in Mexican American families. *Developmental Psychology, 46*(3), 566–578.

Lowell, A. F., Peacock-Chambers, E., Zayde, A., DeCoste, C. L., McMahon. T. J., & Suchman, N. E. (2021). Mothering from the inside out: Addressing the intersection of addiction, adversity, and attachment with evidence-based parenting intervention. *Current Addition Reports. 8,* 605–615.

Luke, M. M. (2020). Imperatives in today's world. In G. L. Ensher, D. A. Clark, & M. M. Luke (Eds.), *Mental health in the early years: Challenges and pathways to resilience* (pp. 19–36). ZERO TO THREE Press.

MacMillan Uribe, A. L., Rudt, H. G., & Leak, T. M. (2022). Cultural influences on infant and toddler feeding among low-income Latinx mothers. *Maternal and Child Nutrition, 18*(4), e13342. https://doi.org/10.1111/mcn.13342

Magee, C. A., Gordon, R., & Caputi, P. (2014). Distinct developmental trends in sleep duration during early childhood. *Pediatrics, 133,* e1561–1566. doi: 10.1542/peds.2013-3806

Mai, T., Fatheree, N. Y., Gleason, W., Liu, Y., & Rhoads, J. M. (2018). Infantile colic: New Insights into an old problem. *Gastroenterology Clinics of North America, 47*(4), 829–844. https://doi.org/10.1016/j.gtc.2018.07.008

Main, M. (1996). Introduction to the Special Section of attachment and psychopathology: Part 2, An overview of the field of attachment. *Journal of Consulting and Clinical Psychology, 64*(2), 237–243.

Malik, N. (2012). The challenging child: Emotional dysregulation and aggression. In S. J. Summers & R. Chazan-Cohen (Eds.), *Understanding early childhood mental health: A practical guide for professionals* (pp. 25–39). Paul H. Brookes Publishing Co.

Mann, K., Gordon, J., & MacLeod, A. (2009). Reflection and reflective practice in health professions education. *Advances in Health Science Education, 14*, 595–621.

Manning, B. L., Roberts, M. Y., Estabrook, R., Petitclerc, A., Burns, J. L., Briggs-Gowan, M., Wakschlag, L. S., & Norton, E. S. (2019). Relations between toddler expressive language and temper tantrums in a community sample. *Journal of Applied Developmental Psychology, 65*, 101070. https://doi.org/10.1016/j.appdev.2019.101070.

Marshall, J., Kihlstrom, L., Buri, A., Chandran, V., Prieto, C., Stein-Elgar, R. Koeut-Futch, K., Parish, A., & Hood, K. (2020). Statewide implementation of virtual perinatal home visiting during COVID-19. *Maternal and Child Health Journal, 24*(10), 1224-1230.

Martin, S. E., Boekamp, J. R., McConville, D. W., & Wheeler, E. E. (2010). Anger and sadness perception in clinically referred preschoolers: Emotion processes and externalizing behavior symptoms. *Child Psychiatry and Human Development, 41*, 30–46.

Martinez-Torteya, C., D'Amico, J., & Gilchrist, M. (2018). Trauma exposure: Consequences to maternal and offspring stress systems. In M. Muzik & K. L. Rosenblum (Eds.), *Motherhood in the face of trauma: Pathways towards healing and growth* (pp. 85–98). Springer.

Maslach, C., Schaufeli, W. B., & Leiter, M. P. (2001). Job burnout. *Annual Review of Psychology, 52*(1), 397.

Maxted, A. E., Dickstein, S., Miller-Loncar, C., High, P., Spritz, B., & Liu, J. (2005). Infant colic and maternal depression. *Infant Mental Health Journal, 26*(1), 56–68.

McAllister, C. L., & Thomas, T. (2007). Infant mental health and family support: Contributions of Early Head Start to an integrated model for community-based early childhood programs. *Infant Mental Health Journal, 28*(2), 192–215.

McClelland, M. M., & Tominey, S. L. (2014). The development of self-regulation and executive function in young children. *Zero to Three, 35*(2), 2–8.

McDermott, J. M., & Fox, N. A. (2019). Emerging executive functions in early childhood. In C. Zeanah (Ed.), *Handbook of Infant Mental Health* (2nd ed., pp. 120–133). Guilford Press.

McGuigan, W. M., Katzev, A. R., & Pratt, C. C. (2003). Multi-level determinants of mothers' engagement in home visiting services. *Family Relations, 52*(3), 271–278.

McKelvey, L. M., Edge, N. C., Messman, G. R., Whiteside-Mansell, L., & Bradley, R. H. (2018). Adverse experiences in infancy and toddlerhood; Relations to adaptive behavior and academic status in middle childhood. *Child Abuse and Neglect, 82*, 168–177.

McKenna, J., & McDade, T. (2005). Why babies should never sleep alone: A review of the co-sleeping controversy in relation to SIDS, bed sharing, and breast feeding. *Paediatric Respiratory Reviews, 6*, 134–152.

McNeil, C. B., & Hembree-Kigin, T. L. (2010). *Parent–child interaction therapy* (2nd ed.). Springer.

Meltzer, L. J., & Mindell, J. A. (2014). Systematic review and meta-analysis of behavioral interventions for pediatric insomnia. *Journal of Pediatric Psychology, 39*, 932–948.

Mena, K. C., & Bailey, J. D. (2007). The effects of the supervisory working alliance on worker outcomes. *Journal of Social Service Research, 34*(1), 55–65.

Mence, M., Hawes, D. J., Wedgewood, L., Morgan, S., Barnett, B., Kohlhoff, J., & Hunt, C. (2014). Emotional flooding and hostile discipline in the families of toddlers with disruptive behavior problems. *Journal of Family Psychology, 28*(1), 12–21.

Mendez-Miller, M., Naccarato, J., & Radico, J. A. (2022). Borderline Personality Disorder. *American Family Physician, 105*(2), 156–161.

Merrick, M. T., Ford, D. C., Ports, K. A., Guinn, A. S., Chen, J., Klevens, J., Metzler, M., Jones, C. M., Simon, T. R., Daniel, V. M., Ottley, P., & Mercy, J. A. (2019). Vital signs; Estimated proportion of adult health problems attributable to adverse childhood experiences and implications for prevention—25 states, 2015–2017. *Morbidity and Mortality Weekly Report, 68*(44), 999–1005.

Mills, A., Schmied, V., Taylor, C., Dahlen, H., Schuiringa, W., & Hudson, M. E. (2012). Connecting, learning, leaving: Supporting young parents in the community. *Health and Social Care in the Community, 20*(6), 663–672.

Mindell, J. A., & Williamson, A. A. (2018). Benefits of a bedtime routine in young children: sleep, development, and beyond. *Sleep Medicine Reviews, 40*, 93–108.

Monahan, C. I., Beeber, L. S., & Jones Harden, B. (2012). Finding family strengths in the midst of adversity: Using risk and resilience models to promote mental health. In S. J. Summers & R. Chazan-Cohen (Eds.), *Understanding early childhood mental health: A practical guide for professionals* (pp. 59–78). Paul H. Brookes Publishing Co.

Mongeau, L. (2020). *Our fragile child care system may be about to shatter*. Retrieved from the Hechinger Report. https://hechingerreport.org/our-fragile-child-care-system-may-be-about-to-shatter

Murphy, E. S., & Lupfer, G. J. (2014). Basic principles of operant conditioning. In F. K. McSweeney & E. S. Murphy (Eds.), *The Wiley Blackwell handbook of operant and classical conditioning* (pp. 167–194). Wiley.

National Research Center for Parents with Disabilities. (2022). *Prevalence of parents with disabilities in the United States*. Brandeis University Press.

Neilsen Gatti, S., Watson, C., & Siegel, C. (2011). Step back and consider: Learning from reflective practice in infant mental health. *Young Exceptional Children, 14*(2), 32–45.

Nelson, C. A., Fox, N. A., & Zeanah, C. H. (2014). *Romania's abandoned children: Deprivation, brain development, and the struggle for recovery*. Harvard University Press.

Norman-Murch, T. (1996). Reflective supervision as a vehicle for individual and organizational development. *Zero to Three, 17*, 16–20.

Norman-Murch, T. (2005). Keeping our balance on a slippery slope: Training and supporting infant/family specialists within an organization context. *Infants and Young Children, 18*(4), 308–322.

Norman-Murch, T., & Ward, G. (1999). First steps in establishing reflective practice and supervision: Organizational issues and strategies. *Zero to Three, 20*(1), 10–14.

Noroña, C. R., Raskin, E., Flores, E., Fernandez-Pastrana, I., Anderson-Phou, S., & Saulnier, M. (2023). Diversity-informed reflective consultation and radical healing: A new paradigm for infant and early childhood mental health providers serving immigrant families. *Zero to Three, 43*(3), 33–54.

O'Donnell, K., Glover, V., Barker, E. D., & O'Connor, T. G. (2014). The persisting effect of maternal mood in pregnancy on childhood psychopathology. *Developmental Psychopathology, 26*(2), 393–403.

Ong, K. K., Emmett, P. M., Noble, S., Ness, A., & Dunger, A. (2006). Dietary energy intake at the age of 4 months predicts postnatal weight gain and childhood body mass index. *Pediatrics, 117*(3), 503–508. doi: 10.1542/peds.2005-1668

Osofsky, J. D. (2009). Perspectives on helping traumatized infants, young children, and their families. *Infant Mental Health Journal, 30*(6), 673–677.

Osofsky, J. D. (Ed.) (2011). *Clinical work with traumatized young children* (pp. 1–8). Guilford Press.

Osofsky, J. D. (2011). Introduction: Trauma through the eyes of a young child. In J. D. Osofsky, *Clinical work with traumatized young children* (pp. 1–7). Guilford Press.

Owens, J. A., & Dalzell, V. (2005). Use of the "BEARS" sleep screening tool in a pediatric residents' continuity clinic: A pilot study. *Journal of Developmental and Behavioral Pediatrics, 6*, 63–69. Patient Protection and Affordable Care Act of 2010, PL 111-148, 42 U.S.C. 18001.

Paradis, N., Johnson, K., & Richardson, Z. (2021). The value of reflective supervision/consultation in early childhood education. *Zero to Three, 41*(3), 68–75.

Parker, A. (2021). Reframing the narrative: Black maternal mental health and culturally meaningful support for wellness. *Infant Mental Health Journal, 42*, 502–516.

Paruthi, S., Brooks, L. J., D-Ambrosio, C., Hall, W. A., Kotagal, S., Lloyd, R. M., Malow, B. A., Maski, K., Nichols, C., Quan, S. F., Rosen, C. L., Troester, M. M., & Wise, M. S. (2016). Recommended amount of sleep for pediatric populations: A consensus statement of the American Academy of Sleep Medicine, *Journal of Clinical Sleep Medicine 12*(6), 785–786.

Patterson, G. R. (1982). *Coercive family process*. Castalia.

Pavkov, T. W., & Wells, L. (2023). The Relationship between reflective supervision/consultation and reduced burnout among early education professionals. *Zero to Three, 43*(4), 50–57. https://doi-org.proxy.ulib.uits.iu.edu/https://www.zerotothree.org/resources/zero-to-three-journal/zero-to-three-journal-archive/

Pavli, A., Theodoridou, M., & Maltezou, H. C. (2021). Post-COVID syndrome: Incidence, clinical spectrum, and challenges for primary healthcare professionals. *Archives of Medical Research, 52*(6), 575–581.

Pawl, J. (2000). The interpersonal center of the work that we do. *Zero to Three, 20*, 5–7.

Pawl, J., & St. John, M. (1998). *How you are is as important as what you do*. ZERO TO THREE Press/National Center for Clinical Infant Programs.

Perera, D. N., Short, L., & Fernbacher, S. (2014). "It's not that straightforward": When family support is challenging for mothers living with mental illness. *Psychiatric Rehabilitation Journal, 37*(3), 170–175.

Petfield, L., Startup, H., Droscher, H., & Cartwright-Hatton, S. (2015). Parenting in mothers with borderline personality disorder and impact on child outcomes. *Evidence Based Mental Health, 18*(3), 67–75.

Pew Research Center. (2020). *COVID 19: Effect on personal life.* https://www.pewresearch.org/pathways-2020/CVCHILDCARE/total_us_adults/us_adults

Pew Research Center. (2022). *COVID Pandemic pinches finances of America's lower- and middle-income families.* https://www.pewresearch.org/wp-content/uploads/sites/20/2022/04/PSDT_04.19.22_covid.finances_report.pdf

Poehlmann-Tynan, J. (2020). Reuniting young children with their incarcerated parents. *Zero to Three, 40*(4), 30–40.

Pohl, A. L., Crockford, S. K., Blakemore, M., Allison, C., & Baron-Cohen, S. (2020). A comparative study of autistic and non-autistic women's experience of motherhood. *Molecular Autism, 11*(1), 3. https://doi.org/10.1186/s13229-019-0304-2

Popp, T. K., & Wilcox, M. J. (2012). Capturing the complexity of parent–provider relationships in early intervention: The association with maternal responsivity and children's social-emotional development. *Infants and Young Children, 25*(3), 213–231.

Potegal, M., Kosorok, M. R., & Davidson, R. J. (2003). Temper tantrums in young children: 2. Tantrum duration and temporal organization. *Developmental and Behavioral Pediatrics, 24*(3), 148–154.

Price, S. K., & Masho, S. W. (2014). What does it mean when we screen? A closer examination of perinatal depression and psychosocial risk screening within one MCH home visiting program. *Maternal and Child Health Journal, 18*(4), 765–771.

Rader, N., & Zukow-Goldring, P. (2012). Caregivers' gestures direct infant attention during early word learning: The importance of dyadic synchrony. *Language Sciences, 34*(5), 559–568.

Ramchandani, P. G., Domoney, J., Sethna, V., Psychogiou, L., Vlachos, H., & Murray, L. (2013). Do early father–infant interactions predict the onset of externalizing behaviors in young children? Findings from a longitudinal cohort study. *Journal of Child Psychology and Psychiatry, 54*(1), 56–64.

Reschke, P. J., Fraser, A. M., Picket, J., Workman, K., Lehnardt, H., Stockdale, L. A., Padilla-Walker, L. M., Cox, K., Holmgren, H. G., Hagen, S., Summers, K., Clifford, B. N., Essig, L. W., & Coyne, S. M. (2023). Variability in infant helping and sharing behaviors across the second and third years of life: Differential roles of target and socialization. *Developmental Psychology, 59*(3), 524–537. https://doi.org/10.1037/dev0001441

Repachouli, B., & Gopnick, A. (1997). Early reasoning about desires: Evidence from 14- to 18-month-olds. *Developmental Psychology, 33*(1), 12–21.

Ribaudo, J., Lawler, J. M., Jester, J. M., Riggs, J., Erickson, N. L., Stacks, A. M., Brophy-Herb, H., Muzik, M., & Rosenblum, K. L. (2022). Maternal history of adverse experiences and posttraumatic stress disorder symptoms impact toddlers' early socioemotional wellbeing: The benefits of infant mental health-home visiting. *Frontiers in Psychology, 12,* 792989. https://doi.org/10.3389/fpsyg.2021.792989

Rice, K. F., & Groves, B. M. (2005). *Hope & healing: A caregiver's guide to helping young children affected by trauma.* ZERO TO THREE Press.

Riley, L. K., Rupert, J., & Boucher, O. (2018). Nutrition in toddlers. *American Family Physician, 98*(4), 227–233.

Riley, S., Brady, A. E., Goldberg, J., Jacobs, F., & Easterbrooks, M. A. (2008). Once the door closes: Understanding the parent–provider relationship. *Child and Youth Services Review, 30,* 597–612.

Roben, C. K. P., Cole, P. M., & Armstrong, L. M. (2013). Longitudinal relations among language skills, anger expression, and regulatory strategies in early childhood. *Child Development, 84*(3), 891–905.

Rodrigues, M., Silva, R., & Franco, M. (2023). COVID-19: Financial stress and well-being in families. *Journal of Family Issues, 44*(5), 1254–1275. https://doi.org/10.1177/0192513X211057009

Rodriguez, V. J., La Barrie, D. L., Zegarac, M. C., & Shaffer, A. (2023). A systematic review of parenting scales measurement invariance/equivalence of by race and ethnicity: Recommendations for inclusive parenting research. *Assessment, 30*(1), 22–36. https://doi-org.proxy.ulib.uits.iu.edu/10.1177/10731911211038630

Roell, T., & Neal-Barnett, A. (2021). A systematic review of the effect of parental adverse experiences in parenting and child psychopathology. *Journal of Child and Adolescent Trauma, 15*(1), 167–180.

Roggman, L., A., Cook, G. A., Innocenti, M. S., Jump Norman, V. K., Boyce, L. K., Olson, T. L, Christiansen, K., & Peterson, C. A. (2019). The Home Visit Rating Scales: Revised, restructured, and revalidated. *Infant Mental Health Journal, 40*, 315–330.

Roggman, L. A., Peterson, C., Cohen, R. C., Ispa, J., Decker, K. B., Hughes-Belding, K., Cook, G., & Vallotton, C. D. (2016). Preparing home visitors to partner with families of infants and toddlers. *Journal of Early Childhood Teacher Education, 37*, 301–313.

Romano, E., Baillargeon, R. H., & Cao, G. (2013). Hyperactive behaviors among 17-month-olds in a population cohort. *Infant Mental Health Journal, 34*(5), 406–416.

Romano, M., & Schnurr, M. (2022). Mind the gap: Strategies to bridge the research-to-practice divide in early intervention caregiver coaching practices. *Topics in Early Childhood Special Education, 42*(1), 64–76.

Rosenblum, K. L., Dayton, C. J., & Musik, M. (2019). Infant social and emotional development: Emerging competence in a relational context. In C. H. Zeanah (Ed.), *Handbook of infant mental health* (4th ed., pp. 95–119). Guilford Press.

Rothbart, M. K., & Bates, J. E. (2006). Temperament. In W. Damon & R. M. Lerner (Series Eds.) & N. Eisenberg (Vol. Ed.), *Handbook of child psychology: Vol. 3. Social, emotional, and personality development* (6th ed., pp. 99–166). Wiley.

Rothbart, M. K., & Posner, M. I. (2006). Temperament, attention, and developmental psychopathology. In C. Cicchetti & D. J. Cohen (Eds.), *Developmental psychopathology: Vol. 2. Developmental neuroscience* (2nd ed., pp. 465–501). Wiley.

Rowell, T., & Neal-Barnett, A. (2021). A systematic review of the effect of parental adverse childhood experiences on parenting and child psychopathology. *Journal of Child and Adolescent Trauma, 15*(1), 167–180. https://doi.org/10.1007/s40653-021-00400-x

Ryan, R., Martin, A., & Brookes-Gunn, J. (2006). Is one good parent good enough? Patterns of mother and father parenting and child cognitive outcomes at 24 and 36 months. *Parenting Science and Practice, 6*(2–3), 211–228.

Sadler, L. S., Slade, A., & Mayes, L. C. (2006). Minding the Baby: A mentalization based parenting program. In J. G. Allen & P. Fonagy (Eds.), *Handbook of mentalization-based treatment* (pp. 271–288). Wiley.

Sama-Miller, E., Akers, L., Mraz-Esposito, A., Zukiewicz, M. Avellar, S., Paulsell, D., & Del Gross, P. (2018). *Home visiting evidence of effectiveness review: Executive summary.* U.S. Department of Health and Human Services, Administration for Children and Families, Office of Planning, Research, and Education.

Samuels, J., Shinn, M., & Buckner, J. C. (2010). *Homeless children: Update on research, policy, programs, and opportunities.* Office of the Assistant Secretary for Planning and Evaluation, U.S. Department of Health and Human Resources.

Sattler, J. (1998). *Clinical and forensic interviewing of children and families: Guidelines for the mental health, education, pediatrics and child maltreatment fields.* Author.

Scarlett, H., Moirangthem, S., & van der Waerden, J. (2023). The impact of paternal mental illness on child development: An umbrella review of systematic reviews and meta-analysis. *European Child and Adolescent Psychiatry.* doi: 10.1007/s00787-023-02261-1.

Schafer, J. K. (2016). Personal characteristics of effective home visitors. *Journal of Social Sciences Research, 41*(1), 84–95.

Sciaraffa, M. A., Zeanah, P. D., & Zeanah, C. H. (2018). Understanding and promoting resilience in the contact of adverse childhood experiences. *Early Childhood Education Journal, 46*(3), 343–353

Scheeringa, M. (2004). Posttraumatic stress disorder. In R. DelCarmen-Wiggins & A. Carter (Eds.), *Handbook of infant, toddler, and preschool mental health assessment* (pp. 377–399). Oxford University Press.

Scheeringa, M., & Zeanah, C. (2001). A relational perspective on PTSD in early childhood. *Journal of Traumatic Stress, 14*, 799–815.

Schellinger, K., & Talmi, A. (2013). Off the charts? Considerations for interpreting parent reports of toddler hyperactivity. *Infant Mental Health Journal, 34*(5), 417–419.

Schilling, L., Spallek, J., Maul, H., Tallarek, M., & Schneider, S. (2021). Active and passive exposure to tobacco and e-cigarettes during pregnancy. *Maternal Child Health Journal, 25*(4), 656–665.

Schneider, J. L., & Iverson, J. M. (2021). Cascades in action: How the transition to walking shapes caregiver communication during everyday interactions. *Developmental Psychology, 58*(1), 1–16.

Schön, D. A. (1983). *The reflective practitioner.* Basic Books.

Schön, D. A. (1987). *Educating the reflective practitioner.* Jossey-Bass.

Seligman, S. (2014). Attachment, intersubjectivity, and mentalization within the experience of the child, the parent, and the provider. In K. Brandt, B. D. Perry, S. Seligman, & E. Tronick (Eds.), *Infant and early childhood mental health: Core concepts and clinical practice* (pp. 309–322). American Psychiatric Publishing.

Sethi, S. (2020). *CLASP.* https://www.clasp.org/publications/report/brief/advancing-racial-equity-maternal-mental-health-policy

Shahmoon-Shanok, R. (2006). Reflective supervision: Its meaning and significance for integrated practice. In G. M. Foley & J. D. Hochman (Eds.), *Mental health in early intervention: Achieving unity in principles and practice* (pp. 343–381). Paul H. Brookes Publishing Co.

Shahmoon-Shanok, R. (2010). What is reflective supervision? In S. Scott Heller & L. Gilkerson (Eds.), *A practical guide to reflective supervision* (pp. 7–24). ZERO TO THREE Press.

Sheridan, A., Murray, L., Cooper, P.J., Evangeli, M., Byram, V., & Halligan, S.L. (2013). A longitudinal study of child sleep in high and low risk families: Relationship to early maternal settling strategies and child psychological functioning. *Sleep Medicine, 14,* 266–273.

Shetty, J., Newton, A. T., & Reid, G. J. (2022). Parenting practices, bedtime routines, and consistency: Associations with pediatric sleep problems. *Journal of Pediatric Psychology, 47*(1), 49-58.

Shivers, E. M., Janssen, J. A., Subramaniam, A., Parker, A. L., Noroña, C. R., Lara, C., Best, D., Yazzie, D. A., Cimino, J., Kohchi, J., & Fitzgibbons, S. (2022). Digging deeper: De-colonizing our understanding and practice of reflective supervision through a racial equity lens: First-wave findings. Prepared by Indigo Cultural Center for the Alliance for the Advancement of Infant Mental Health. With funding from Perigee Fund. https://static1.squarespace.com/static/5884ec2a03596e667b2ec631/t/6410b334e4ab1e59d42eef25/1678816062872/22_29_digging+deeper+design+Final.pdf

Shonkoff, J., & Phillips, D. A. (2000). *From neurons to neighborhoods: The science of early childhood development.* National Academies Press.

Siegel, D. J. (2013). *Reflections on the mindful brain.* http://www.openground.com.au/OG-SITE-ARTICLES-2013/Siegel-article.pdf

Simpson, T. E., Robinson, J. L., & Brown, E. (2018). Is reflective supervision enough? An exploration of workforce perspectives. *Infant Mental Health Journal, 39*(4), 478–488.

Slade, A. (2005). Parental reflective functioning: An introduction. *Attachment and Human Development, 7*(3), 269–281.

Slade, A. (2007). Reflective parenting programs: Theory and development. *Psychoanalytic Inquiry: A Topical Journal for Mental Health Professionals, 26*(4), 640–657.

Slade, A., Sadler, L. S., Eaves, T., & Webb, D. L. (2023). *Enhancing attachment and reflective parenting in clinical practice: A Minding the Baby Approach.* Guildford.

Slomski, A. (2012). Chronic mental health issues in children now loom larger than physical problems. *Journal of the American Medical Association, 308*(3), 223–225.

Smith, L. E., Weinman, J., Yiend, J., & Rubin, J. (2020). Psychosocial factors affecting parental report of symptoms in children: A systematic review. *Psychosomatic medicine, 82*(2), 187–196. https://doi.org/10.1097/PSY.0000000000000767

Sparr, M., Morrison, C., Joraanstad, A. Cachat, P., & West, A. (2022). *Home visitor professional well-being: What it is and why it matters.* OPRE Report No. 2022-102. Office of Planning, Research, and Evaluation; Administration for Children and Families; U.S. Department of Health and Human Services.

St. James-Roberts, I., Sleep, J., Morris, S., Owen, C., & Gillham, P. (2001). Use of a behavioural programme in the first 3 months to prevent infant crying and sleeping problems. *Journal of Paediatrics and Child Health, 37,* 289–297.

Stacks, A. M., Jester, J. M., Wong, K., Huth-Bocks, A. Brophy-Murphy, H., Lawler, J., Ribaudo, J., Muzik, M., & Rosenblum, K. L. (2021). Infant mental health home visiting: Intervention dosage and therapist experience interact to support improvement in maternal reflective functioning. *Attachment & Human Development, 24*(2), 1–23.

Steele, M., Murphy, A., & Steele, H. (2015). The art and science of observation: Reflective functioning and therapeutic action. *Journal of Infant, Child, and Adolescent Psychotherapy*, 14(3), 216–231.

Substance Abuse and Mental Health Services Administration (SAMHSA). (2009). *Family psychoeducation: The evidence*. Rockville, MD: Center for Mental Health Services, Substance Abuse and Mental Health Services Administration, U.S. Department of Health and Human Services. Author.

Substance Abuse and Mental Health Services Administration (SAMHSA). (2021). *SAMHSA announces national survey on drug use and health (NSDUH) results detailing mental illness and substance use levels in 2021*. https://www.samhsa.gov/newsroom/press-announcements/20230104/samhsa-announces-nsduh-results-detailing-mental-illness-substance-use-levels-2021

Substance Abuse and Mental Health Services Administration (SAMHSA), Center for Behavioral Health Statistics and Quality. (2014). *The NSDUH report: State estimates of adult mental illness from the 2011 and 2012 National Surveys on Drug Use and Health*. Author.

Suchman, N., DeCoste, C., Castiglioni, N., Legow, N., & Mayes, L. (2008). The Mothers and Toddlers Program: Preliminary findings from an attachment-based parenting intervention for substance abusing mothers. *Psychoanalytic Psychology*, 25(3), 499–517. 10.1037/0736-9735.25.3.499

Susman-Stillman, A., Lim, S., Meuwissen, A., & Watson, C. (2020). Reflective supervision/consultation and early childhood professionals' well-being: A qualitative analysis of supervisors' perspectives. *Early Education and Development*, 31(7), 1151–1168.

Swigonski, N., James. B., Wynns, W., & Casavan, K. (2021). Physical, mental, and financial impacts of COVID-19 on early childhood educators. *Early Childhood Education Journal*, 49, 799–806.

Tandon, S. D., Mercer, C. D., Saylor, E. L., & Duggan, A. K. (2008). Paraprofessional home visitors' perceptions on addressing poor mental health, substance abuse, and domestic violence: A qualitative study. *Early Childhood Research Quarterly*, 23, 419–428.

Thompson, R. A. (2008). Early attachment and later development: Familiar questions, new answers. In J. Cassidy & P. R. Shaver (Eds.), *Handbook of attachment: Theory, research, and clinical applications* (pp. 348–365). Guilford Press.

Thompson, R. A., & Goodvin, R. (2007). Taming the tempest in the teapot. In C. A. Brownell & C. B. Kopp (Eds.), *Socioemotional development in the toddler years: Transitions and transformations* (pp. 320–341). Guilford Press.

Thompson, R. A., Simpson, J. A., & Berlin, L. J. (2022). Taking perspective on attachment theory and research: nine fundamental questions. *Attachment & Human Developmental* 24(5). 543–560.

Tomlin, A. M. (2002). Partnering with parents with personality disorders: Effective strategies for early intervention providers. *Infants and Young Children*, 14(4), 68–75.

Tomlin, A. M., & Heller, S. (2016). Measurement development in reflective supervision: History, methods, and next steps. *Zero to Three Journal*, 37(2), 4–13.

Tomlin, A. M., Hines, E. N., & Raches, C. M. (2023). Overactivity disorder of toddlerhood: Kaiden 32 months old. In K. Mulrooney, M. Keren, & J. D. Osofsky (Eds.), *DC:0-5 Casebook* (pp. 35–46). ZERO TO THREE Press.

Tomlin, A., Ruprecht, K., & Arditti, J. (2020). Promoting resilience with children impacted by parental incarceration. *Zero to Three*, 40(4), 5–13.

Tomlin, A. M., Sturm, L., & Hines, E. (2016). Reflection in home visiting: The what, why and a beginning step toward how. *Infant Mental Health Journal*, 37(6), 617–627.

Tomlin, A. M., & Viehweg, S. A. (2003). Infant mental health: Making a difference. *Professional Psychology: Research and Practice*, 34(6), 617–625.

Tomlin, A., Weatherston, D., & Pavkov, T. (2014). Critical components of reflective supervision. Responses from expert supervisors from the field. *Infant Mental Health Journal*, 35(1), 70–80.

Touchette, E., Petit, D., Paquet, J., Boivin, M., Japel, C., Tremblay, R. E., & Montplaisir, J. Y. (2005). Factors associated with fragmented sleep at night across early childhood. *Archives of Pediatrics and Adolescent Medicine*, 159(3), 242–249.

Tracey, T. J., Bludworth, J., & Glidden-Tracey, C. E. (2012). Are there parallel processes in psychotherapy supervision? An empirical examination. *Psychotherapy*, 49(3), 330–343.

Traube, D., Gozalians, S., & Duan, L. (2022). Transition to virtual early childhood home visitation during COVID-19. *Infant Mental Health Journal, 43,* 69–81.

Tremblay, R., Nagin, D., Seguin, J., Zoccolillo, M., Zelazo, P., Boivin, M., Perusse, D., & Japel, C. (2004). Physical aggression during early childhood: Trajectories and predictors. *Pediatrics, 114,* 43–50.

Trivette, C. M., Dunst, C. J., & Hamby, D. W. (2010). Influences of family-systems intervention practices on parent–child interactions and child development. *Topics in Early Childhood Education, 30*(1), 3–19.

Ursache, A., Blair, C., Stifter, C., & Voegtline, K. (2013). Emotional reactivity and regulation in infancy interact to predict executive functioning in early childhood. *Developmental Psychology, 49*(1), 127–137.

van den Akker, A., Hoffenaar, P., & Overbeek, G. (2022). Temper tantrums in toddlers and preschoolers: Longitudinal association with adjustment problems. *Journal of Developmental and Behavioral Pediatrics, 43*(7), 409–417.

Vallotton, C. D., & Ayoub, C. A. (2011). Use your words: The role of language in the development of toddlers' self-regulation. *Early Childhood Research Quarterly, 26*(2), 169–181.

Wakschlag, L. S., Choi, S. W., Carter, A. S., Hullsiek, H., Burns, J., McCarthy, K., Leibenluft, E., & Briggs-Gowan, M. J. (2012). Defining the developmental parameters of temper loss in early childhood: Implications for developmental psychopathology. *Journal of Child Psychology and Psychiatry, 53*(11), 1099–1108. 10.1111/j.1469-7610.2012.02595.x [PubMed: 22928674]

Wakschlag, L. S., Perlman, S. B., Blair, R. J., Leibenluft, E., Briggs-Gowan, M., & Pine, D. S. (2018). The neurodevelopmental basis of early childhood disruptive behavior: Irritable and callous phenotypes as exemplars. *American Journal of Psychiatry, 175*(2), 114–130. 10.1176/appi.ajp.2017.17010045

Walsh, B. A., & Mortensen, J. A. (2020). *Transforming Early Head Start home visiting: A family life education approach.* Routledge.

Watson, C., with Harris, M., Hennes, J., Harrison, M., & Meuwissen, A. (2022). *RIOS guide for reflective supervision and consultation in the infant and early childhood field.* ZERO TO THREE Press.

Watson, C. L., Bailey, A. E., & Storm, K. J. (2016). Building capacity in reflective practice: A tiered model of statewide supports for local home-visiting programs. *Infant Mental Health Journal, 37,* 640–652.

Watson, C., & Gatti, S. N. (2012). Professional development through reflective consultation in early intervention. *Infants and Young Children, 25*(2), 109–121.

Watson, C., Gatti, S. N., Cox, M., Harrison, M., & Hennes, J. (2014). Reflective supervision and its impact on early childhood intervention. *Early Childhood and Special Education, Advances in Early Education and Day Care, 18,* 1–26.

Weatherston, D. (2000). The infant mental health specialist. *Zero to Three, 21,* 3–10.

Weatherston, D. (2001). Infant mental health: A review of the relevant literature. *Psychoanalytic Social Work, 8*(1), 39–69.

Weatherston, D. (2005). Returning the treasure to babies: An introduction to infant mental health service and training. In K. M. Finello (Ed.), *The handbook of training and practice in infant and preschool mental health* (pp. 3–30). Jossey-Bass.

Weatherston, D. J., & Barron, C. (2010). What does a reflective supervisory relationship look like? In S. Scott Heller & L. Gilkerson (Eds.), *A practical guide to reflective supervision* (pp. 63–82). ZERO TO THREE Press.

Weatherston, D., Kaplan-Estrin, M., & Goldberg, S. (2009). Strengthening and recognizing knowledge, skills, and reflective practice: The Michigan Association for Infant Mental Health competency guidelines and endorsement process. *Infant Mental Health Journal, 30*(6), 648–663.

Weatherston, D., & Ribaudo, J. (2020). The Michigan infant mental health home visiting model. *Infant Mental Health Journal, 41,* 166–177.

Weatherston, D., & Tableman, B. (2015). *Infant mental health home visiting: Supporting competencies/reducing risks.* Michigan Association for Infant Mental Health.

Weatherston, D., Weigand, R. W., & Weigand, B. (2010). Reflective supervision: Supporting reflection as a cornerstone for competency, *Zero to Three, 31*(2), 22–30.

Webster-Stratton, C. (2019). *The incredible years(R): A trouble-shooting guide for parents of children aged 3–8 years* (3rd ed.). Incredible Years.

Weinfield, N. S., Sroufe, L. A., Egeland, B., & Carlson, E. (2008). Individual difference in infant-caregiver attachment: Conceptual and empirical aspects of security. In J. Cassidy & P. R. Shaver (Eds.), *Handbook of Attachment: Theory, research, and clinical applications* (pp. 78–101). Guilford Press.

Weitzman, C., Edmonds, D., Davagnino, J., & Briggs-Gowan, M. (2014). Young child socioemotional/behavioral problems and cumulative psychosocial risk. *Infant Mental Health Journal, 35*(1), 1–9.

Weitzman, C., & Wegner, L. (2015). Promoting optimal development: Screening for behavior and emotional problems. *Pediatrics, 135*(2), 384–395.

Weldum, J. R., Songer, N. S., & Ensher, G. S. (2009). The family as foreground. In G. L. Ensher, D. A. Clark, & N. S. Songer (Eds.), *Families, infants, and young children at risk: Pathways to best practice* (pp. 39–58). Paul H. Brookes Publishing Co.

Wesley, P. W., & Buysse, V. (2001). Communities of practice: Expanding professional roles to promote reflection and shared inquiry. *Topics in Early Childhood Special Education, 21*(2), 114–123.

Wessel, M., Cobb, J., Jackson, E., Harris, G., & Detwiler, A. (1954). Paroxysmal fussing in infancy, sometimes called colic. *Pediatrics, 14,* 421–435.

Weston, D. (2005). Training in infant mental health: Educating the reflective practitioner. *Infants and Young Children, 18*(4), 337–348.

Wiggins, J. L., Briggs-Gowan, M. J., Estabrook, R., Brotman, M. A., Pine, D. S., Leibenluft, E., & Wakschlag, L. S. (2018). Identifying clinically significant irritability in early childhood. *Journal of the American Academy of Child & Adolescent Psychiatry, 57*(3), 191–199. 10.1016/j.jaac.2017.12.008 [PubMed: 29496128]

Wiggs, L. (2001). Sleep problems in children with developmental disorders. *Journal of the Royal Society of Medicine, 94,* 177–179.

Wight, V., Chau, M., & Aratani, Y. (2010). *Who are America's poor children? The official story.* National Center for Children in Poverty Policy Brief. http://www.nccp.org/publications/pdf/text_912.pdf

Wilcoxon, L. A., Meiser-Stedman, R., & Burgess, A. (2021). Post-traumatic stress disorder in parents following their child's single-event trauma: A meta-analysis of prevalence rates and risk factor correlates. *Clinical Child and Family Psychology Review, 24*(4), 725–743. https://doi.org/10.1007/s10567-021-00367-z

Williams, D. S., & Fraga, L. (2011). Coming together around military families. In J. D. Osofsky (Ed.), *Clinical work with traumatized young children* (pp. 172–199). Guilford Press.

Williamson, A. A., & Mindell, J. A. (2020). Cumulative socio-demographic risk factors and sleep outcomes in early childhood. *Sleep, 40*(3), 1–13.

Wittmer, D. (2008). *Focusing on peers: The importance of relationships in the early years.* ZERO TO THREE Press.

Wolke, D. (2019). Persistence of infant crying, sleeping and feeding problems: Need for prevention. *Archives of Disease in Children, 104*(11), 1022–1023.

Woods, J. J., Wilcox, M. J., Friedman, M., & Murch, T. (2011). Collaborative consultation in natural environments: Strategies to enhance family-centered supports and services. *Language, Speech, and Hearing Services in Schools, 42,* 379–392.

Wymer, S. C., Corbin, C. M., & Williford, A. P. (2022). The relation between teacher and child race, teacher perceptions of disruptive behavior, and exclusionary discipline in preschool. *Journal of School Psychology, 90,* 33–42.

Xie, W., Bathelt, J., Fasman, A., Nelson, C. A., & Bosquet Enlow, M. (2022). Temperament and psychopathology: The "community" to which you belong matters. *Child Development, 93*(4), 995–1011.

Xu, X., Spinrad, T. L., Eisenberg, N., & Eggum-Wilkens, N. D. (2021). Longitudinal transactional relations among young children's defiance and committed compliance and maternal assertive control. *Infancy, 26,* 686–704.

Yamashiro, A., & McLaughlin, J. (2021). *Early childhood homelessness state profiles: 2018–19.* U.S. Department of Education, Office of Planning, Evaluation and Policy Development, Office of the Chief Data Officer. https://www2.ed.gov/about/offices/list/opepd/ppss/reports.html

Yavuz-Muren, H., Korucu, I., & Selcuk, A. B. (2022). Temperament and social development in childhood. In P. K. Smith and C. H. Hart (Eds.), *The Wiley-Blackwell handbook of childhood social development* (3rd ed., pp. 297–315). Wiley-Blackwell.

Yeh, M., Zerr, A., & McCabe, K. (2022). Personalizing PCIT for culturally diverse families: Outcomes from a pilot trial utilizing the Persin framework. *Behaviour Therapy and Research, 159*, 1–10.

Yoches, M., Summers, S. J., Beeber, L. S., Jones Harden, B., & Malik, N. M. (2012). Exposure to direct and indirect trauma. In S. J. Summers & R. Chazan-Cohen (Eds.), *Understanding early childhood mental health: A practical guide for professionals* (pp. 79–98). Paul H. Brookes Publishing Co.

Zeanah, C. H., Berlin, L. J., & Boris, N. W. (2011) Practitioner review: Clinical applications of attachment and research for infants and young children. *Journal of Child Psychology and Psychiatry, 52*(8), 819–823.

Zeanah, P. D., & Korfmacher, J. (2019). Infant mental health and home visiting: needs, approaches, opportunities, and cautions. In C. H. Zeanah (Ed.), *Handbook of infant mental health* (4th ed., pp. 610-625). Guilford Press.

Zeanah, P. D., Korfmacher, J., Lim, I., Steier, A., & Zeanah, C. H. (2023). Introduction to special section doing the "right" thing: Ethical issues in infant and early childhood mental health. *Infant Mental Health Journal, 44*(5), 611–613.

Zeanah, P. D., Larrieu, J. A., & Boris, N. W. (2006). Nurse home visiting: Perspectives from nurses. *Infant Mental Health Journal, 27*(1), 41–54.

Zeanah, P. D., Steier, A., Lim, I., Korfmacher, J., & Zeanah, C. H. (2023). Current approaches and future directions for addressing ethics in infant and early childhood mental health. *Infant Mental Health Journal, 44*(5), 625–637.

ZERO TO THREE Press. (2005). *Diagnostic classification of mental health and developmental disorders of infancy and early childhood* (revised ed.). Author.

ZERO TO THREE Press. (2021). *DC:0-5, Diagnostic classification of mental health and developmental disorders of infancy and early childhood* (Version 2.0). Author.

Zhang, Q., Liu, S., Wang, Z., & Cheng, N. (2023). Developmental cascades of behavior problems and cognitive ability from toddlerhood to middle childhood: A 9-year longitudinal study. *Early Human Development, 179*, 105731. https://doi.org/10.1016/j.earlhumdev.2023.105731.

Zimmerman, M., Rothschild, L., & Chelminski, I. (2005). The prevalence of DSMIV personality disorders in psychiatric outpatients. *American Journal of Psychiatry, 162*, 1911–1918.

Zubler, J. M., Wiggins, L. D., Macias, M. M., Whitaker, T. M., Shaw, J. S., Squires, J. K., Pajek, J. A., Wolf, R. B., Slaughter, K. S., Broughton, A. S., Gerndt, K. L., Mlodoch, B. J., & Lipkin, P. H. (2002). Evidence-informed milestones for developmental surveillance tools. *Pediatrics, 149*(3). e2021052138

Index

Page numbers followed by *t* and *f* indicate tables and figures, respectively.

ABC model of behavior, 59–60
ACEs, *see* Adverse childhood experiences
Adaptive parenting style, 139
ADHD, *see* Attention deficit/hyperactivity disorder
Adverse childhood experiences (ACEs), 161, 234
Aggressive behaviors, 107–108
　attention deficit/hyperactivity disorder (ADHD) and, 110–111
　child, caregiver, and home visitor perspectives on, 117
　examples of, 117–121
　exploring the provider's feelings and reactions to, 122–123
　family risk factors and maintenance of, 113–121, 114*t*
　physically, 110
　and supporting positive behaviors through teaching and reflection, 121–122
　when to worry about, 108–112, 109*t*, 112*t*
Alliance for Infant Mental Health, 239
Alliance for the Advancement of Infant Mental Health, 237
American Academy of Pediatrics, 53
　campaign for Safe Sleep, 88
American Academy of Sleep Medicine, 87
Anxiety, 181–182
　caregiving styles and, 158–159
　communication and cognitive milestones and, 156–157
　inhibited temperament and, 155–156, 155*f*
　red flags for, 160
　what helps infants and children with, 163–168

Appendices
　Exploring Challenging Behaviors-Pulling It Together Worksheet (Appendix 4A) and, 66–70*f*, 72–76*f*
　PAUSE Worksheet (Appendix 3A), 31, 37, 38–39*f*, 49–51, 100–101*f*, 124–125*f*, 144–145*f*, 169–170*f*, 200–201*f*, 221–222*f*
　Practice Discussing Difficult Topics (Appendix 9A), 205–206
　Practice Reframing Commands (Appendix 7A), 149–150
　Reflection on Work–Life Balance (Appendix 10A), 227–228
　Timely Tips for Tolerating Challenging Behaviors (Appendix 6A), 129
　Tips for Calming Your Baby (Appendix 5A), 105
Attachment and Biobehavioral Catchup (ABC) parenting program, 6
Attachment in first relationships, 2–7, 4*t*, 6*t*
Attention deficit/hyperactivity disorder (ADHD), 110–111
Autism, 32, 87, 91, 183, 192
Aversive control tactics, 114
Avoidant behavior, 159–160

Babies, understanding perspective of, 35
Behavior, 53–55
　ABC model of, 59–60
　with changes to environment, outcome, or response of other people, 60–63
　as communication, 57–58
　consequence of, 61
　co-regulation and, 57
　Exploring Challenging Behaviors-Pulling It Together Worksheet (Appendix 4A) and, 66–70*f*, 72–76*f*

267

Behavior—*continued*
  pulling everything together regarding, 64–65
  punishment for, 61
  reinforcing, 60–61
  as response to changes, 58–59
  as sign of development or temperament style, 55–57
  social learning theory and, 61–62
  support of positive, through teaching and reflection, 121–122
  teaching different, 63–64
  thinking differently about, 55–59
  see also Aggressive behaviors
Biases, 190–191
Biting, *see* Aggressive behaviors
Borderline personality disorder (BPD), 176, 179, 180–181
Boundaries and ethics in early childhood work, 210–213
BPD, *see* Borderline personality disorder
Burnout, 215–217

Calming, 93, 96–97
Caregivers
  accepting the unexpected, 195–196
  attachment to, 3, 4*t*
  bad match with home visitor, 13–14
  barriers to relationships with home visitors, 12–13
  building problem-solving skills, 194–195
  depression in, 179
  with disability, 178–179, 182–183
  engaging with, to face family challenges, 197–198
  exploring feelings and reactions of, in response to aggressive behaviors, 122–123
  family risk factors and maintenance of aggression by, 113–121, 114*t*
  giving commands, 140–141, 149–150
  home visitor's attention on, 4–5
  parental reflective functioning (PRF) and, 23
  reflective functioning capacity in, 24–26, 24*t*
  sleep and, 85–87
  strategies for supporting early relationships between home visitors and, 5–7, 6*t*
  strengths of, 6
  styles of, 116, 139, 158–161
  substance use disorder (SUD) in, 178–179, 183–186
  trauma of losing, 162–163
  understanding perspective of, 35
  working alliance between providers and, 7–11, 9–11*t*
  see also Family challenges
Centers for Disease Control (CDC), 83, 183
Change, behavior as response to, 58–59
Chess, S., 56
Coaching of home visitors, 14–16
Colic, 96
Commands, giving, 140–141, 149–150
Communication
  behavior as, 57–58
  and cognitive milestones and anxiety, 156–157
  managing missteps in, 214–215
Compliance, 133–137, 135*t*
Consequence, 61
Cooperation, *see* Prosocial behaviors
Co-regulation, 57
Co-sleeping, 88
COVID-19 pandemic, 8
  anxiety increased during, 153, 165, 181
  changes in environment due to, 6
  social determinants of health and, 189
  as trauma event, 59
Crying, 93, 96–97

Depression, 179
Detached caregiving, 116
Development, behavior as sign of, 55–57
Diagnostic Classification of Mental Health and Developmental Disorders of Infancy and Early Childhood, 111
Direction following, *see* Prosocial behaviors
Disability, 178–179, 182–183
Dozier, Mary, 6
Dysregulation, 108–109

Early Head Start, 211
Early intervention, 1–2
Early Relational Health-Conversation (ERH-C) intervention, 5
EF, *see* Executive functioning
Emotional regulation, *see* Self-regulation
Evaluating outcomes using reflective processes in PAUSE framework, 37, 40, 43
Executive functioning (EF), 78–81, 80*t*, 132–133
  compliance and, 133
Exploring Challenging Behaviors-Pulling It Together Worksheet (Appendix 4A), 66–70*f*, 72–76*f*

Family challenges, 175–178
  accepting the unexpected with, 195–196
  borderline personality disorder (BPD), 176, 180–181
  building problem-solving skills for, 194–195
  caregivers with disability, 178–179, 182–183
  depression and caregiving, 179
  environmental risk factors, 189
  having reasonable expectations about, 192–193
  home visitors supporting parents and caregivers through, 190–196
  how to engage with families to address, 197–198
  knowing your limits in dealing with, 196
  mental illness and disability, 178–179
  sharing information about, 193–194
  sorting through myriad possible family risk factors and, 178–189, 178t
  stress and mental health conditions during pregnancy, 187–189
  substance use disorder (SUD), 178–179, 183–186
  traumatic experiences, 186–187
  see also Anxiety
Fears and separation issues, 151–152
  caregiver loss as form of trauma and, 162–163
  caregiving style and responses to, 158–161
  normal, 152–155, 154t
  temperament and, 155–157, 155f
  trauma and, 161–162
  what helps anxious infants and children deal with, 163–168
Feeding skills, 89–93, 94–95t
Fonagy, Peter, 22
Friedlander, M. L., 214
Fussy Baby Network, 98

Ghosh Ippen, C., 166
Gibbons, J., 155
Goldberg, S., 238
Gopnik, Allison, 142

Hardy, K. V., 238
Hitting, see Aggressive behaviors
Home visitors, 1–2
  assisting in control of aggressive behaviors, 115–116
  attachment in child's first relationship and, 4–5
  bad match with caregivers, 13–14
  barriers to relationships with caregivers, 12–13
  benefits of reflective skills for, 21
  boundaries and ethics for, 210–213
  child action and, 9t
  clarity of roles and responsibilities of, 211–212
  common problems for, 43–45
  COVID-19 pandemic effects on, 8
  discussing self-regulation with families, 81–82, 81t
  encouragement for, 229–230
  filling up the family's emotional tank, 11, 11t
  finding balance between competing needs, 19–20
  frustration of, 209
  gaining skills with difficult topics, 191–192
  having reasonable expectations for family challenges, 192–193
  helping infants and children with anxiety, 163–168
  knowing your limits, 196
  managing missteps, 213–215
  mentoring, coaching, and supervision in, 14–16
  navigating problems in self-regulation, 84–97
  observing feeding, 91–93
  parallel process and, 10, 10t
  providing emotional support, 190–191, 209–210
  secondary trauma and burnout in, 215–217
  sharing information, 193–194
  strategies for supporting early relationships between caregivers and, 5–7, 6t
  supporting parents and caregivers through family challenges, 190–196
  training for, 208–209
  understanding perspective of, 35
  virtual, 8
  working alliance between caregivers and, 7–8
  see also Provider Reflection Worksheet (Appendix 3B); Reflective supervision and consultation (RSC)

Information gathering in PAUSE framework, 33–34
Inhibition to novelty disorder, 159

Kagan, J., 155

Labeled praise, 140
Learn the Signs. Act Early., 183
Lieberman, A., 166
Listening, *see* Prosocial behaviors; Observing and listening in PAUSE framework

Meltdowns, *see* Aggressive behaviors
Mental illness (MI), 176, 178–179
  biases toward, 190–191
  and stress during pregnancy, 187–189
Mentoring of home visitors, 14–16
MI, *see* Mental illness
Michigan Infant Mental Health Home Visiting Model, 186
Mindfulness, 20–22
Minding the Baby model, 2
Mind-mindedness, 80
MIO, *see* Mothering from the Inside Out
Missteps, managing, 213–215
Mothering from the Inside Out (MIO), 185
Multicultural Relational Perspective (MRP) approach, 238

Neonatal abstinence syndrome (NAS), 184
Normal fears in young children, 152–155, 154t

OADT, *see* Overactivity Disorder of Toddlerhood
Object permanence, 153
Observing and listening in PAUSE framework, 31–33
Overactivity Disorder of Toddlerhood (OADT), 111

Parallel process, 10, 10t, 44, 147f, 214, 218, 232, 238
Parental reflective functioning (PRF), 23
Patterson, Gerard, 114
PAUSE framework, 4, 29–31, 30f, 47f, 220
  asking questions in, 33–34
  common challenging issues with, 43–45
  evaluating the outcomes using reflective processes in, 37, 40, 43
  family challenges and, 199
  fears and separation issues and, 168
  perceive step in, 31–33
  prosocial behaviors and, 143
  provider reflection worksheet in, 41–42 (Appendix 3B)
  reflection on reflection in, 45–46
  self-regulation and, 99
  strategizing in, 36–37
  understanding each participant's experience or viewpoint in, 34–36
PAUSE Worksheet (Appendix 3A), 31, 37, 49–51
  examples of, 38–39f, 100–101f, 124–125f, 144–145f, 169–170f, 200–201f, 221–222f
Pawl, Jeree, 46
Perceive step in PAUSE framework, 31–33
Potegal, M., 110
Practice Discussing Difficult Topics (Appendix 9A), 205–206
Practice Reframing Commands (Appendix 7A), 149–150
Prosocial behaviors, 131–133
  compliance, 133–137, 135t
  methods to help young children build self-regulation of feelings and, 137–141, 138t
  supporting other social and emotional skills and, 141–143
Provider Reflection Worksheet (Appendix 3B), 37, 51–52, 102–103f
  examples of, 41–42f, 51–52f, 102–103f, 126–127f, 146–147f, 171–172f, 202–203f, 223–224f
Provider Reflective Process Assessment Scales (PRPAS), 237
Punishment for behavior, 61

Questions in PAUSE framework, 33–34

Rapid eye movement (REM) sleep, 85
Reflection
  for dealing with common problems, 43–45
  and finding balance between competing needs, 19–20
  mindfulness and, 20–22
  PAUSE framework and, 30
  reflecting on, 45–46
  reflective capacity and, 22–26
  for supporting positive behaviors, 121–122
Reflection on Work–Life Balance (Appendix 10A), 227–228
Reflective Interactive Observation Scale (RIOS), 238
Reflective skills, 15
Reflective supervision and consultation (RSC), 30, 186, 208, 217–218
  benefits of, 218–220, 235
  Black and Latinx supervisors and, 233–234
  caveat regarding, 241

continuing throughout the career, 239
delivery of, 236
evaluations in, 237–238
features of, 231–234
high-quality, 237
how to prepare for, 239–240, 242–243
necessity of, 234–235
taking the next steps in, 241
Reflective Supervision Rating Scale (RSRS), 238
Reflective Supervision Self-Efficacy Scale
  for Supervisees, 238
  for Supervisors, 238
Regulation, *see* Self-regulation
Relationship-based practice, 7
Relationships
  attachment in first, 2–7, 4t, 6t
  barriers to caregiver and home visitor, 12–13
  between caregivers and providers, 7–11, 9–11t
  communication problems and, 214–215
  early intervention and, 1–2
  strategies for supporting early, 5–7, 6t
Reznick, J. S., 155
Routines for self-regulation, 82–84
  challenges with, 97–98
RSC, *see* Reflective supervision and consultation

Scaffolding, 142
Schön, Donald, 21
Secondary trauma, 215–217
Self-regulation, 77–78, 133
  crying, calming, and soothing and, 93, 96–97
  executive functioning foundations in infancy and, 78–81, 80t
  feeding and, 89–93, 94–95t
  first steps in discussing about, with families, 81–82, 81t
  methods to help young children build, 137–141, 138t
  mind-mindedness and, 80
  navigating problems in, 84–97
  preventing problems in, through routines, 82–84
  sleep and, 85–89, 86t
  what to do when routines and caregiver education are not enough for, 97–98
Self-soothing, 85, 96
Shahmoon-Shanok, Rebecca, 231
Shea, S. E., 238
Shivers, E. M., et al., 217, 220, 232, 233
Shyness, 156

SIDS, *see* Sudden infant death syndrome
Sleep, 85–89
  analyzing overall family, 89
  co-sleeping and, 88
  problems with, 87–88
  recommended patterns for, 86t
  responding to concerns about, 89, 90
Social anxiety disorder, 158
Social determinants of health, 189
Social learning theory, 61–62
Social skills, *see* Prosocial behaviors
Soothing, 93, 96–97
Special Supplemental Nutrition Program for Women, Infants, and Children (WIC), 93
Stranger anxiety, 153–154
Strategizing in PAUSE framework, 36–37
Stress and mental health conditions during pregnancy, 187–189
Substance use disorder (SUD), 178–179, 183–186
Sudden infant death syndrome (SIDS), 88
Supervision of home visitors, 14–16

Tantrums, *see* Aggressive behaviors
Temperament, 155
  anxiety and inhibited, 155–156, 155f
  behavior as sign of, 55–57
  communication and cognitive milestones and, 156–157
Thomas, A., 56
Three-term contingency model of behavior, 59–60
Throwing, *see* Aggressive behaviors
Timely Tips for Tolerating Challenging Behaviors (Appendix 6A), 129
Tips for Calming Your Baby (Appendix 5A), 105
Trauma, 161–162
  burnout and secondary, 215–217
  caregiver loss as form of, 162–163
  family challenges with, 186–187

Understanding each participant's experience or viewpoint in PAUSE framework, 34–36

Van Horn, P., 166
Virtual home visiting, 8

Watson, Christopher, 237–238
Weatherston, D. J., 238
Working alliance, 7–8